A Clim

G000115984

The case of the Tottenham Three – the men convicted of the murder of PC Keith Blakelock in the 1985 Broadwater Farm riot – is the most shocking of the recent scandals that have rocked the English legal system to its foundations. It dates not from the 1970s era of unreformed law but from the contemporary world of the late 1980s. And Winston Silcott, falsely demonised by the police and the media as the monstrous ringleader in the killing, still languishes in prison on another murder charge.

Using confidential police reports and legal papers, *A Climate of Fear* presents dramatic new evidence proving that Silcott deserves to be freed. Silcott's defence to this earlier murder was critically prejudiced by the pending Blakelock case: he was not a monster but a victim, while his true case against the charge was never heard.

David Rose has researched the Blakelock case more closely than any other journalist and was the only national newspaper correspondent to question the verdicts even as they were announced. He helped organise electrostatic deposition analysis (Esda) of Silcott's police statement, which led directly to Silcott's leave to appeal. In *A Climate of Fear* Rose traces the case from its origins, demonstrating that the murder convictions were only one aspect of a police investigation – the largest in the history of the force – that ran wildly out of control. Not since the witch trials of the seventeenth century had such wholesale use been made of uncorroborated confessions, extracted under duress, or civil liberties been abused on such a scale.

A Climate of Fear identifies a cancer of racism at the heart of English criminal justice, which the quashing of the Blakelock convictions in 1991 has done nothing to excise.

David Rose is Home Affairs Correspondent for the *Observer*. He has also worked as a reporter for the *Guardian* and *Time Out*. He is the co-author, with Richard Gregson, of *Beneath the Mountains: Exploring the Deep Caves of Asturias*. He lives in London with his wife and baby daughter.

A Climate of Fear

The Murder of PC Blakelock and the Case of the Tottenham Three

David Rose

BLOOMSBURY

First Published in Great Britain 1992
Bloomsbury Publishing Limited, 2 Soho Square, London W1V 5DE

Copyright © David Rose 1992

The moral right of the author has been asserted

PICTURE SOURCES

Bob Gannon: page 5 *top*
Guardian: page 6
David Harden/*Observer*: page 4 *top*
Roger Hutchings/*Observer*: page 3
David Jacobs: page 1 *top & bottom*
Neil Libbert: page 4 *bottom*
David Mansell/*Observer*: page 8 *top*
Press Association: pages 2 *top*, 5 *bottom*, 7, 8 *bottom*

Map on page 20 by Neil Hyslop

A CIP catalogue record for this book
is available from the British Library

ISBN 0 7475 1184 5

Typeset by Hewer Text Composition Services, Edinburgh
Printed and bound in Great Britain by
Cox & Wyman Ltd, Reading, Berkshire

For Shyama and Anyusha

INNOCENT
I'LL ALWAYS BE
IN SORROW
UNTIL DEATH
SETS ME FREE
FORWARD TO TOMORROW

Winston Silcott
Gartree Prison, 1989

Contents

Acknowledgements

My first and greatest debt is to the *Observer* newspaper, and its editor Donald Trelford, assistant editor David Randall, news editor Paul Routledge, and features editor Bob Low. Since I joined the paper in September 1990, they have given me unstinting support in my inquiries into the miscarriage of justice endured by the three men convicted of PC Blakelock's murder. At a time when this was a brave and controversial thing to do, they proved their commitment with a magnificent front-page display disclosing the new evidence about Winston Silcott's confession, supported with a whole page inside. They also allowed me generous leave of absence in order to write this book. In general, the *Observer* has provided me with the happiest and most stimulating working environment of my career.

I must also thank my agent, Anne McDermid, who has been a hospitable and encouraging friend over years when I only talked about writing books rather than got on with the job, and Penny Phillips and David Reynolds of Bloomsbury, who made herculean efforts to publish this book within weeks of its late delivery.

Many people have assisted my researches, and if I inadvertently fail to mention some of them, I apologise. The families of the three men all put up with my questions over the years, though at times they must have been tiresome and intrusive. I must especially mention Sharon Raghip, who campaigned tirelessly for her husband and George, Mary and Bill Silcott who are still fighting for Winston's release. Andrew Hall, Winston Silcott's solicitor, now a barrister, has become a close friend through this case. He worked on it unpaid for long periods when few were sympathetic, and it was he who found the key to unlocking it by commissioning the Esda tests. He has been a constant point of reference for me, commenting on crucial passages and putting up with my telephone calls late at night and early on weekend mornings. I must also thank Gareth Peirce, Engin Raghip's solicitor, and Danny Simpson and Steve Kamlish, Mark Braithwaite's legal team, who lent me documents, time and advice. Sir Derek Hodgson, who tried the Blakelock murder case, granted me an interview. In rereading transcripts of the trial, particularly his courageous and forthright rulings in respect of the juveniles, I am humbled by the size of that privilege.

The Broadwater Farm Defence Campaign no longer exists, but I was given access to the invaluable resource of its voluminous files. Stafford Scott, who arranged this, has helped me in many other ways: without him this book could not have been written. Delroy Lindo filled in many of the blanks of Winston Silcott's childhood.

I have drawn extensively from published materials, particularly Lord Scarman's report on the Brixton disorders, and the report of the inquiry by Lord Gifford and others into the riot at Broadwater Farm. My friends at the *Observer* library provided cuttings at short notice. Tony Bunyan of the new Statewatch library assisted with digging out the crucial texts of Sir Kenneth Newman. Gabriel Black found time to see me between feeding her hungry daughter. A. Sivanandan and the staff of the Institute of Race Relations, from whom I have long derived intellectual nourishment, sandwiches and gossip, soothed my brow and faxed me documents.

I have received much help from serving and retired members of the Metropolitan Police. Mike Granatt and David Rangecroft of the Department of Public Affairs were, as ever, courteous, helpful and efficient. Like many journalists, I have often had cause to wish other press offices were as useful and well organised. The former Commander Alec Marnoch gave generously of his time and deep wisdom, as did Colin Couch, Tottenham's former chief superintendent. There are other officers to whom I owe an equal debt, whom it would be prudent not to name. Special mention must be made of Chris Sallon, who gave of his valuable time to read the manuscript for legal mantraps.

Finally I must thank my darling wife, Shyama, who kept a husband absent in the study fed, watered and inspired, and our daughter Anyusha, who occasionally slept for more than two hours at a stretch. To them this book is dedicated. It goes without saying that its errors are entirely my own.

Introduction

The miscarriage of justice which befell Winston Silcott, Engin Raghip and Mark Braithwaite ended not with a bang but with a murmur, a judge's cryptic comment so faint that for several minutes their families had no idea what had happened. All Lord Justice Farquharson said, or rather muttered, was: 'That speaks for itself.'

'That', just after noon on 25 November 1991, was the beginning of the Crown's capitulation in the PC Keith Blakelock murder case, in the shape of a few brief comments by the leading counsel for the prosecution, Roy Amlot QC.

Four and a half years earlier, he had chilled the blood of an Old Bailey jury with his clinical exposition of Blakelock's death, bringing in guilty verdicts, against the expectation of many police officers. Now, in the cramped but cosier precincts of the Royal Courts of Justice in the Strand, Amlot had had to respond to submissions by Anthony Scrivener QC, for Silcott, regarding new forensic evidence about Winston Silcott's 'confession'. The police, the tests suggested, had lied on oath when they claimed to have written it down contemporaneously as Silcott spoke in a police interview room less than a fortnight after the killing in October 1985. According to the scientists, the most important passages appeared to have been added later.

'It goes without saying that the matter has been fully investigated, not only on the part of the defence but by the Crown,' Amlot said, speaking with a quiet, understated dignity that served only to emphasise the magnitude of his remarks. 'Taking all the factors into account, we cannot ask you to rely on the only evidence that was presented against Winston Silcott at the trial. The expert evidence Your Lordships have heard today casts such doubt upon the assertion by Detective Chief Superintendent Graham Melvin that the notes were contemporaneous notes, that we can no longer ask the court to rely on that evidence.'

'That speaks for itself,' responded Lord Justice Farquharson. Silcott's conviction, his thirty-year minimum sentence, his characterisation by the Old Bailey judge as 'a very vicious and a very evil man' were void.

He sat in the dock in a smart green tracksuit. What he called his 'justice beard', grown from the day of his conviction until now it reached his waist, was tied in an exotic bow with the pink ribbon used to bundle barristers' documents. He looked down, a hint of tears in the corners of his eyes: he had grasped the point of Farquharson's comment at once. Then he turned to the packed public gallery and broke out a huge, delighted grin.

It would be right, Lord Justice Farquharson was saying, to allow Silcott's appeal straightaway, before coming to the other two, given the wholly exceptional nature of the case. Silcott waved furiously at his friends and family, mutely signalling his satisfaction. Then, with a last clenched-fist salute, he gave himself up to his prison officer escort, ready to return to Gartree Prison, where he had still to serve another life sentence for murder.

The deliverance of Engin Raghip and Mark Braithwaite was more complete, and was announced by Amlot two days later. Michael Mansfield QC, for Raghip, had argued at length that whatever view the three judges took of his other grounds of appeal, the evidence that Silcott's confession had not been properly recorded 'contaminated' the other convictions.

Amlot's reply was one of the more sensational speeches in English legal history, a body blow to the Metropolitan Police, and to a criminal justice system that was already in disarray. One could take a narrow view, he said, and consider that Chief Superintendent Melvin played only a small part in the cases of Raghip and Braithwaite. But, he went on, 'It seems to the Crown that the proper way to view it is from the broad picture. The broad picture is that Mr Melvin was in charge of the case, the senior officer in the case, in control of the case, the officer to whom all the junior officers looked for all significant decisions.'

Mansfield, Amlot recalled, had asked whether the Crown would have pursued the prosecutions if it had known of the new forensic evidence: 'It seems to us that this is an appropriate question . . . and the answer is, unequivocally, we would not have gone on against Braithwaite, against Raghip, against any other defendants, having learned of the apparent dishonesty of the officer in charge of the case. I say that because the Crown has to depend on the honesty and integrity of officers in a case, especially where he has close control of the case. The impact,' Amlot concluded, 'is obviously severe.'

With that, the court rose for a short adjournment. The judges returned to say that they had better hear all the arguments on other points, and would deliver a full, considered judgement later. But it would be wrong to keep Raghip and Braithwaite in jail a moment longer. In an unprecedented step, Lord Justice Farquharson granted two men who were still technically convicted killers of a policeman unconditional bail, and they were swept in tumult into the street, to be jostled not by prison warders but by camera crews, asked not for fingerprints but for their autographs.

This is a bleak and dismal story, on which much ink has already been spilled, in newspapers, a public inquiry report, and other sundry documents. Nor is it over yet: at the time of writing, Graham Melvin and his colleague, Detective Inspector Maxwell Dingle, face criminal charges of perjury and conspiracy to pervert the course of justice. Melvin and Dingle have let it be known that they plan to resist the charges with the utmost vigour. I am constrained, therefore, from commenting on their actions in respect of their interviews with Winston Silcott, beyond what lies on the record of the Court of Appeal.

But although the allegations against them have been central in law to the collapse of the convictions of Silcott, Raghip and Braithwaite, they are only peripheral to the wider story of the Blakelock murder and Broadwater Farm. The dramatic scenes in the Court of Appeal in the autumn of 1991 leave big questions of criminal justice, policing and race unresolved.

Not the least of them is this: why is nobody now convicted of PC Blakelock's murder?

The answer, this book will argue, raises profound issues about policing in a democracy. The investigation of Blakelock's murder, a horror almost without equal in peacetime Britain, was flawed from the outset, proceeding in a manner that ensured vital witnesses never came forward, nor evidence to light. A community that was already alienated from the law enforcement authorities saw not bridges built but the deepening of the abyss. From the outset, the path followed by Detective Chief Superintendent Melvin and his colleagues led from waves of arrests to detention incommunicado, interrogation, denial of legal advice, and very serious charges based, in case after case, on confessions alone.

In the process, the rights of suspects, many of them juveniles, were widely abused. At times, the Blakelock murder investigation had more in common with the witch hunts of the seventeenth century than with an orthodox attempt to solve a murder.

Cross-examined in the witness box, Melvin was asked repeatedly why he relied so heavily on admissions, and why there were so few witnesses ready to identify the perpetrators of these terrible crimes. The reason, he said, was that the inhabitants of Broadwater Farm had hidden behind a 'wall of silence', and this, in turn, had been engendered by the 'climate of fear' which the rioters and their friends imposed. The proposition of this book is that while there was fear, and crime and criminals, on Broadwater Farm before the riot of 6 October 1985, the climate of fear was fostered by the methods of the murder inquiry. Melvin and his colleagues, who had the firm endorsement of the highest echelons of the Scotland Yard hierarchy, were largely to blame for the shortage of material witnesses.

However, we need to go back a stage beyond this, and ask why the investigation was allowed to proceed in such a manner? Why was this the mode so swiftly adopted, apparently without consideration of an alternative approach?

The riot at Broadwater Farm took place during the reign of that most academic and theoretical of commissioners, Sir Kenneth

Newman; and if few of his subordinates followed the details of his reasoning about inner-city, multiracial areas like Broadwater Farm, it nonetheless had a strong influence on events. In public, most of the time, Sir Kenneth endorsed Lord Scarman's report on the Brixton disorders of 1981, with its emphasis on consultation and what became known as 'community policing'.

It will be argued here that his apparent support for this kind of approach masked an underlying instinct which was wholly authoritarian. In reality, conditioned by his experience as chief constable of the RUC, Sir Kenneth believed that the problems for the police of places like Broadwater Farm were in key respects analogous to those caused by the IRA. Consultation, in his mind, was a process to be endured, or rather used, not as a democratic end in itself but as a way of exercising what he called 'social control'.

His more sensitive subordinates were alive to these philosophical currents, which dovetailed neatly with the cruder opinions of many street officers. I believe they are a key to understanding much of what happened at Broadwater Farm, before and after the riot. At the same time, the conflicts of outlook within the police, and their sometimes vague understanding of contemporary thinking about public order in the inner cities, led to inaction at crucial moments and were important factors behind the outbreak of the riot.

Looking at the Blakelock case in this way suggests that the confidence expressed by senior Met officers after the Appeal Court rulings of 1991, that miscarriages of justice of this type 'could not happen again', was too optimistic. These officers, led by the present commissioner, Sir Peter Imbert, and his deputy, John Smith, based their belief on legal and technological change: the Police and Criminal Evidence Act, with its insistence on access for suspects to legal advice, and the tape recording – soon even the video recording – of interrogations.

These developments may help prevent some kinds of abuse, including that of which Graham Melvin and Maxwell Dingle now stand accused. But they do not touch the underlying problem of treating whole communities, particularly black communities, as beyond the legal pale, to be alternately squeezed and patronised. Nor do they go into the matter of the possible inherent unreliability of *all* confessions obtained under the stressful conditions of interrogation in police custody. From their very different points of view, it is beginning to dawn on jurists and psychologists that however fairly admissions are recorded, the risk of false confessions may be too great to allow them to be the basis for any criminal conviction.

Another issue the case throws up is the unfashionable matter of 'institutionalised racism'. There was a long pre-history to the conviction of Winston Silcott as the 'ringleader' of the killing, in which discrimination in education, employment, housing and the criminal justice system played their parts. In the end, he was served up to the waiting media, themselves so conditioned to expect the worst of his kind that few commentators questioned the tenuous basis of the case.

Even as I heard and saw the jury return its verdict within the Old Bailey's forbidding number two court in 1987, it was my belief – soon to be shared in reports by eminent American jurists and Amnesty International – that the case should never have got past a magistrate. It certainly should not have required a *deus ex machina* in the shape of allegations of the most serious kind of impropriety before its final collapse. Winston Silcott went down because his face had been made to fit for years before a wider public first came to hear of Broadwater Farm.

Under Sir Peter Imbert, the Metropolitan Police has officially abandoned the authoritarian tendencies of the Newman era. The ideology embodied by his 'Plus' programme of internal reform, based on new ideals of public service, is essentially democratic, thanks in no small part to the remarkable man who led Sir Peter's Plus policy team for three years, the lately retired Commander Alec Marnoch. But as Marnoch and other candid officers will admit, the process of reform is far from complete, while its success is patchy at best. Nor do all senior officers share Sir Peter's philosophy, in London or nationally. There is an intense, often subterranean, debate in progress, whose outcome remains uncertain.

In the course of researching this book, I have spoken to many police officers; some have become my friends. I know from experience over several years that there are many officers of the highest calibre and integrity in the United Kingdom police service. Yet still there seem to be many internal barriers to real change, too many divisions across the country where the old 'canteen culture' prevails. Sometimes, when senior officers close ranks to justify a fiasco, or the disclosure of scandal in court, one senses a belief in police infallibility, not shared by all officers, but nevertheless a frequent background refrain.

In the last years of Mrs Thatcher, the heat of an iconoclastic Prime Minister was turned on the police as never before, as careful leaks to newspapers suggested the way forward might be a root and branch purge, with the introduction of an 'officer class'. This threat to the established structure of the police has receded. But if public trust is to be fully restored, and the police shown to be capable of reforming themselves, it seems to me they have to do two things: to listen to their own voices of dissent, so matching their outward commitment to a wider democratic society with democracy within; and to cast out the infallibility principle for ever.

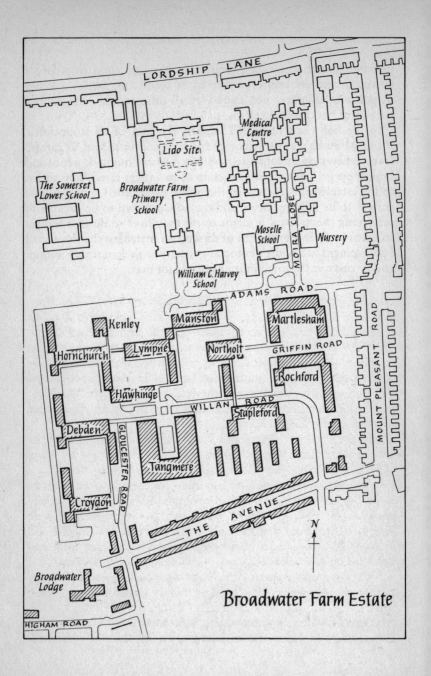

Broadwater Farm Estate

1

Black Boys and Boys in Blue

It begins in the 1960s, when the Beatles played 'She Loves You' and King Pleasure played calypso, and three little boys lived in Tottenham: Winston Silcott, Delroy Lindo and Stafford Scott. They had all been born at the close of the fifties to parents from the West Indies, members of the great, hope-filled immigration which began when the students of London University welcomed with garlands the passengers off the first boat, the *Empire Windrush*, and continued with labour-recruitment tours of Jamaica by a junior health minister, Enoch Powell.

Winston's parents, Mary and Walter, known to most people as Bill, came to Britain in 1957 from the island of Montserrat. They were Seventh Day Adventists, and their faith helped them cope with the swift realisation that conditions in their adopted country were a lot less rosy than they had envisaged before departure. They were an educated, intelligent couple but, like all too many West Indians, they found that the only work available was menial and routine. They took a set of furnished rooms in the East End, and Bill worked as a labourer, Mary in a factory producing cakes.

After Winston's birth in 1959, Mary went back to work. George, his brother, arrived in 1964, and the family settled in Tottenham, again in a rented flat. Architecturally, Tottenham, well to the north of central London, was attractive, built mostly of Victorian and Edwardian redbrick, and endowed with its share of parkland.

But it was markedly poorer than the other, Highgate, side of the new London borough of Haringey, and already it was attracting a high immigrant population, not only West Indians but Greek and Turkish Cypriots and, to a lesser extent, south Asians. By the mid-sixties it had become a centre for the rag trade in which thousands of women cutters and stitchers scraped a living as homeworkers and in sweat shops, turning the sketches of Mary Quant into off-the-peg reality. Here Mrs Silcott found a job, working overtime to earn the industry's notoriously exploitative piece rates.

At primary school, where Winston did well, reading easily and displaying an outstanding talent for football, he met Delroy, with whom he forged an enduring friendship. 'He was just a normal kid, popular, easy-going, rarely inn trouble with the teachers,' Delroy recalls. 'He used to go to church a lot and he would force me to come as well.' The two boys went to different comprehensives but stayed in close touch, living as they did on adjoining roads, and Winston's attempts to improve Delroy's soul continued for several years.

At eleven, Winston went to the now defunct William Foster School, where for the first time he encountered Stafford Scott. At first they were brought together by football: both were highly competitive but they displayed complementary skills. Winston was the genius with the ball, a master dribbler who could outfox all comers, but he lacked discipline; sometimes Stafford, less technically gifted but a better tactician, would score more goals.

If football was the one area where Winston and Stafford visibly excelled, part of the reason was the ugly presence of racism. 'Any time you got a detention,' says Stafford, 'you had only to look around the room. Black guys would outnumber the whites by ten to one. In fact it was rare to see a white boy at all.' Some teachers, Stafford and Winston agree, openly picked on the minority of black children. When Winston was about thirteen, he saved his pocket money and bought his mother a bottle of perfume on his way to school as a birthday present. Seeing the chemist's bag on his desk, a teacher asked him what it was. Winston showed her the bottle and explained why he had bought it. At once, the teacher accused him of stealing it and, ignoring his protestations, dragged him away from his open-mouthed classmates to the school office. There, she telephoned the shop which, luckily for Winston, remembered the black youngster who had bought perfume for his mother. For a boy raised at the Seventh Day Adventist congregation every Saturday, this was not a trivial experience.

Stafford, who now directs a successful employment agency near Tottenham, has written for the *Guardian* and spent a long time as the highly articulate spokesman of the Broadwater Farm Youth Association, came up against school racism and the stereotype of the West Indian 'underachiever' in a different, no less wounding, way. 'I was academically successful. In my early teens my parents talked of my becoming a lawyer and, all things being equal, it was not an unreasonable ambition. I could have done A levels and gone to university. Then I was told: no way was I going to be allowed to join the O level class and sit for GCEs; I was going to be with the slow, CSE stream. I was hurt, believe me. That was something which took a long time to recover from. It changed my life. Whatever I said, they wouldn't change their minds.'

For his part, Winston was urged by Bill and Mary to consider medicine as a career. He was more down to earth than Stafford: it seemed, he thought, an utterly unattainable objective.

In his report on the Brixton riot of 1981, Lord Scarman stated: 'There is overwhelming evidence that they [young black people] have failed to benefit from our society to the extent that they might reasonably have expected. In particular, the underachievement of West Indian children at school has been well chronicled.' The causes, Lord Scarman went on, were a matter for controversy, but he cited not discrimination within the educational system but 'the failure of black youths to acquire sufficiently early the skills of language and literacy' and other cultural differences.

This analysis reflected orthodox thinking in the 1970s, when Stafford, Delroy and Winston were at school. It does not, says Stafford Scott, reflect the experience of black youth at the William Foster School in Tottenham. 'Just that label, underachievement, caused untold damage. There was no expectation that we would achieve, and so we didn't. You know how schoolkids are: they always rail against discipline, and being given work to do. So if they bung you in a class where no one really asks you to work, to stretch yourself, and where the discipline is lax, then you become a layabout, which is how they picture you anyway.'

There were other appalling incidents. Even after being placed in the CSE class for other subjects, Stafford was allowed to remain on the O level drama course. When he was fifteen, he had a session with the school careers adviser. 'He told me I was obviously extremely artistic and had a great future. For a few moments I felt proud, started to preen myself. Then he suggested I should think about becoming a hairdresser. I just walked out.'

On another occasion, an Australian supply teacher on temporary attachment to the school hauled Stafford and two other black children out of the drama class and harangued them in a classroom. 'She seemed to have gone completely mad. She kept shouting that we had no place in Britain, and why didn't we go back to where we came from. We had been born here and she, an Australian, was telling us to go back home!' This was too much even for William Foster, and after a complaint from Stafford's parents, no more was seen of the young Australian.

The cumulative effect was serious. Stafford says: 'Inside of you, a youngster growing up, this kind of thing touches some nerves. After a while, it starts off what white people call a chip on your shoulder. We would describe it as a well-founded grudge.'

Winston, Delroy and Stafford all left school at fifteen to find a variety of meaningless jobs, young Winston first earning £55 a week as an apprentice cabinet maker at a firm called Beautility. He stuck it for fifteen months, until a foreman wrongly accused him of theft from the canteen. It did not take long before the three youths began to find themselves in trouble with the law.

Lord Scarman understood something of the hostility that black youths felt towards the police. They were, he said, 'tempted by deprivation' into street crime. The result was that 'the recipe for a clash with the police is therefore ready mixed: and it takes little, or nothing, to persuade them that the police, representing an establishment which they see as insensitive to their plight, are their enemies.'

Elsewhere in his report, Lord Scarman considered the question of police racism, finding that it did in fact manifest itself in the 'ill-considered, immature and racially prejudiced actions of some officers . . . it may be only too easy for some officers, faced with what they must see as the inexorably rising tide of street crime, to lapse into an unthinking assumption that all young people are potential criminals.' Every instance of racism, he said, had an enormous impact: 'The damage done by even the occasional display of racial prejudice is incalculable.'

He also considered the question of harassment by police. Some of the many allegations must be true, he said, even if others were founded on no more than the self-interested gossip of criminals. He added: 'I do not doubt harassment does occur . . . many believe that the police routinely abuse their powers and mistreat alleged offenders. The belief here is as important as the fact.'

Eventually, Winston and Stafford turned to burglary, and perhaps their perceived position of relative deprivation had a part to play in this, although at the time they were in employment. But none of the three was convicted of any criminal offence until after the police and the law had already classified them as offenders. From their perspective, Scarman failed to make a crucial link: between his description of prejudice and harassment and the criminalisation of black youth.

In Winston's case, it started with an offence of mind-boggling triviality. On his way to work one morning, he was stopped, searched and eventually charged with having faulty brakes on his bicycle. He was fined £15. His mother observes: 'If he was a white boy, they would just have given him a caution and let him go.'

Stafford Scott's first brush with the police was altogether more frightening. One day in the scorching summer of 1976, his record clean, he went with four black friends to Bow Street Magistrates' Court, where another friend was being tried for theft. At lunchtime, they left the court and walked into Covent Garden – followed by four detectives who had been involved with the case. To Stafford's bewilderment and horror, all were arrested under the old 'sus' (suspected persons) law: their presence in the area, the police claimed in court, had been suspicious.

They in turn now came before the magistrates and were convicted. Two were sent to borstal; Stafford and the others were each fined £40 – 'a hell of a lot of money for us in those days'. They appealed to the Crown Court, where the judge heard the evidence of the defence solicitor in the original case, that at the time the youths had supposedly been seen acting suspiciously by the four police officers, all concerned had been securely within the precincts of the court. The magistrate disregarded this account and upheld the convictions.

'The knock-on effect of that was that I lost my chance of joining the RAF,' Stafford says, 'because I now had a criminal record. I had been interviewed and was on their books, waiting for an opening. I had wanted to do an apprenticeship in telecommunications and radar. I thought I could do that for a few years, then come out with a skill with which I could make a good life for myself. It was not to be.' He added: 'If you're told enough times that crime is something your kind do, eventually any reservations about going ahead and doing it start to disappear.'

Delroy Lindo also fell foul of 'sus'. He had gone with friends to Oxford Street: 'That was a big thing for us in those days; it was a big day out, to walk around and look at the shops. They claimed I had jostled someone's bag and locked me up, and from that day on, my record was marked. That seemed to me the objective of the whole thing, to blacken your record. It was like a conspiracy, the way I saw it. Then I started looking around and saw that every black kid my age had been done for sus, and the next time we got done, if there was a next time, it would be that much easier to get a tough sentence.'

In any event, Stafford and Winston now turned to crime in earnest: not to street robbery, the offence examined by Lord Scarman in the background of the Brixton disorders of 1981, but to housebreaking and burglary. From the autumn of 1976 through the first months of 1977 and beyond, they went on a wild spree. Partly, according to Winston, it was a sense of 'getting something back' from white society. But also it was the sheer, unadulterated thrill. Sometimes there were close shaves, when occupiers returned and they had to dash for cover. 'It was a group thing,' Winston says, 'and basically we did it for the excitement. We certainly never made much money.'

They came down to earth with a bang when they tried to fence some stolen property through a chef at a local fast food outlet, who was known throughout the area. He asked them to come back a few hours later, and when they did, the police were waiting. Another of those arrested named many of their associates, and by the time the matter came to trial at Snaresbrook Crown Court in December 1977, there were sixteen in the dock. Winston pleaded guilty to nine counts of burglary. All went to borstal for varying terms: in Winston's case, it was a few months, but Stafford, who the prosecution claimed was the ringleader, was jailed for three years.

In the eyes of the police, they had lived up to expectation – as 'scrotes', police slang covering individuals considered to be worthless members of society or villains. The officers of Tottenham Division were rapidly coming to expect no better from the estate where the Scott, Silcott and Lindo families had by now been living for several years, Broadwater Farm.

The many millions of pounds that have been poured into Broadwater Farm over the years cannot disguise the fact that it is an eyesore. It now has remembrance gardens, bizarrely equipped with granite boulders, to mark the spot where PC Blakelock was hacked to death; new security systems, strong outside lighting and a few jolly murals on the sides of the concrete blocks. Inside, the flats are spacious, and in winter unusually, even oppressively, warm thanks to a souped-up communal heating system. But these features are largely cosmetic. Broadwater Farm remains a bleak and brutal indictment of the follies of 'slum clearance' and the dumps in which governments and local authorities saw fit to 'decant' people in the 1960s and early 1970s.

There is still graffiti, and an air of decay, of buildings old before their time. It is dominated by its high-level outdoor walkways, by stark rubber-matted corridors within, and by the chilly winds which blow around the two high-rise blocks in the middle. However deep the coffers of the Department of the Environment, it is still a place that people want to leave.

The Farm sits in a marshy basin, and so remains invisible from much of Tottenham. But as one approaches the estate along one of the side roads from the thoroughfare of Philip Lane, it starts to loom over the brow of the basin's lip, huge and solid, its massive white structures merging with the grey sky, and jarring with the redbrick all around. Seen from across the sports ground which borders it to the north, particularly in the rosy glow of sunset, the effect is more pleasing; with a little imagination, it can even start to resemble a science-fiction city of the future, with a striking and impressive skyline. That, according to Steve Gould, a contemporary Haringey planner, was probably how its designers saw it, and intended it to be seen. 'Unfortunately,' he added, 'once you get in there it's more like the inside of some kind of nightmarish Nintendo computer game.'

I have not been able to discover who came up with a name for the estate. There had been allotments on the land, and there was also water, in the shape of the Moselle River. Prone to occasional flooding, the watercourse forced the designers to build every block on stilts, with car parks at ground level. They gave Tangmere, the central block, a big, open area surrounded by shops at the first-floor level. This, staying with aquatic imagery, they called the 'deck'.

The estate was constructed by Taylor Woodrow using one of the industrialised, pre-fabricated systems in vogue in the late 1960s. Salem El-Doori, the head of the architects' team, told the public inquiry chaired by Lord Gifford after the riot: 'For local authorities, such systems were very attractive, because of the speed of building, economy of resources, and the difficulty of finding skilled labour.' The inquiry also heard from the Haringey chief executive, Roy Limb: 'The chair of planning in those days thought Broadwater Farm would be an everlasting memorial to him and his committee.'

The building took six years, with the last of more than one thousand flats opened in 1973. The Silcott family had moved into the Martlesham block two years before. At first, they found life a great improvement: there were other children to play with Winston and George, comfort, and congenial neighbours. But contrary to reports at the time of the riot, the Farm never won any prizes or awards. It would not have deserved them: within a few years of its opening, like many system-built estates, the blocks were facing leaks, damp and other structural problems.

Lord Gifford's inquiry report gave a compelling account of the estate's rapid decline. By 1976, it was already being described in the local press as a 'sink' estate, terrorised by violent criminals – a characterisation vehemently contested at the time by some residents. Another newspaper story in 1978 quoted the beat PC as saying that crime was no worse on the Farm than elsewhere in Tottenham, and that 'you are more likely to get mugged at Bruce Grove than you are here'. But this came towards the end of a sensational piece describing the estate as 'terror flats'. Its dismal image was rapidly emerging.

In 1980, less than ten years after it was built, it figured under the pseudonym 'Lakeside estate' in a DoE report on hard-to-let housing. Its slide in popularity had been catastrophic; the council might make it 'tolerable' for the next decade, but after that, 'the possibility of demolition is one that will have to be considered'. The same year, Joanne George, who became chair of the Tenants' Association, arrived on the Farm for the first time. She said in her evidence to the Gifford inquiry:

> The first thing that actually hit me was the condition of the estate and the flat that I was first offered myself. The estate was dirty, there was lots of vandalism, lots of glass, the flat I was allocated was in a really bad state of repair. There was no kitchen sink, there was no kitchen cupboard, there was a hole in the floor . . . all the passages had graffiti and stains. It was absolutely disgusting and I was told, 'sorry, no money for decorations'.

As Gifford's report stated, real grievances, such as poor maintenance, were combining with a lurid and exaggerated public image to the point where 'labelling became attached not just to the buildings but to the people, as if they too were undesirable'. It appears that some local businesses were adopting the illegal practice of 'redlining', denying people facilities because of their address, for the report went on: 'Residents on the estate had severe problems with hire purchase or TV hire facilities, or obtaining goods from catalogues.'

By 1976, the proportion of residents who wanted a transfer was double the borough average at 20 per cent, and many of those offered flats there were turning them down. As a result, the council's housing officers told the inquiry, 'dwellings tended to be left to those whose need was most urgent'. Three-quarters of all tenancy acceptances were from homeless, usually single-parent, families, compared with a Haringey average of 24 per cent. The proportion of Afro-Caribbean and Asian families rose steadily: 42 per cent at the 1981 census, and 52 per cent by the time of the inquiry in 1986, of whom nearly all were of West Indian origin or descent.

But to the Silcotts, Scotts and Lindos, Broadwater Farm was home. If holes in floors went unmended and roofs let in water, the decline of the estate was only another facet of the racial discrimination evident in other spheres of their lives. There was a further manifestation right under their noses: the Tenants' Association bar and social club which opened beneath a walkway at the Willan Road side of the estate in 1972. For years this was the only social facility of any kind on the Farm, and according to the Gifford inquiry it operated a *de facto* colour bar. Black residents were refused membership without reason, racist remarks were overheard. Stafford Scott says: 'The social club actually became a pub. There were several occasions where black people were assaulted and badly beaten in there, badly beaten.'

In 1981 it was forced to take steps to clean up its act. Financial irregularities came to light, and after a council investigation, several staff were sacked.

2

The Theory and Practice of 'Symbolic Locations'

To the Metropolitan Police, Broadwater Farm was a den of iniquity, a nest of crime and criminals almost without equal. Deputy Assistant Commissioner Michael Richards, in charge of the whole of north London, said on television soon after the riot: 'It's long been a haven for the wrongdoer. It's long been the place to which people go from outside to gain comfort and support of a like ilk.' Chief Superintendent (now Commander) Colin Couch, who led Tottenham Division from 1984 to 1986, tended to be more diplomatic in his language. But his opinion differed only in degree. Interviewed in 1992, he spoke of the three-mile maze of walkways, which allowed those pursued by police to escape, and the problems posed by the sale of drugs in the garages. Like Richards, he believed the estate was a focus for criminality in the surrounding area.

To Sir Kenneth Newman, Commissioner of Police for the Metropolis from 1982 to 1987, Broadwater Farm was something else again: a 'symbolic location'. This was a term he coined, and its meaning is the key to understanding his attitude to the inner city. In 1983, according to his annual report to the Home Secretary, there were four such locations in London, including Railton Road in Brixton, All Saints Road in Notting Hill, and Broadwater Farm. By 1985, the list had grown to eleven.

In various speeches and articles, Newman defined this singular term. In October 1983, for example, he delivered the Sir George

Bean Memorial Lecture, under the rubric 'Policing London, post Scarman'. He said:

> Throughout London there are locations where unemployed youths – often black youths – congregate; where the sale and purchase of drugs, the exchange of stolen property and illegal drinking and gaming is not unknown. The youths regard these symbolic locations as their territory. Police are viewed as intruders, the symbol of authority . . . they equate closely with the criminal rookeries of Dickensian London.

His view of the inhabitants of such locations was unashamedly dim:

> A neighbourhood bobby who does not see too much and does not interfere is tolerated. But if he arrests someone for an offence, the thin veneer of that tolerance is likely to be exposed; he will find himself surrounded, assaulted, and his prisoner released. If reinforcements are called in to assist him, the chances are that numbers will escalate, and confrontation become a full-blooded riot. This kind of scenario and others like it, once the daily routine of London's police at the start of the century, is again one of the realities in policing London.

Drugs and drink, he added, were a special problem: 'They more than anything are responsible for confrontations between police and black people.'

Some of the same analysis and, in places, whole sentences went into another speech by Sir Kenneth which went further, and was of great significance although ignored by the media at the time. Delivered in 1983 to the right-wing European Atlantic Group, it provides a fascinating guide to the thinking of Britain's most senior policeman. Entitled 'Public Order in Free Societies', it began with a somewhat rambling discussion of the relationship between freedom and order at various times and places. Then he turned to the meat of his discourse:

There are two particular problems in the Western societies which have the potential to affect the balance between order and freedom. The first problem is concerned with the growth of multi-ethnic communities. The second is related to indigenous terrorist movements engaging in terrorism to promote separatism or an extreme ideology.

This was a breathtaking equation, especially coming from the lips of Sir Kenneth Newman, who as a former Chief Constable of the Royal Ulster Constabulary knew all about terrorism firsthand. He seemed to be saying that the challenges posed to policing and to society by areas with large black communities were analogous, if not identical, to those posed by the IRA. As terrorism had required measures limiting individual liberty such as the Prevention of Terrorism Act, so areas with large black populations might require similar sacrifices.

Turning to 'multi-ethnic societies' in detail, Newman found that they had produced an underclass, 'a class that is beneath the working class and subject to underachievement and other forms of disadvantage'.

Newman was fond of quoting Lord Scarman's Brixton report, and went on to do so here. But his reading was selective, and came to markedly different conclusions. Where the thrust of Scarman was towards democratic accountability, Newman's arguments resonated with the smack of authoritarianism.

Scarman was criticised at the time his report was issued for not going far enough in the democratic direction. He rejected, for example, the idea of an elected police authority for London (not that such a proposal stood the remotest chance of making headway with Mrs Thatcher's government at the time of the hated Greater London Council led by Ken Livingstone), but he did declare himself strongly in favour of a London-wide 'advisory board' to curb the Home Secretary's unfettered power over the Metropolitan Police.

There was a deep commitment to accountability and the democratic process running through Lord Scarman's recommendations, which went well beyond the measures which were eventually adopted. On the matter of complaints against police, for example, he found the system extant in 1981, in which the police had more or less a free hand in investigating themselves, wholly unsatisfactory. He said:

> My own view is that if public confidence in the complaints procedure is to be achieved, any system falling short of a system of independent investigation available for all complaints which are not withdrawn, is unlikely to be successful.

In Scarman's view, 'a package of more limited measures' might help boost confidence but would be very much second best. That second best was what eventually emerged in the 1984 Police and Criminal Evidence (PACE) Act: a new lay Police Complaints Authority whose members could only 'supervise' investigations by police officers, rather than an independent free-standing agency with its own inquiry teams.

Scarman was scathing about the failure to consult the local community before the 'Swamp 81' anti-mugging operation which precipitated the riots at Brixton, and stated:

> Consultation and accountability are the mechanisms – in part administrative, and in part legal – upon which we rely to ensure that the police in their policies and operations keep in touch with, and are responsible to, the community they police.

Consultation, Lord Scarman said, had to be statutory, and eventually, after a voluntary liaison body had been in existence in Lambeth for two years, consultative groups became another part of the 1984 PACE Act. But Scarman did not envisage them as the sterile, often boycotted forums which eventually came to pass. He found the greatest flaw in the constitutional position of the police to be that there was no link between the distant electoral accountability of governments and consultation over the policing of communities. He went on:

> It is essential that any local machinery should not simply be a statutory talking shop but should have real powers, which I envisage might include a role in the complaints procedure, and the inspection of detention areas within police stations, and the

right to make representations to a Metropolitan Advisory Board, if, as I suggest, such a board were to be established. Any aspect of police policy should be regarded as a matter appropriate for discussion through the machinery, including operational questions.

To Sir Kenneth Newman, such measures were anathema. Above all, they would mean ceding authority over the police to Labour politicians in London's 'loony' local authorities, whom Newman frequently criticised, and whose relationship with the Metropolitan Police was extremely poor. This was the era when some councils went so far as to ban traffic bobbies from schools. Neither side found much joy in Lord Scarman's proposals. But while the left simply attacked him as a mealy-mouthed liberal, Newman was more subtle. In public, he was often to be found quoting the Scarman report with apparent approval, as in his talk to the European Atlantic Group.

Discussing the problems of public order in 'multi-ethnic' areas, Newman quoted Scarman extensively: on the risk of jeopardising tranquillity through excessive use of force, and the need to secure 'community assent'. But instead of going on to stress the need for accountability, Sir Kenneth now shifted the focus of the argument entirely, to symbolic locations.

He was, he said, in general agreement with Scarman's call for balance between crime prevention and civil tranquillity. But he went on: 'It is a strategy which raises difficult moral, legal and political problems for the police.' In symbolic locations, with their 'proprietorial' youths who regarded the police as intruders, and on the 'ethnically mixed housing estates', Newman believed that 'the police acting alone are faced with the gloomy prospect of being constantly at war with a section of the community'.

He was, he said, in favour of consultation as a way of re-ducing the heat of confrontation – although here 'the patience and restraint required from the police should not be underesti-mated'. But not for him the consultative group as a means of establishing democratic accountability. As far as Newman was concerned, the input was the other way: from police into com-munity, not from community to police. The very last thing he had in mind was giving the people of the 'rookeries' a say in police policy:

> In the circumstances of today, it is quite clear that problems of this kind cannot be handled by police alone. They must be addressed on a multi-agency basis and within the framework of a clear social policy which provides alternative options to straightforward law enforcement.
>
> It is not sufficient to think only in terms of crime control. We need to lift the problems to a higher level of generality, encompassed by the expression 'social control', in a benign sense, in order to provide a unifying concept within which the activities of police and other agencies can be co-ordinated.

That the people who needed controlling might also deserve some say in the matter does not seem to have occurred to Newman, who displayed severe disdain for his critics in multiracial areas. He reflected that police operations around symbolic locations 'will almost certainly attract the attention of the media and community activists'. Questions would be asked: had the police overreacted? Did they use oppressive numbers? Were they engaged in needless harassment? These, he said, were legitimate questions. However: 'Truthful, rational answers may not be what some people are looking for.'

Unfortunately, it was in the multi-ethnic areas particularly that 'political agitators exploit civil liberties issues, play down the issue of general communal security and make it difficult for the police to promote that feeling of security and confidence that is the precondition for economic investment'. Later he added:

> Individual liberties are important, but we must not become so obsessed by them that we overlook the importance of communal freedom and security.

Sir Kenneth believed this 'communal security' could be increased by the addition of a few 'social control' measures, including identity cards, and an obligation on everybody to inform the government of their place of residence; and government files on individuals' employment, income, education, hospital treatment and psychoanalytic treatment. This wise example, he claimed, had been adopted in Scandinavia, but such measures would not affect the core freedoms of parliamentary democracy.

Returning to the comparison between multi-ethnic communities and terrorism, he said:

> There is one thing that policing terrorism has in common with policing ethnic ghettos. Policing activities must be accompanied by social and economic measures and the policies of the police and civil administration must be co-ordinated with a coherent strategy.

In other words, in places like Broadwater Farm, the police should be consulted over issues which had little to do with law and order.

A year after Newman's retirement in 1987, an example of how far this analysis could take the police occurred around the 'symbolic location' of the All Saints Road part of Notting Hill. The then divisional Chief Superintendent, Clive Pearman, wrote to the local council leadership and lobbied the Home Office in an effort to bring about the end of grant aid to, and consequently the closure of, the district's principal campaigning black organisation, the Mangrove Centre, a persistent thorn in the side of the police. As his critics remarked at the time, in a period of weakening local government, it was as if the police were trying to fill the vacuum.

Whatever their shortcomings as a blueprint for democratic policing, Sir Kenneth's ideas were at least coherent, and as one approach to the prevention of large-scale public disorder, they were potentially effective. Aware of the dangers of starting a riot by being over-zealous, the police needed 'special techniques' for symbolic locations. One approach now being followed by the Met, which minimised the abrasive contact of stopping and searching people in the street, was based 'on a more sophisticated system of intelligence and surveillance'. This, Newman said, 'concentrates on the accurate targeting' of suspects.

Here again he was drawing on his Northern Ireland experience.

In initiating various surveillance and intelligence mechanisms, he made it clear to his colleagues that Ulster had shown him the way. At multi-ethnic symbolic locations:

> Immediate pursuit or arrest of offenders is sometimes unwise. Police officers are encouraged to note the description of the offender and arrest him (or her) later in less conspicuous circumstances; or action may be delayed until reinforcements can be called and a careful, controlled and swiftly executed operation mounted.

Emphatically, this was not a recipe for 'softly, softly' policing. Behind the velvet glove of multi-agency consultation was to be the iron fist of specialist public order squads and instant response units. No commissioner was more determined to see the police well-equipped for riot than Newman. Under his auspices, the Met became one of the first forces to have plastic bullets, and behind the scenes he waged a constant war of attrition with the Treasury and the Home Office for more resources.

Detailed 'contingency plans' were drawn up for all the symbolic locations, providing for the swift control of strategic points. The plan for Broadwater Farm was kept at Tottenham Police Station, with a copy at the radio communications control room at Wood Green where riot operations were eventually directed. It was divided into several sections, headed 'rendezvous points', 'forward control', 'fire brigade control', 'tactics' and 'deployments' on the walkways and at ground level. Detailed down to the number of units needed at each place, it was very specific as to strategy:

> It is essential that in order to contain and isolate disorder, police should quickly gain control of the walkways connecting the flats on the estate. Unless this is carried out effectively, units at ground level may be subjected to missiles thrown from above and roaming crowds could move about the estate, thus rendering police mobility in vehicles ineffective. Once the walkways have been secured, pockets of disorder may be contained and dealt with.

These were prescient words.

There was friction between police and the inhabitants of Broad-water Farm for a long time before the autumn of 1985, with an abundance of harassment allegations of the type predicted by Sir Kenneth Newman.

In 1982, Delroy Lindo took a job as a youth worker with the fledgling Broadwater Farm Youth Association. This had been formed a year earlier by Dolly Kiffin, an influential and enterprising woman on the estate, to remedy the lack of social facilities for black people, and to provide an alternative to the depressing social club. Before long it was serving meals daily to (mainly white) pensioners from a permanent base, a disused chip shop on Tangmere. Later, having attracted central and local government grants, it grew to include a child day care centre, music and cultural events, and a series of co-operative businesses: a launderette, hairdressers and greengrocers, and workshops for sewing and photography.

Delroy was not on a high salary, but he was proud of his cars, a series of old but powerful models: 'My cars were always flashy and clean.' Like most black drivers, he was stopped regularly – often, he believed, without cause – and given a 'producer', an instruction to come to the police station with insurance, MOT etc. within seven days. 'Sometimes my friends and I would get one or two these things *every week*,' he says. On one occasion, he was challenged with unusual aggression by an officer in Tottenham High Road: 'He was abusing me, calling me nigger, black bastard.' They ended up fighting in the gutter, but the inevitable charge of assaulting police was dropped before it reached the magistrates' court.

'It was a way of keeping up the pressure, the harassment, making sure we still knew our place,' Delroy says. 'It was sus when I was a teenager and on my feet: now, when I had a job, and a car, it was producers. As far as I was concerned, it typified the attitude of the police to people from Broadwater Farm and black people in general.'

Lord Gifford's inquiry reported a lengthy history of mutual hostility between Tottenham's black community and the police. In 1975, a black sixth-form student was charged with assaulting police, but at his trial many witnesses gave evidence that the police had beaten him up. According to Gifford:

> Witness after witness to our inquiry spoke of the indignities which they have suffered at the hands of police officers for no other reason than that they are black.

Lord Gifford was well known as a socialist lawyer, and Newman forbade police participation in the inquiry, although at least two very senior officers, one of them a possible future commissioner, did talk to him in private. But it is worth quoting the response to the publication of the report in 1986 by Alan Stainsby, then the Tottenham Divisional Chief Superintendent. Racism was being eradicated from the police, he said. But he added: 'I view the report as a valuable contribution to police/community relations in Tottenham.' He ordered fifty copies for his officers to study.

In 1981, there were two violent confrontations between youths and police. At Easter, trouble broke out at a funfair in Finsbury Park, in which a police commander suffered a broken nose. Then in July, as Toxteth, Moss Side and other inner-city ghettos erupted in riot, Tottenham saw its own disturbances at the Wood Green shopping centre, with eight policemen injured and fifty-nine shops damaged or looted. There was a smaller recurrence in 1983.

At Broadwater Farm, there were further violent challenges to police authority. It would be foolish to claim that these actions had nothing to do with wider criminal activity, or that they were solely a response to heavy-handed policing. But if those who initiated attacks on the police may have been motivated by the basest kind of self-interest, the blanket criminalisation of other young black residents ensured they were supported, not reviled.

In August 1982, a beat officer on the Farm was hit with a bottle while on patrol. The following November, Roger Scott, Stafford's younger brother, was arrested in Tangmere by police who claimed he had burgled the social club. According to Lord Gifford's report, 'there were dozens of other youths present who had been watching a film with Roger and knew he could not have done it.' In any event, a large picket swiftly gathered outside the police station. A unit of riot police waded into the demonstration and, among others injured, Clasford Sterling, co-founder of the

Youth Association, sustained a broken nose. Four people were charged with obstruction as a result of the picket, but Roger Scott was released the same evening without charge.

Next day, someone dropped two steel beer kegs on a police car from one of the Farm walkways. Miraculously, no one was hurt. The same day, a home beat officer was beaten about the head with a billiard cue when he answered a call inside the Manston block. Police in riot gear came on to the estate in force and stayed for two days. Here was the Newman doctrine being scrupulously observed: a 'careful, controlled and swiftly executed operation' to prevent further disorder.

From this time on, the Farm was policed by a special team of eight beat officers. There were also regular surveillance teams who did not always operate with maximum discretion. Once, Millard Scott, his suspicions aroused by strange glinting reflections from an empty flat window, trained a pair of binoculars on the premises to find a police officer looking back, also armed with binoculars.

The worst incident took place in August 1983. Youths gathered at the scene of an arrest and fighting broke out, in which PC Graham Betts was stabbed and seriously wounded.

Few police officers will have read Sir Kenneth Newman's thoughts about symbolic locations in any detail, although the use of the phrase in relation to Broadwater Farm in his annual report cannot have passed unnoticed. But just as they stood him in good stead with Mrs Thatcher's government, so they fitted comfortably with the gut reactions of many PCs and senior officers when dealing with Broadwater Farm. Until 1985, the commander in charge of the district which included Tottenham Division was Jim Dickinson, whose reputation was of an old-fashioned hardliner. In 1983, he was interviewed for the Channel 4 Afro-Caribbean programme *Black on Black*. He was asked whether the reduction in the crime rate for Broadwater Farm that year was due solely to the higher level of policing, or whether – as the youths claimed – it might have something to do with self-help projects of the Youth Association. He replied contemptuously: 'Well, if they claim that, very good . . . but it only proves they were responsible for it in the first place.'

After the riot, another Channel 4 programme, *Diverse Reports*, also carried interviews with policemen who expressed very low opinions of the Farm and its inhabitants, albeit that by this time a policeman had been hacked to death there. Inspector David Hudson said that the Youth Association members 'identify strongly with the black criminal and the white criminal elements that come on to the estate', many of whom used Broadwater Farm to deal in drugs because they knew they could rely on this source of local support. The estate was a 'safe haven' for pushers, he said.

PC Mark Greaves said the people of the estate were terrified to go outside, but the police had turned their backs on them while they were 'mobbed, burgled and sexually assaulted'.

The Gifford inquiry quoted some cruder examples of police officers' views of the estate. White witnesses recalled racist remarks by officers called out to burglaries: 'Oh, so you've had some coons breaking in, have you'; 'If we could have gone into the Youth Association we might have found the person who did this.'

It is a curious fact that reported crime on Broadwater Farm actually fell substantially in the years before the riot: a total of 266 offences in the six months June–November 1982, rising to 418 for the equivalent period in 1983, before easing to 173 in 1984 and 161 in 1985. The harsh comments of the police might have seemed more justified if there had been evidence to show that a disproportionate number of offences committed elsewhere were the work of residents of Broadwater Farm. It ought to be possible to collate this information from addresses given in police charge sheets. Unfortunately, this has never been done.

The extent of the gulf between the estate and the police received statistical confirmation in the form of an opinion poll of the Farm's residents for the Gifford inquiry, carried out by the highly respected Middlesex Polytechnic Centre for Criminology. This took place after the riot, which hardened attitudes on both sides. But as a picture of perceptions, the results were striking.

Asked whether the police sometimes, often or very often used unnecessary force, fabricated statements or used violence at police stations, nearly twice as many replied in the affirmative as in London as a whole: about 65 per cent to 38. On the estate, 60 per cent claimed to have suffered personally or to have witnessed police malpractice, five times the London average.

This, then, was the reality of Sir Kenneth's symbolic location: a place where residents harboured bitter grievances against the police, who returned them in kind, and where a number of violent clashes had already taken place.

Newman's formula was a self-fulfilling prophecy. As the sus law could criminalise an individual, so to treat a whole estate as a rookery, a symbolic location, risked bringing just that about. Each new confrontation and each 'reprisal' by the youths added another twist to the vicious spiral. As 1985 dawned, there was an urgent need for retreat from the brink.

3

Riots and Rumours of Riot

In June 1984, a new man took charge of Tottenham's police: Chief Superintendent Colin Couch. It was clearly a troubled posting – Couch was the third divisional chief in seven months.

Born and raised in north London, he had the look of a high flyer. He did not, unlike an increasing number of police officers, have a degree, but he was an alumnus of the special course at the police staff college at Bramshill. Entry to this highly competitive institution explicitly marked out young officers as the chief constables of the future. Couch had served as a community liaison officer in Camden, an area which, like Tottenham, had both a multiracial population and a trenchant Labour council. Interviewed in 1992, he put himself firmly on the democratic side of the democratic/authoritarian divide: 'You have to police by consent. That is the only way we are going to remain one of the few unarmed forces in the world.'

Like other disciplined services, the preferred public face of the Metropolitan Police is of unity, obedience, of agreement with shared and understood objectives. The reality is that it seethes with dissent, debate, and the jostling of competing factions. The policy priorities of the man at the centre may be ignored, or misapplied, or simply never get through.

Colin Couch did not fully share Newman's outlook on the inner city. In the mid-1980s, the conclusions of the Scarman report were popularised under the term 'community policing'. Couch says he was determined to follow its precepts: 'When I arrived in Tottenham, there was no community policing, and I tried to put that right. Community policing doesn't mean you do exactly what people want. But you should try to find out what they do want, and try to achieve those goals within the context of effective policing.'

Within weeks, Couch reorganised his officers. Previously, there had been only six home beat officers for the whole division. The rest of its complement of 179 were rostered on three rotating 'reliefs', or shifts, and so had no firm links to any particular area or group of streets. Couch took twenty-eight away from the reliefs and made them 'community cops', each with a beat for which they bore responsibility. The eight officers dedicated to the Farm remained.

Throughout London, among the older, sometimes cynical ranks of PCs and sergeants represented by the Police Federation, community policing was not well-regarded. Frequently the term was taken as a euphemism for 'soft policing', in which certain 'no-go areas' were sanctioned as the price of avoiding disorder. Their attitude was expressed in a phrase that became something of a slogan: 'Police duty is not negotiable.'

After the riot, Couch was to become the target for sustained and bitter criticism from officers who blamed him for PC Blakelock's death, and for having failed to take firm action to nip the incipient disturbances in the bud. Today, with hindsight, he admits that he should have made more strenuous efforts to carry his junior staff along with his way of thinking: 'I should have spent more time explaining it to the ground floor.' Nevertheless, he says, 'I never expected to get one hundred per cent support. When I left, the Federation rep told me I'd got seventy per cent. Other than the 5 and 6 of October 1985, my two years in Tottenham were the happiest of my career.'

Six months after taking over, Couch seemed to have scored a number of successes. From nothing, the number of neighbourhood watch schemes had grown to more than a hundred. He had developed personal contacts with various so-called 'community leaders', prominent Jews, Cypriots and Afro-Caribbeans.

However, the black leaders cultivated by Couch were generally of the older generation: Hyacinth Moody, chair of the Community Relations Council police liaison committee, and members of the Tottenham West Indian Centre. Inevitably, perhaps, his main contact on Broadwater Farm was Dolly Kiffin, founder of the Youth Association.

More formal consultative arrangements were running into the sand. There was no voluntary, pre-PACE Act consultative group in Haringey, but in 1983, Haringey's Labour council set up a police committee to monitor police activity in the borough. It was bitterly resented by the district commander, Jim Dickinson, who refused to attend the committee, saying 'my constitutional position . . . debars me from involvement in these schemes'.

In January 1985, the new council leader, Bernie Grant, asked the police to attend meetings of a forum called the Broadwater Farm Panel, which met regularly under his chairmanship to air the problems of the estate. Couch and his energetic community liaison officer, Superintendent Dick Stacey, who was well-known and respected on the Farm, saw this as an excellent opportunity. Among Grant's requests was that the police should present a written report to panel meetings. In Brixton, Commander Marnoch had been doing just that at meetings of the consultative group, finding this by far the easiest way to order its business.

The request for reports was vetoed by Commander Dickinson, and Couch was obliged to reject the council's invitation. His letter to Grant stated: 'I and my officers attend numerous meetings to respond to community issues and demands, and never has a request been made for a written report. If we did, I and my staff would be permanently preparing reports instead of combating the crime rate, racial harassment and the problems of minority groups.'

In April, Grant suggested 'talks about talks', and wrote asking Couch to meet himself, leaders of the Youth and Tenants' Associations, and council officers from the police unit and the Farm. Again Couch declined, saying: 'I would like to know what you require of the police before I meet what appears to me to be a vetting group.' If Couch was inspired by the Scarman report, this was not the way to implement it. Not for another year did Tottenham's divisional chief, by then Alan Stainsby, attend the Broadwater Farm Panel.

At the same time as this sad exchange, Commander Dickinson contacted the council about setting up a consultative group as now required under the PACE Act. There were, as we have seen, very narrow limits set by the legislation on these statutory groups, which were left without powers, the 'talking shops' which Scarman had expressly warned against. But talking was better than no contact at all. Narendra Makanji, chair of the police committee, told Dickinson that his committee already provided an 'appropriate basis' for consultation. Understandably, the commander gave him short shrift: 'I am not able to discuss consultative arrangements on this basis further.'

Sir Kenneth Newman's nickname in the Metropolitan Police was 'ET', a tag that derived from his prominent ears and general resemblance to Hollywood's favourite alien. Whatever one thinks of his thoughts on inner cities, there are times when any critic has to pause and admire his ET-like powers of extrasensory perception. In April 1985, all was quiet on Broadwater Farm, and at the other symbolic locations. But in his office high above the traffic, Sir Kenneth called a meeting. For the first time since 1981, he was seriously worried by the prospects for violent disorder.

He may have been concerned by the continuing high rate of unemployment in the inner cities, at a time when the economy as a whole was beginning its leap from the Geoffrey Howe recession to the yuppy boom of the late eighties – on the Farm, half the heads of household were without work. London's crime rate, meanwhile, was still rising steeply. Whatever his reasoning, he called together a group of senior officers with experience in public order work and asked them to review the existing arrangements and produce recommendations.

The group consisted of Bob Innis, a DAC (deputy assistant commissioner) in charge of operations; David Polkinghorne, commander of Q district in west London, which included the troubled Chalkhill and Stonebridge Park estates; Larry Roach, the community liaison commander at Scotland Yard; Commander Alec Marnoch, from Brixton; and Ken Masterson, an ex-RUC man who was now a training commander. They met seven or eight times through 1985's damp summer and long, hot autumn.

No copies of their eventual report appear to have survived. Among their main conclusions was that if rioting ever broke out on an estate, the police would be in grave difficulty. Faced with an increase in 'tension indicators', they added, the answer would be to take firm action at once: to increase the number of patrols with 'ongoing intensive coverage'. At the same time, contacts with tenants' bodies should be stepped up, and contingency plans for disorder laid down and rehearsed.

The vast size of the Met, with more than 28,000 officers and 17,000 civil staff, has always made the implementation of policy somewhat haphazard, leaving aside the question of internal dissent. Working against Sir Kenneth and his public order specialists was a considerable inertia. Its results were to be disastrous.

From May 1985 on, police faced a deteriorating situation at Broadwater Farm, with a dangerous escalation in the frequency of violent incidents. They could have dealt with it in three ways: through the pre-emptive use of force; with effective consultation; or as the committee of public order men suggested, with a combination of the two. In the end they did nothing.

Complicating the picture was Sir Kenneth's enduring legacy to the Metropolitan Police, the most radical reorganisation in its history. The old districts, borough-sized layers between the divisions and the four huge areas, were abolished altogether, and with them the jobs of the commanders who used to control them. The areas were split into two, requiring the creation of four new headquarters. At the same time, all the central departments at Scotland Yard went through an equally convoluted process of merger, demerger and redefinition.

It did not take place overnight. There was an official 'block change' day in March, and then on 23 September the new areas supposedly came into being. In fact, throughout 1985 and into the following year, the whole of the Metropolitan Police was in a state of flux, and the new structures did not fully replace the old until well into 1986. The purpose of the reforms had been to create clearer lines of command. For the time being, while the changes went through bewildering intermediate stages, the opposite was true.

Some officers with long service felt there was no place for them in the new set-up. Like Commander Jim Dickinson, who departed the Haringey district in May 1985, they resigned. 'Love him or loathe him, he had experience, and you knew where you were with him,' said one senior colleague. His replacement, while the district tier eked out the last months of its existence, was not another fully-fledged commander, or indeed a uniformed man at all, but a detective chief superintendent 'acting up', Ted Hodge. A career CID man, he cannot be blamed for the negligible extent of his experience of public order policing and the inner city. The same applied to Mike Richards, late of the Anti-terrorist Squad, the Deputy Assistant Commissioner at the helm of the new north London 'one area'.

Despite the efforts of Colin Couch, by the spring of 1985, there had been no real improvement in the relationship between the police and the youth of Broadwater Farm. Delroy Lindo says: 'It was essentially broken. They used to come in van loads, often early in the morning, just to make a simple arrest.' On one occasion in March, three vans of public order specialists, known as district support units, came on to the Farm for no apparent reason, spreading out in what the Gifford inquiry described as a show of force. Later, Superintendent Stacey, the community liaison officer, apologised, saying they had been at a Tottenham Hotspur football match where their presence had been unnecessary.

It appeared that in part owing to the old district structure, Couch's control over events was limited. Delroy says: 'There would be meetings between Miss Dolly and senior officers, and we'd be promised that everything was going to be cool. Then next day they'd be back to their nonsense, showing aggression. The senior officers promised they would tone it down, work together. But the bobbies on the street had their own ideas, and they didn't seem to be being monitored.'

Despite the underlying tension, there were no major incidents after the stabbing of the PC in 1983 until May 1985. But from then onwards, when a youth was 'liberated' on the Farm from the police who had come to arrest him, they began to come thick and fast.

In June, there was a large picket of Tottenham Police Station following another arrest, and the circulation of a rumour that the prisoner had been beaten up. On this occasion, Dolly Kiffin was allowed to see the youth and was able to reassure people that he had not been injured, whereupon the crowd dispersed.

On 13 July, Kiffin, together with Stafford Scott, Clasford Sterling and the entire leadership of the Youth Association, went to Jamaica. The purpose of the trip was somewhat vague, but it included liaison and community work with the youth association of a place in Kingston called West Park. Accompanying them was Roy Limb, the council chief executive, who had become a useful intermediary between the police and youth on the Farm. Kiffin was to stay away until late September, the rest returning at the end of August.

To adopt, for a moment, the language of Sir Kenneth Newman, there is no doubt that the trip removed an important source of 'social control' on the Farm. On the one hand, it gave rise to some envy on the part of those who were left behind, whose confidence fell in the people who had come to represent them. At the same time, while even Dolly Kiffin's friends would concede that she could be a difficult, demanding woman, her influence was undeniably immense. She had the power to declare certain activities, such as the sale of hard drugs, as 'off limits' on Broadwater Farm, and to see that her instructions were carried out.

Her absence, together with that of Roy Limb and Kiffin's subordinates, left the police in a quandary. With no formal consultative mechanisms in place, such contact as they had with the black community had relied on personal relationships alone. But now, Couch later complained in a *World in Action* programme, 'I had no one to talk to.'

The risks of relying too heavily on 'community leaders' had been exposed. As a *Guardian* leading article stated after all the 1985 riots, when there had been endless media comment about such individuals, the phrase always had a certain patronising sterility. 'What is your community, who is your leader?' the paper asked its readers.

Dolly Kiffin's departure saw several ominous developments. Increasing numbers of youths who did not live on the Farm began to use the Youth Association, apparently because of the cheap West Indian food available there at lunchtime. At the same time, the pushers moved in. Broadwater Farm became an open-air drugs market. And the hostile confrontations with the police began to mount.

On the very day after the departure of the junket to Jamaica, there was another mêlée around an arrest. According to the *Public Order Review*, a police internal study of the 1985 riots at Brixton and Tottenham and their backgrounds, 'officers were surrounded by an extremely hostile crowd of black people. Abuse and racial insults were directed in the main at one of the constables, who is himself black.' Three days later, on 17 July, police chasing a stolen car were attacked by youths with milk bottles: 'The situation was judged so serious that all police were withdrawn from the estate, until the area quietened down.'

In the next ten weeks, there were another ten incidents, ranging from the trivial, the shouting of abuse, to the hurling of bottles. On 4 and 5 September, there were attempts to attack the Post Office van, and next day missiles were thrown at firemen. On 7 September, a council team trying to remove abandoned cars came under fire.

On 9 September, another factor was added to the increasingly febrile atmosphere: the destructive and bloody riot in Lozells Road, in the Handsworth area of Birmingham.

I arrived there within a couple of hours of its outbreak. None of the other mainland disorders of 1981 or 1985 came close in terms of environmental devastation to the mayhem wrought that night. Early in the proceedings, the police lost all effective control and were forced to withdraw. By 10 pm, huge fires raged unchecked along the entire length of what had been a major shopping street. Next day, it resembled the worst scenes from Beirut. Nearly £40 million of property had gone up in smoke, much of it small businesses owned by Asians operating at the very margins of profitability. Two men had died horribly, choked and burnt in the blazing shell of their Post Office.

Nor, as the TV news showed vividly, did the West Midlands police restore effective order next day. The Home Secretary, Douglas Hurd, and Chief Constable Geoffrey Dear were almost lynched when an ill-conceived publicity stunt went very badly wrong. The idea had been for Hurd and Dear to meet a few sample families and ask them their concerns. They arrived in two Daimlers, each sporting full-beam headlights in broad daylight, and travelled the length of the ruined high street through an angry mob at least a thousand strong. Their protection, when they disembarked, was minimal, and within a few minutes the thin cordon of police caved in completely, exposing the chief constable and the secretary of state to a hail of missiles. They were saved only by the quick thinking of a police van driver, who reversed at high speed from round a corner and rescued them in the nick of time.

Handsworth had a considerable impact on the youth of Broadwater Farm. The day after Hurd's misadventure, two policemen were cornered on the fourth floor of Tangmere block by a group of youths. The *Public Order Review* claimed that one of the youths threatened: 'If you start to touch that radio, you're dead.' The officers fled down the stairs, to shouts of 'Birmingham, Handsworth, riot.' They were subjected to a barrage of bottles and bricks, and both were seriously injured.

After the riot, Couch was to be pilloried for his alleged lack of action to deal with the apparently mounting crisis. A 'diary' kept by the Broadwater Farm officers – in fact, no more than an informal message book – was published in *Police*, the Federation magazine. It described the incidents later detailed in the *Public Order Review*, giving a vivid flavour of the fear the Farm beat officers felt: 'Very tense atmosphere when patrolling tonight. BE CAREFUL OUT THERE!!' The day after the riot, one of the officers wrote: 'IT HAPPENED! SURPRISE, SURPRISE!'

A few weeks later, a bitter memorandum by the Farm police team leader, Sergeant Gillian Meynell, was leaked to the *Daily Mail*. A briefing paper intended for her Police Federation representatives only, it was harshly critical of Couch, claiming that his devotion to community policing had led him to ignore the rising 'tension indicators'. On one occasion, she claimed, her officers collected fifty drugs packets, but still nothing was done.

The lack of action was later to be criticised at Scotland Yard, in a still-secret report on the riot by David Williams, a former Tottenham chief superintendent. South of the river in Brixton, Commander Marnoch also noticed an increase in tension. After discussions with his consultative group, he doubled the number of foot patrols. Interviewed in 1992, he was unequivocal that the same thing should have been done in Tottenham.

In fact, Colin Couch shared his view. At the end of August, before Handsworth, he submitted a brief memorandum to acting Commander Hodge, asking for resources to increase the foot patrol complement on the Farm from eight to twenty-two, with the back-up of district support units if necessary. His request, the Williams report confirmed, merely gathered dust. 'With hindsight, I made a mistake at that point. I should have gone to the next man up, to DAC Richards,' he says. His request for reinforcements has never been disclosed in public, while he took the flak in silence. But he fully shared Sergeant Meynell's concern about the estate, and was filled with foreboding. Without reinforcements, he says, 'I was left hoping it would rain: it needed something to break the chain of events. I also realised that if anything happened, I would get the blame.'

Riots rarely start in a downpour. On 6 October there was some drizzle, but the heavens did not open until late in the evening, by which time Keith Blakelock was already dead.

Dolly Kiffin returned from Jamaica on 23 September. She told the Gifford inquiry that she was immediately struck by the multitude of strangers on the estate. Within hours of her return, she was called to a meeting by Superintendent Stacey. Her impression, supported by Neale Coleman, the senior council officer for the estate, was that the police were 'waiting for her to call them in'. Citing the risk she might run in asking for action against drug pushers who might well be armed and dangerous, she declined.

Five days later there was another riot, in Brixton, triggered by the shooting in bed of a black woman, Cherry Groce, by a police inspector looking for her son. The rioters were armed with petrol bombs, sledgehammers, and knives. During the evening a photographer was killed by a breeze block dropped on to his head, and one group of rioters committed a terrible gang rape. But by comparison with the later events in Tottenham, Brixton '85 was a small, self-contained riot, in which police dispersal tactics limited the scale of both damage and injury. Estates where the police might have faced a pitched battle on unfavourable terms were sealed off. Small squads of riot police harried the participants ceaselessly, preventing them from concentrating anywhere where they might confront police in numbers.

Commander Marnoch helped to reduce the scale of the violence with an immediate announcement − for which he took full responsibility − that the officer who shot Mrs Groce would be suspended, pending an inquiry by the new Police Complaints Authority. Afterwards, the value of his democratic approach to policing in the preceding months paid dividends. Not only had Marnoch met the 'community leaders' and council through Lambeth's experimental consultative group, he had made a point of walking at least once a week with Brixton's chief superintendent, Tony Speed, down the 'front line' of Railton Road, one of Commissioner Newman's symbolic locations. 'It was important to show the ground floor it could be done,' he says, 'so giving our approach credibility. We were making ourselves available to people, and were ready to take the flak if it came.' The *Public Order Review* commented:

> The situation was brought under control in a relatively short time . . . the Lambeth community/police consultative group and the law-abiding public of Brixton played a major part in restoring normality. Lay visitors were offered access to the several charge centres where prisoners were being held and their favourable comments on the disciplined and orderly nature of the police arrangements for handling prisoners were helpful . . . the speedy restoration of normality in Brixton is tangible evidence of the value of this approach.

Calm as things were in Brixton in the aftermath of its riot, the same cannot be said for other parts of the region covered by the Metropolitan Police. In every area with a large black community, rumour was rife. Responding to one such story, the police became convinced a riot had been 'planned' for the Pepys estate in Bermondsey. Like Broadwater Farm, it had overhead walkways linking the blocks, and the police had a contingency plan for occupying them. It was put into operation from about 9 pm on 1 October: police in riot uniform sealed off the estate to all but those who had proof of their residence there. The dog did not bark: there was no riot in Bermondsey.

Similar rumours were sweeping Tottenham, where the confusions inherent in the chain of command and the differing approaches of senior officers were creating an apparently erratic response. On 1 October, there was a 'day of action' on the Farm, with cars being stopped entering and leaving. This operation, a far cry from 'targeting and surveillance', did not appear to have any obvious purpose, save to add to the grievances of both the youth and Sergeant Meynell's home beat team, who thought 'firm policing' had come to an end as soon as it had got underway.

It is a cliché of military history that generals making preparations for future hostilities always plan to fight the last war. A classic example was the building in the 1930s of the French Maginot Line, impregnable fixed defences undertaken in the belief that a future conflict with Germany would be fought mainly by infantry in trenches. When Hitler's highly mobile, mechanised *Blitzkrieg* arrived in 1940, it simply went round the Maginot Line.

In similar fashion, senior police officers were convinced by the example of the disturbances in the Wood Green shopping centre of 1981 and 1983 that any rioting in Tottenham would be there, not at Broadwater Farm. By the middle of the week, DAC Richards had decided to open the radio communications room at Wood Green on Saturday, 5 October, in case of trouble, and to have riot units standing by.

On 2 October, the day after the car search operation, a petrol bomb was found on the Farm. In her memorandum, Sergeant Meynell described meeting Couch, warning him that there was a risk of serious disorder on the estate. He confirms that he disregarded this possibility: 'I never thought they would dirty their own home. She thought they would.'

But while she claimed she was sure there would be a riot on the Farm the following weekend, her real evidence was slim. As the Gifford report commented, there had been rumours of riot in Tottenham every year since 1981. In the normal course of events, the hostility between the youth and the police could have been expected to persist: a hoax call claiming officers were under attack on 3 October was just another event in the depressingly familiar pattern. As in Brixton, without a 'trigger event' there would probably have been no riot.

One was not long in coming.

4

The Wheel Comes Off

If Detective Constable Michael Randall had not turned up for work on his day off, perhaps there would have been no disturbances at Broadwater Farm. It was his decision to search the home of Cynthia Jarrett, and it was he, according to the verdict at her inquest, who accidentally pushed against her, causing her to fall to the ground. It was Randall who vainly attempted mouth-to-mouth resuscitation after her sudden collapse. Her death turned the situation from crisis to emergency. It was the trigger for the Tottenham riot.

Randall, twenty-four, a recent arrival at the Tottenham CID, went to the police station on Saturday, 5 October, at about 4 pm to tidy up some paperwork. On at least one previous occasion, the enthusiasm he displayed for his job had got him into trouble. In the summer of 1985, a black family had complained about his conduct of a search of their home, and while not formally disciplined, he had been given strong words of advice by a senior officer.

While Randall was at the station, he learnt that his uniformed colleagues were holding Mrs Jarrett's son Floyd in the cells. He went to investigate.

Floyd Jarrett had moved away a few miles up the Great Cambridge Road to Enfield, but he was still well known in Tottenham and on Broadwater Farm, where for years he had been a stalwart of the Youth Association. His arrest, at around one o'clock in

Tottenham's Rosebery Avenue, was reminiscent of all too many encounters between young black people and the police.

PC Christopher Casey noticed that the tax disc on Floyd's ancient BMW had expired at the end of August, and gave him a 'producer'. He also ran a check on the car using his radio with the police national computer. The vehicle was not recorded as stolen, but there was one letter on the number plate different from that on the tax disc – UGX50F, as against WGX50F. On that flimsy basis, Casey announced that Floyd was under arrest on suspicion of stealing the car. Unwisely, Floyd started to run across the road. Casey and two other officers caught him, and there was a short struggle.

Floyd was charged with assaulting the police. At his trial at Tottenham Magistrates' Court two months later, Casey claimed Floyd punched him in the face. An architect called Ralph Harris told the court he saw the three officers seize Floyd from behind, and that he saw no punches. Floyd was acquitted, with the magistrates indicating their displeasure by awarding costs of £350 against the police.

At the police station, Floyd gave a false name, but by the time DC Randall arrived, his true identity was known, as was the fact that the car had not been stolen. He should have been released. But about fifty minutes after getting to the police station, Randall decided to search his family's house. He claimed later he had reason to believe Floyd was dealing in stolen goods. The basis for this intelligence remains obscure. Nothing, in any event, was ever found.

As the search party – consisting of Randall, PC Casey and two other officers – left, the duty officer, Inspector Clarke, told them he hoped they 'would not cause any riots'. Randall asked the station radio controller to keep an open channel in case he needed support.

Puzzling discrepancies emerged later over the timing of the search and the obtaining of a warrant. In the first of two statements, the magistrate who issued the warrant said he did so between 6 and 6.30 pm – by which time Mrs Jarrett was dead. Later, he changed his mind, saying in a second version that the police came to his house for the warrant, a drive of slightly more than a mile from the Jarrett home, between 5.30 and 6.15. There were other, less striking, discrepancies in the accounts given of the timing of events by different police officers.

It is easy to be imprecise over the exact timing of events that did not seem particularly important at the time, and the issue of the warrant has never been conclusively resolved. What is certain, however, is that the officers failed to show it to the Jarretts.

The family lived in Thorpe Road, not far from Broadwater Farm. The police turned up at 5.45 pm, carrying Floyd Jarrett's keys. They made no attempt to knock on the door or ring the bell, but let themselves in. They had not told the station custody sergeant they had taken the keys; this, he confirmed at the inquest, was contrary to the correct procedure. Inside the house were Cynthia, her daughter Patricia, and two babies, watching television. Mrs Jarrett heard a noise and went into the passage. Her daughter heard her exclaim: 'Oh Lord, oh Lord, there are some police in the house.' The officers' response to Patricia's appearance was to lie, claiming they had found the front door open. At the inquest, they said they did so 'in order not to aggravate the situation'.

DC Randall and his colleagues told the inquest that Patricia had been abusive and aggressive from the time of their arrival, and suggested that the stress to her mother was caused not by the fact that her house was being searched, or that she was pushed over, but by Patricia's 'anti-police attitude'. A radio call from Randall to Inspector Clarke back in the police station at 5.55 casts doubt on these claims: he said there were 'no problems', giving Clarke the confidence to stand down the officers waiting in reserve.

Later, both Randall and another officer, PC Allan, said in evidence that Patricia failed to telephone an ambulance. According to Randall, she had dialled 999 but then slammed the receiver down and continued swearing at the police. These statements were contradicted by the timed logs of the emergency services switchboard. The coroner described them as 'contrary to the facts'. After hearing PC Allan's evidence, he told the jury that the matter went directly 'to the credit of the police officers . . . it is important for you to be able to assess the truthfulness of the witness.'

The police denied Cynthia Jarrett had been pushed at all. But Patricia said Randall entered the dining room, where her mother was putting one of the babies into an armchair. He shouldered her aside, and she fell to the ground. He ignored Mrs Jarrett and carried on with his search: 'Randall came back past us and saw me assisting my mother off the floor, and went to the sideboard. He was looking through the sideboard while Mother was gasping for breath. I helped Mother up into the chair. She was gasping for breath and breathing heavily. She said "I don't feel well," she said I should phone for an emergency doctor.'

After calling the ambulance, Patricia said, she sat cradling her mother's head in her arms, 'talking to her, trying to get her to tell me what was the matter. The police did not offer to help.'

Michael, her brother, arrived home at this point, and ordered the police to leave. There was an eleven-minute delay before the ambulance appeared, and after telling the family that he had first-aid qualifications, DC Randall was re-admitted, to attempt the kiss of life. Cynthia Jarrett was carried into the ambulance at 6.20 pm, but was dead on arrival at the North Middlesex Hospital.

The inquest heard medical evidence from Dr Walter Somerville that Mrs Jarrett had a heart condition so severe that she probably had only months to live. But he added that a fall by a woman with a condition of this kind might well have been an 'additional precipitating factor' in her demise. The shock of seeing the police in her house had probably started the train of events in which her heart went from being 'an organ doing its duty to one fading rapidly towards the last few minutes of her life'.

The coroner spelt out to the jury what a verdict of accidental death would mean: that Mrs Jarrett had been pushed, but they could not be sure this was a deliberate act. If they believed the police claim that she collapsed spontaneously, they should return a verdict of death by natural causes. Unanimously, the jurors opted for accidental death. Four months later, the Essex police completed an inquiry into the incident supervised by the new Police Complaints Authority. Like all PCA investigations, its full report was secret, but there were no disciplinary or criminal charges against any of the officers involved in the search at Thorpe Road.

Colin Couch was ill with flu on 5 October, and knew nothing of the death of Mrs Jarrett until he heard it on the eight o'clock news next morning. He was not slow to recognise its implications. Prising himself from his sickbed, he went to the police station, to find DAC Richards already there with Commander David Polkinghorne, a member of Sir Kenneth Newman's summer public order group, who was due soon to be transferred to the north London 'one area' headquarters. They told Couch that for the rest of the day, there would be substantial reserves of police in riot gear available at Wood Green.

Already, during the night, the first signs of trouble had been manifest. At 1.30 am, the Jarrett family had gone with friends to Tottenham Police Station for a meeting with Chief Superintendent Stainsby, who had come to Tottenham from his post at Edmonton in Couch's absence. They had been given only a copy of the warrant used in the search and demanded, unsuccessfully, to see the original. As their discussions were in progress, missiles were hurled at the police station, breaking four windows. It took all the persuasive efforts of the Jarretts and some of the older 'community leaders' to disperse the gathering crowd.

Given the feverish background, it is questionable whether confrontation could by this stage have been avoided. But as the day wore on, events drifted further and further out of control, acquiring a momentum of their own.

Characteristically, Couch at once organised a meeting of his community contacts, including the council's chief executive Roy Limb, Jeff Crawford, senior worker at the Community Relations Council, Hyacinth Moody and Dolly Kiffin. At her insistence, Floyd and Michael Jarrett were also in attendance. It began at 12.45, chaired by DAC Richards. In response to demands to suspend DC Randall and the other officers involved in the Jarrett search, he would give no ground, saying only that the matter was now in the hands of the Police Complaints Authority. It would, in fact, have been well within his powers to announce a suspension, pending the inquiry. He was asked about his decision more than a year later, as he gave evidence to the murder trial, and said only: 'We do not suspend police officers in order to appease the public.' The community elders left with nothing to offer those with more militant opinions.

As the meeting broke up, a crowd was gathering outside the police station. The initial reaction of the officer in charge outside the building was to use the riot reserves to disperse it, but

Crawford, soon endorsed by Couch, persuaded him to allow the demonstration to proceed. For nearly an hour, a thin line of officers in ordinary uniforms stood unflinchingly, absorbing vehement abuse. 'I thought if I let them vent their spleen, it would help,' says Couch. 'When they moved off peacefully I thought we had won.' He went back to his office with Hyacinth Moody, joined for a time by Crawford, giving orders that no officers were to go on to the Farm without an inspector reviewing the position. The two duty members of the home beat stayed on the estate's periphery.

Already, the lines of command and control were becoming blurred. Couch confirms that he was unaware of what was happening a mile away in the radio control room at Wood Green, and was unsure of both the current deployment of riot units and the number available. At Wood Green, fresh information about the evolving situation, local knowledge and experience all seem to have been in short supply.

At 3.15, just before the demonstration outside Tottenham Police Station came to an end, the two Farm beat PCs were called to an address in The Avenue, which runs outside the south side of Broadwater Farm. A crowd of youths gathered, and as the police left the house, they were bombarded with bricks and pieces of broken paving stone. Roger Caton was pulled to the ground and held face down while his attackers hurled a rock at his back. When they ran off, he crawled in agony to the main road, seeking help. His spleen was ruptured and bleeding profusely into his abdomen.

In the view of later assessments at Scotland Yard, crucial mistakes were already being made. The secret report by David Williams (now Surrey's chief constable) concluded that far from withdrawing to the periphery, before the Avenue attack the police should have gone on to the estate in numbers, mounting visible foot patrols, with riot back-up if necessary. And if there was a time to try to implement the contingency plan, to take the kind of swift and decisive action recommended by Sir Kenneth Newman, it would have been after this first attack.

The lack of action was the cause of later outrage among the lower ranks of the Metropolitan Police, where it was seen as the defeatist continuation of 'community policing'. Many PCs and sergeants said they had been convinced there would be rioting from the mid-afternoon onwards, and at Broadwater Farm, not the Wood Green shopping centre. Astonishingly, the Wood Green control room, where DAC Richards and Commander Polkinghorne were now in command, remained unaware of the incident in The Avenue. For at least two hours, there were no emergency calls, and at 4 pm, a two-hour changeover period began between the first and second shifts of riot officers waiting in reserve. The first shift of more than two hundred constables – who once the riot began in earnest were to be swiftly recalled – was sent home.

Meanwhile, two meetings were in progress: at the Tottenham West Indian Centre, and at the Youth Association on Broadwater Farm. The first was attended mainly by older people, including most of the 'community leaders': Bernie Grant, Dolly Kiffin, Roy Limb, and key figures from the West Indian Leadership Council and other organisations. The mood was bitter, with sharp calls made for the suspension of Randall and his colleagues, and the resignation of DAC Richards. But many of those present realised that in this volatile and perilous situation, it was no use passing resolutions, no matter how heartfelt, and at about 5.30 most headed for Broadwater Farm.

Many of those who had demonstrated at the police station had gone back to the Farm and gathered at the Youth Association where they continued to vent their feelings until the arrival of the West Indian Centre contingent. Even then, the proceedings remained confused. Some called for the physical avenging of Mrs Jarrett's death – at the murder trial, Roy Limb stated he had heard demands for 'an eye for an eye, a tooth for a tooth'. The mood was ugly. Bernie Grant was shouted down. He told the Gifford inquiry: 'People were really hyped up. I have never seen anything like it. People were very, very threatening. They were very aggressive.'

Finally it was decided to return to the police station for another picket. The meeting ended between 6.30 and 6.45, and in little groups those in attendance emerged from the Youth Association on to the deck of Tangmere and down the narrow concrete staircase on to the grass outside.

There is still no definitive, agreed version of what happened next. At the murder trial, defence counsel Michael Mansfield (who has since become a QC) spent several days cross-examining the police, in an attempt to prove that the riot began when the path of the would-be picketers was blocked by officers in riot vans. Mansfield said that when they saw the first police vehicle, which was stationed outside a day nursery in Willan Road, they did no more than slap on its sides. Only when they realised they were being prevented from leaving the estate by larger numbers of police did they begin to attack them. The police, he suggested, were arriving at the estate either to occupy it, in accordance with the contingency plan, or to stop a further demonstration from reaching the police station.

The police, then and since, are equally vehement that the disturbances began when a police van answering a 999 call came under unprovoked attack by youths armed with staves, knives and machetes. In their version, the officers in this van, identified by the call sign Y32, were lucky to escape with their lives. By the time additional forces arrived, flaming barricades were already in position at the four main entrances to the estate.

The ugliness of the mood around the Farm is not in doubt. At 6.25, a police inspector was attacked by two youths on a motorbike in The Avenue. They drew alongside his car, and the pillion rider smashed a bottle through the side window. Glass went into the inspector's eyes, and he was lucky to escape. The two riders, it would appear, had not been present at the Youth Association.

In his summing up of the murder trial, Mr Justice Hodgson drew attention to the evidence of Victor Broughton, who came to the Farm planning to visit his daughter's boy friend. He arrived at the estate's main, Gloucester Road, entrance shortly before 7 pm and was turned out of his car, which was then set on fire by a large group of youths. At this time, he said, no police were in evidence. However, this happened a considerable distance from the roughly simultaneous 'contact' at Willan Road, four hundred yards away. The attack on the officers at 3.15, and that by the motorcyclists later on, suggest there were people bent on violence who took no part in any of the demonstrations or meetings. Possibly the firing of Broughton's car was their work.

To follow the argument any further becomes a distinctly arcane exercise. Some of the discrepancies may be capable of resolution: as well as Y32, which at some stage early in the evening was unquestionably attacked and badly damaged, there was another van in the vicinity, Y31. This may have been the vehicle that was only slapped. But by this stage the multiplicity of factors coming into play at Broadwater Farm – deep-seated social and racial tension, the confusion of police ideology and operational policy, the recent examples of Handsworth and Brixton, the absence of redress for Mrs Jarrett's death – probably made violent disorder inevitable. In the down-to-earth language of police slang, 'the wheel was coming off'.

On one point, however, the evidence suggests Mansfield must certainly have been wrong. Giving evidence at the murder trial, Superintendent David French, who spent the day at Wood Green and later took charge of part of the estate, poured scorn on the idea that DAC Richards and Commander Polkinghorne were trying to activate the contingency plan without telling their immediate subordinates such as himself. Had they done so, he said, they would not have sent the early shift home; while he, together with units of the Special Patrol Group, was actually having dinner when the first urgent messages requesting assistance crackled over the airwaves.

In any event, as was soon to be shockingly clear, the one thing lacking from the police operation as the riot developed was any clear idea of what to do.

The first senior officer to the scene was Colin Couch, who had stayed at Tottenham, still talking to Hyacinth Moody, when he heard the radio distress call from Y32. 'I thought I would be going to assist officers senior to me but I found myself in charge,' he says.

He arrived with two van loads totalling about thirty officers at the junction of Mount Pleasant Road and The Avenue, and nothing, he says, could have been further from his mind than occupying walkways. His fear was that the emerging riot might engulf the whole of the surrounding area, and he gave the order for 'containment', to keep the youths inside Broadwater Farm. In those first few minutes, he and his officers pushed one hundred yards into the estate.

From that point on, at the four road entrances to the Farm – Griffin Road, Adams Road, Willan Road and Gloucester Road –

containment was the policy adopted, apart from a single attempt to advance beneath the Martlesham block, which was swiftly beaten off. Its consequence, as units poured into the area in ever-increasing numbers, was to make the police sitting targets.

A black youth present at Griffin Road describes the outbreak of hostilities in that part of the estate:

> People had taken different routes, moving in several groups through the estate after leaving the meeting. From where I was standing, hand on heart, the community took no precipitate action: nothing was done until we found our exit was blocked by police. We got up towards Mount Pleasant, and then we could see three or four police vans on the other side, parked in a turning. The police were decanting, wearing their riot gear, and they were running towards us, banging their truncheons on their shields, shouting 'get back in there, you black bastards'.
>
> The rumour went round that the rec [the recreation ground to the north of the estate] was full of police dogs, that we were trapped. Then we heard a loud noise from under Martlesham: the police were advancing, still banging their shields. Just as suddenly, for no apparent reason, they withdrew. I don't know what was happening elsewhere at this time, not long after seven. But where we were, at first people were just curious. The crowd started to move under the block, still thinking of getting out. There might have been a hundred of us.
>
> We moved forward a little and there were lines and lines of policemen, just standing there. Someone picked up a rock and threw it at the police. There was this eerie silence for a moment. We saw the rock fly through the air and time seemed to stand still. It went over the shields and you heard a policeman groan.
>
> Everyone moved away from the guy who'd thrown the rock: we expected a snatch squad any second. But they just carried on standing there. Someone threw a second rock: again there was this groan. Finally there was a third rock, and that was like the signal. It just went off. I can't describe what happened: the suddenness; the frustration and the bitterness were just all coming out. The riot had begun.

Griffin Road and Adams Road saw the most intense violence that night, because the rioters were able to hurl their rocks and petrol bombs at the police lines from the overhead walkways. By eight o'clock, according to the *Public Order Review*, a pattern of behaviour by the rioters was established:

About 200–300 youths would emerge from under the tower blocks and attack one or more of the barricaded locations . . . after each attack, when the ammunition was exhausted, the rioters withdrew to re-arm, and then attack again, either in the same location or at one of the other main locations.

It was with simple accuracy that the secret Williams report stated that the rioters were 'delighted' that the police continued to be such an easy target. The youth's account continues:

As time went on, it became clear the police were taking a ferocious beating. Euphoria is too strong a word, but there was a feeling of wellbeing. The Met was getting fucked over, and there were no qualms being felt about attacking the officers. Sometimes injured officers dropped their shields, and the real hotheads tried to get them for souvenirs, they stashed them and planned to collect them later. People's chests were puffed up. They had been taking it all these years, and now they were giving some back.

Jeff Crawford, the senior Haringey community relations officer, who lived in south London, saw evidence of just how ferocious the beating was soon after he arrived, having been driven to Tottenham in a police car. Behind the police lines was 'a shifting convoy of ambulances: as soon as one was loaded up with injured officers, another would move up to take its place'. The police cleared all the roads to speed traffic to the North Middlesex two miles away, but eventually the hospital could no longer cope and casualties were taken to the Whittington in Archway, four miles distant. Two hundred and fifty-five officers were eventually to need treatment.

At Griffin Road, the rioters had three firearms, including a revolver and a shotgun, which was fired at least thirty times. PC Stuart Patt took a bullet in the stomach and required emergency surgery. From the Wood Green control room, DAC Richards sought and obtained the permission of Commissioner Newman to use plastic bullets, and at 10.20 Scotland Yard's tactical firearms unit appeared outside the Farm. However, the violence was on the wane by then, and no plastic bullets were fired. It also seems that none of the four chief superintendents or superintendents in charge at each of the four road entrances wished to go down in history as the first policeman to use plastic bullets on the UK mainland.

Some of the PCs in riot gear were much more experienced in public order policing than the senior officers at the four locations, being veterans of the miners' strike and the battles at places such as Orgreave. The SPG units at Griffin Road begged in vain to be allowed to make an advance against the rioters, claiming that with their NATO flameproof overalls, they could subdue the riot in two hours.

Others seem to have been told the purpose of the operation was to seal the estate. But the whole of its lengthy northern flank, bordering the recreation ground, was left open. Hearing the news through radio and television, or simply attracted by the noise and the frenetic to-ing and fro-ing of police vans, there were many who joined the rioters who did not live on Broadwater Farm, and whose connection with the Jarrett family was tenuous at best. Among the rioters throughout the evening were many white youths.

DAC Richards insisted later that the contingency plan was available at Wood Green, but a forward strategy was considered impossible because the rioters had formed 'lakes of petrol' in basement garages on the estate, which could have been turned into firetraps. This allegation, made in a written report, was to be the subject of fierce criticism, from within both the Metropolitan Police and the community of Broadwater Farm, where no basement garages exist. Richards was forced to clarify his point, saying he had meant pools or sheets of petrol. That claim too was strongly denied.

Whatever the position at Wood Green, the copy of the contingency plan at Tottenham Police Station stayed locked in a safe all night. Many policemen continue to believe that underlying the 'strategy' of standing in lines, absorbing punishment, was still an obsession that there might be trouble in the Wood Green shopping centre. Even while the riot was at its worst, reserves of more than two hundred riot-equipped officers were kept at Wood Green. They endured a long agony of frustration as they tuned into the police radio to hear their colleagues being pounded. Repeatedly, inspectors from these reserve 'serials' (units of an inspector, two sergeants and twenty or more PCs) went into the control room from their vans, pleading to be allowed to join the fray. Each time they were overruled.

Possibly there may still have been fears for the shopping centre, but the failure to engage the reserves points as conclusively to more general chaos. Once the violence was fully underway, the police communications system collapsed. The *Public Order Review* stated:

> The failure to create [separate] command and support channels at an early stage led to considerable congestion on networks . . . personnel on the ground had great difficulty in hearing transmissions because of background noise and because of the protective helmets which cover the ears. A real need has been identified for radio receiver/transmitters to be fitted to helmets of supervisors and work is in hand to carry this out.

The Williams report was more emphatic about the problems of using only one radio channel. When the commanders of the four different sectors at the Farm wanted to communicate with Wood Green, they were swamped by the dozens of calls being made by the units in the field.

This was made frighteningly clear to Colin Couch. After his initial engagement in The Avenue, he took charge of the south-western entrance to the estate, at Gloucester Road. Despite the early arson attack on Mr Broughton's car, for most of the evening this sector was peaceful. Couch could hear some of the noise of the fighting centred on Griffin Road and Adams Road. But the breakdown in communications gave him only a dim picture of its ferocity. Early in the evening, he had two fully-fledged, riot-trained serials at his disposal. As it was clear they were unnecessary at Gloucester Road, he sent them to reinforce their colleagues on the other side of the estate.

By 9.30, Couch had only a 'scratch' serial, number 502, consisting of eleven officers led by Sergeant David Pengelly. A few of its members were trained in the use of shields and other public order tactics, but many were not. They included PC Keith Blakelock, a home beat officer who worked in the attractive, predominantly middle-class suburb of Muswell Hill.

At this point in the evening, three men from the West Indian Centre committee, Arthur Lawrence, George Martin and Vernon Moore, spoke to Couch and Superintendent Stacey at the entrance and went on to the estate to see what was happening at Tangmere. They found the shops on the deck were being looted, partly in a hunt for further ammunition. They went over to Griffin Road, and then returned, noticing that a fire had started in the Tangmere newsagents.

Tangmere is a big, squat building, shaped in conscious imitation of a Babylonian ziggurat. The fire had already been noticed by Colin Couch, and by ten o'clock, smoke was billowing around Tangmere's roof. There were two senior firemen at Gloucester Road, and he discussed the prospects of the fire spreading, so endangering people in the four floors above the deck.

At the same time, gripped by a mounting sense of urgency, Couch made a series of calls for assistance. Superintendent French later told the murder trial that two full serials had tried to reach him from the other side of the estate, but found it impossible – like every police unit throughout the evening – to penetrate the rioters' lines.

Another failure of the police organisation now came tragically to bear. At least two serials *did* set off from Wood Green in answer to Couch's messages. But like most of the units deployed on the Farm that night, they were strangers to the area. More compellingly, they had no map. Leaving Wood Green in their vans, they knew only to make for Broadwater Farm; they did not know the names of the roads at each end. Seeing the huge build-up of emergency service vehicles at the wrong, eastern end of the estate, they assumed they had reached their destination.

Couch was now faced with the dilemma of his life. Twice, in an attempt to test the water, he walked from his post at the roadway on to the estate, advancing, in his ordinary uniform, until he stood in the gloom beneath Tangmere. Nothing happened. 'I was faced with this conundrum,' he says, 'either doing nothing and seeing the flats burn down, or giving the order to go in with what I had.'

The firemen now believed the risk was substantial. The two senior fire officers followed Couch's example, but instead of stopping
at ground level they climbed the concrete stairway to the deck. At
once they encountered a group of rioters, most of them masked,
who abused them, and chased them away with bottles. At the trial,
much was to be heard of the possibility that a signal was given in
some way to draw rioters to Tangmere. Possibly some of those
involved in this first attack on the firemen went to tell their fellow
rioters of the pickings that might shortly be had on the deck.

In any event, Couch gave the order to go in. With great bravery,
Sergeant Pengelly led his men into the Farm with the fire crew, who
lugged their hoses and other equipment across the ground and up
the stairs. As soon as they reached the deck they came under fierce
attack. Pengelly shouted, 'Get out, get out.' They began to run for
their lives.

Somehow, pursued by the swelling mob, which numbered at
least thirty, perhaps fifty or more, the police and firemen got down
the stairs in good order, through the blackness of the car park and
on to the grass beyond. There Keith Blakelock slipped and fell.

The rioters came at Blakelock from all sides. At the beginning of
their attack, someone removed his helmet, and desperately he tried
to protect his face with his arm. He was kicked on the ground and
stabbed again and again. In the words of PC Richard Coombes,
the mob were like vultures, pecking at his body as their arms rose
and fell to deal their blows. One of the residents who watched in
horror from his flat described them as 'a pack of dogs, attacking
its prey'. For a short time, Blakelock was hidden by his assailants
from view.

One of the fire officers described the scene in court: 'At first people were kicking and punching him, and then, directly afterwards,
a number of instruments were used. The instruments were going
up and down, being flayed at him. The last I saw of PC Blakelock
was he had his hand up to protect himself.'

Blakelock's hands and arms were cut to ribbons as he tried feebly
to resist the fury of the rioters and their weapons, subjected all the
while to brutal kicks. He had no chance: no protection. His head
seems to have turned to one side, exposing his neck. There he took
a savage cut from a machete.

As Sergeant Pengelly ran towards safety, his way was suddenly cut off in front. He turned and saw one of his men – he had no idea who – being attacked on the ground. His statement, made soon after the riot, conveyed in full the horror of the attack, which he single-handedly brought to an end with an act of great courage:

> I do not know where the rest of my men were. On looking to my right on the edge of the grass area just by the flats I saw a large group, 20 to 30 strong, of coloured men, some bending over. Instinctively I knew that they surrounded someone who was on the ground. I believed at first it was a fireman. I attacked them, shouting. After covering a distance of about 15 yards I hit the nearest of them with my truncheon on the head. He was about 45 to 50 years, with short, curly black hair, going grey. As he fell away to my right I hit another coloured person to my left and the group broke up and ran off.
>
> I could see then it was a police officer lying motionless on the ground by a fire hydrant coupling. Defending with my shield, I tried to drag him away, shouting for assistance . . . I was facing youths and stumbled over on the ground, I believe having been hit in the right knee by a stone or a brick. I regained my footing quickly as I saw someone with a sword or a machete, amongst others, running about. A coloured youth threw a rock, which hit me full on the visor of my helmet, partly stunning me. I continued retreating, facing off the youths following me. I could not see any of my officers and I believed there was one left behind. I was trying to check the ground for bodies. A coloured youth then caught hold of my truncheon, and I tried to pull it away from him without success. To effect escape I released the thong from my hand and he ran off.

Two other policemen fell: Coombes, who was dealt a terrible wound to his face, and PC Michael Shepherd, whose helmet was pierced with an iron spike. Coombes had also been running to Blakelock's aid. He said he remembered running along the grass, and then nothing until he came to in hospital, his jaw smashed, his face half destroyed.

Colin Couch dashed across the grass from the roadway. After Pengelly, followed shortly with equal bravery by PC Richard

Pandya, had dispersed the group around Blakelock, Couch tried with PC Maxwell Roberts to pick up the fallen officer. In court, the psychological trauma Couch suffered was apparent; his evidence sounded like the description of a nightmare, or a painting by Hieronymus Bosch. As he ran towards him, he said Blakelock was bathed in a 'silvery light'. He added: 'I ran 35 yards. I could see the silver light most of that time. When 20 to 25 feet away, I realised it was the policeman.'

Couch and PC Roberts grabbed Blakelock's overall and dragged him to his feet, shouting, 'Run, bloody run.' Somehow, Blakelock was still alive and managed to take two or three strides before collapsing. His face was a formless red mass; he was recognisable only by his moustache. Roberts could see a wooden-handled knife sticking from the back of his neck.

The attack, as Mr Justice Hodgson was to remark at the murder trial, lasted only seconds. Blakelock slipped on the run and was immediately overwhelmed, but the attack was seen by Pengelly almost at once and speedily dispersed.

As the youths ran off, Keith Blakelock was dragged to the roadway, where his colleagues tried vainly to revive him. Like Cynthia Jarrett some twenty-seven hours earlier, by the time the ambulance carrying him reached the North Middlesex Hospital, he was dead.

5

Enter the Serious Crime Squad

Every murder detective knows that in catching a killer, there is no time more important than the first hours after the murder, when the body is still warm, the forensic evidence fresh, and the scene, with its multitude of potential witnesses, still confused. Scotland Yard wasted no time in getting the PC Blakelock investigation under way. In the early hours of Monday, 7 October, Assistant Commissioner Jeff MacLean went personally to Broadwater Farm, while Sir Kenneth Newman, DAC Richards and John Dellow, the Assistant Commissioner in charge of the Yard's elite Specialist Operations departments, held a hurried discussion. At 2 am, the man who was arguably Scotland Yard's top operational detective, Chief Superintendent Graham Melvin of the Serious Crime Squad, was asked to go to Tottenham and take charge.

Melvin had missed the news that night, and knew nothing of the bloody events at Broadwater Farm. An officer of more than twenty-five years' service, he seemed the ideal choice. Like Colin Couch, he had been marked as a high flyer at the outset of his service and attended the special course at Bramshill.

Melvin was a detective through and through, famous throughout the Metropolitan Police and beyond. He had served successively 'on division' in some of London's toughest postings: in the Flying Squad, hunting armed robbers and the perpetrators of organised crime; as the leader of a murder squad in south London where he had arrested the notorious dwarf gangster 'Little Legs' Smith; and finally in the Serious Crime Squad, as one of a tiny roster of detective chief superintendents asked to take charge of only the biggest cases. His most recent 'result' was the arrest of the Stockwell Strangler, a serial killer who preyed on the elderly.

The waves of scandal which broke over Scotland Yard from the late 1960s on left Graham Melvin unscathed. Sir Robert Mark, Commissioner from 1972 to 1977, had purged the CID root and branch, determined to obliterate a culture in which bribery, favours and compromise with criminals had become the norm. Throughout the period, when more than five hundred detectives were forced to leave the Met, Melvin remained free from the slightest taint. At the start of the following decade, Operation Countryman subjected the CID to renewed scrutiny. It left Melvin alone.

He was a dominating physical presence: a big, powerful man, with piercing blue eyes and a bone-crunching handshake. Eschewing the flashy suits and special squad ties favoured by many detectives, he dressed soberly, often in dark blue. On casual inspection he could have been a successful industrialist. The single-minded zeal with which he applied himself to his work could lead him, on occasion, to speak sharply to subordinates. But he was known throughout the force as a copper's copper who would not shrink from the responsibility of leadership, and as an organiser who had taken pains to keep up with developments in forensic technology. Unlike many of his colleagues of equivalent rank in the autumn of 1985, he was already experienced in the use of the HOLMES (Home Office Large Murder Enquiry System) computer, a package for correlating evidence and interviews designed after the fiasco of the Yorkshire Ripper case.

Chief Superintendent Melvin did not greet his new task with relish. He was five years from the crunch point in any police officer's career: the thirty-year mark when the excellent force pension reaches its maximum value. Financially, it would be to his advantage to leave then, perhaps to join the numerous ex-policemen at work in the security industry. The only effective alternative was to make the leap to the highest echelons of the force: the rarefied heights of commander, deputy assistant commissioner and above in the Met or their equivalents in provincial forces of assistant and deputy chief constable. To do so meant passing the highly competitive selection procedures for the six-month senior command course at Bramshill. Melvin nursed hopes he might achieve this and so continue to serve as a policeman for years to come. But as he listened to the details of PC Blakelock's death, he had a sinking feeling that he was in for a very great deal of trouble, an investigation which would inevitably, whatever he did, attract furious controversy inside and outside 'the job'.

Police officers at all levels share the belief, which all too often seems entirely justified, that promotion depends less on flair than on the successful retention of a low profile, on having the appearance of a 'safe pair of hands'.

Later on the morning of 7 October, before heading for Tottenham, Melvin went to Scotland Yard to collect his things. A few of his colleagues emerged briefly from their offices to wish him luck. Melvin later said he had the unpleasant sensation they were commiserating: that they knew he had drawn a short straw which could end only, as police slang puts it, by 'doing his legs'.

The inquiry now set in motion was to be exceptional in many ways. At a time when the police were beginning to feel the chilly breezes of Thatcherism for the first time, with a new emphasis on value for money and statistically quantifiable 'performance indicators', Newman made it clear that the resources available to the Blakelock inquiry would effectively be limitless. It rapidly grew to become the largest in the history of the Met, with 150 officers assigned full time for many months, and scores of uniformed constables assisting with house-to-house questionnaires and other inquiries.

To have even one detective chief superintendent in a murder case is unusual; most murder squads, organised in London in 'area major investigation pools', are led by detective superintendents. On the Blakelock-Broadwater Farm case, there were to be two chief superintendents. In parallel with Melvin's murder inquiry, Detective Chief Superintendent Andrew Gallagher, a local north London officer, was to co-ordinate the investigation of the many other offences committed during the riot.

The pressure on Melvin's team was ferocious. The tabloid newspapers' treatment of the riot and murder adopted a pitch which had perhaps not been seen since the Guildford and Birmingham pub bombings of 1974. Then, as in 1985, media coverage at the lower end of the market was a not insignificant factor in the eventual miscarriage of justice.

The horror of the killing needed no embroidery. But it got it just the same. Racism was not so much a subtext, more an overt theme, in which the 'alien' nature of all those who lived on Broadwater Farm became the explanation of their 'savagery'. The first paragraph of the front-page report in the *Daily Express* of 7 October described the disturbances as 'Britain's most horrific race riot'. It went on to quote an unnamed 'senior police officer' in paragraph seven, who said: 'This is not England. This is just madness.' A story in the *Daily Mail* the following day published under the byline of the Asian Amit Roy began with almost the same phrase: 'The plain fact of the matter is it isn't England any more.'

The papers were hard-pushed to keep up with the pace of events on the evening of 6 October. As always when a very big story breaks late in the daily production cycle, most reports were largely factual, collated from staff and news agency dispatches which had been filed at high speed. By the morning of 8 October, there had been more time to stir the brew.

Whites, according to *Mail* reporter Tim Miles, were 'prisoners in their own homes – prisoners of crime, of fear, of an ever-present fear of attack'. Notwithstanding the recent steep decline in the Farm's crime figures, he claimed there was 'a daily war being waged against white families by the younger members of a burgeoning black community who occupy virtually all the flats in the twelve blocks of grey, stained concrete that make up the divided zone'. In fact, as we have seen, whites outnumbered Afro-Caribbeans by 49 to 43 per cent on Broadwater Farm. Mr Miles's report went on:

> The nights, say white residents, are the worst. That is when gangs of black youths flock to the estate's social clubs and crowd the walkways and the pavements. It is when the flats are taken over for illegal blues parties and the reggae decibels make sleep impossible . . . from behind many doors come the menacing growls of newly-acquired Alsatians and Dobermanns. There is one united cry: 'Get us out of here before it is too late.'

The article continued with descriptions of an alleged multiple rape and a brutal mugging. One white resident was quoted as saying that the police were ineffective because 'if they come into the estate, they're accused of harassment'. The piece ended with a remarkable call to arms:

> A white pensioner, Mrs Dorothy Watkins, looked at the scorched walls of the flats, the shattered windows of the special school for mentally handicapped children. 'What kind of a country are we living in when these thugs can destroy our lives for us?' she asked. 'I don't care what methods are used to bring some law and order back to Broadwater Farm. Are we to live forever in a jungle where neighbourliness and care is spat on?'

One target for the venom of the tabloids was Bernie Grant, the prospective Labour candidate for Tottenham. On the day after the riot, he very foolishly, if accurately, stated that the reason Newman was prepared to use plastic bullets in any future riot was that the police had been given 'a bloody good hiding'. His remarks were widely interpreted as condoning the violence, and he was forced to endure a barrage of attacks which was to last for many months. The *Sun* set the tone by likening him to an ape, claiming he had been peeling a banana and juggling an orange while he spoke to reporters.

Some stories were pure fiction. The *Daily Mail* indicated the direction Fleet Street sub-editors' minds were moving, unconsciously echoing Sir Kenneth's thoughts on symbolic locations with its headline 'Ambush . . . IRA Style'. But it was left to the *Express* to plumb the lowest depths with its front-page splash of 8 October, published under the heading 'Kill! Kill! Kill!' A sub-head screeched: 'Moscow-trained hit squad gave orders as mob hacked PC Blakelock to death'. The main piece began:

> The thugs who murdered policeman Keith Blakelock in the Tottenham riots acted on the orders of crazed left-wing extremists. Street fighting experts trained in Moscow and Libya were behind Britain's worst violence. The chilling plot emerged last night as detectives hunted a hand-picked death squad believed to

have been sent into north London hell-bent on bloodshed . . . the killers' charge was orchestrated by sinister men with whistles and loudhailers behind the main riot pack. The same men could have sparked the Brixton and Handsworth terror. A senior Scotland Yard officer said yesterday: 'There is no doubt the main body were martialled [sic] in military style.'

Five or six million people read the *Express* in October 1985, two or three for each of the two million copies sold every day. Few of them, it can be assumed, were aware that this bizarre story was a straightforward con: an untrue, unchecked invention by the notorious Fleet Street hoaxer Rocky Ryan. But Ryan, and the handful of others who specialise in gulling newspapers, sometimes for substantial sums of money, achieve their surprising success rate by tailoring their stories very carefully. Newspapers, they know, are unlikely to bother to ascertain a story's veracity if it is the kind of thing they want to hear. And there was a ready market for claims that PC Blakelock's murder was a cold-blooded, well-planned act, perpetrated by political extremists.

Commissioner Newman gave the lead at a press conference on the day after the killing, claiming that 'groups of Trotskyists and anarchists had been identified as orchestrating the disturbances in Tottenham and in Brixton a week earlier. They are both black and white and come from within and outside London.' On 9 October the *Daily Telegraph* struck fear into the heart of middle England with the headline: 'More riots call by Trotskyites and allies':

Trotskyites, socialist extremists, Revolutionary Communists, Marxists and black militants from as far away as Toxteth descended on Tottenham yesterday to take part in a meeting called because of Sunday's riot on the Broadwater Farm estate. They cheered speakers who declared: 'This war is just beginning,' and supported calls for the police to be put under the control of the local community . . . white bearded men in sandals, many accompanied by girls, rubbed shoulders with the local black people and supported calls for more violence on the lines of that on Sunday night, when a policeman was hacked to death.

It was left to the London *Standard* to report ten days later: 'No evidence of agitation before the riot by politically inspired agitators has been found by police.'

A different line in fantasy was peddled by the *Daily Mirror* in its splash of 15 October: 'Gloating Thugs Raid Riot Cops' Hospital'. The text went on:

> Gloating rioters burst into a hospital ward to taunt their police victims as they lay injured and helpless. The thugs mockingly tossed red roses on to the beds of the officers, who were unconscious or sedated. Then they shouted: 'We done you up good and proper. There are some lovely cuts round here. Next time we'll do an even better job on you lot.'

Sensational coverage of this kind had a powerful impact. The reflex of outrage was one aspect of the pressure on Chief Superintendent Melvin and his team of detectives. At the same time, the tenor of reports unconsciously endorsed Sir Kenneth Newman's analysis of the inner city, and his suggestion that the measures required to deal with black youth were analogous to those required to fight the IRA. At this early stage, without a scrap of evidence, newspapers – even if they hadn't fallen for the charms of Mr Ryan – described the riot and murder as 'organised' and 'planned'. The ground was being laid for the notion of a 'ringleader'.

Press reports – and there are many other examples – were portraying the estate as something 'other', alien, 'not England', a jungle. As Tim Miles had hinted in his article in the *Mail*, in such a place, the niceties of civil liberties need not apply. The usual rules of criminal investigation might have to be suspended, or as his interviewee put it, 'I don't care what methods are used to bring some law and order back to Broadwater Farm.'

There was, however, a further element to the intense pressure on the Blakelock investigative team, which had not been present in the Guildford Four or Birmingham Six cases: the overwhelming need to 'get a result' generated by a crisis of discipline within the ranks of the Metropolitan Police. PC Blakelock's murder was the cause of a catastrophic loss of morale.

Not without reason, the junior ranks of the Met blamed not only the black inhabitants of the estate but their own superiors for the killing. Among the thousands of sergeants and PCs, it symbolised what they perceived as a yawning gulf between themselves and the senior ranks of 'deskmen', with their accumulations of 'pizza' (the silver badges of rank) on their collective epaulettes. Blakelock's death seemed to prove what the canteen lawyers and Police Federation representatives had been saying for years: that most senior officers were opportunists largely ignorant of the realities of policing on the streets, whose priority was their own careers, not the care of those under their command.

The anger of the police rank and file found several targets in which the unfortunate figure of Chief Superintendent Colin Couch was prominent. 'PC Blakelock's serial, they were, well, crap,' one PC told me not long after the riot, referring to their lack of public order training and experience, and the folly of their being sent into the estate at a time when Couch was unaware of the peril they faced.

Ten days after the riot, Sir Kenneth Newman addressed the annual meeting of the Metropolitan Police Federation. For the first time in living memory, a commissioner was heckled, as he defended the performance of his senior officers and promised the future availability of CS gas and plastic bullets.

However, his hostile reception was only the merest hint of the fury within the service. Some of it surfaced in the 24 October issue of *Police Review* magazine, in an article headlined 'Gradually losing the war with the left', under the name of Detective Constable Noel Bonczoszek, an officer from Newham, whose beat included the policing of racial violence. Earlier in the year, he had figured prominently in the trial of the Newham Seven, a group of Asians charged with affray after an ugly brawl with a group of thugs who had been cruising east London and picking on Asian youths. Over the article the magazine's editor included this statement: 'The views expressed below are representative of a number of letters and telephone calls we have received [since PC Blakelock's death].' The article began:

For the past ten years the Metropolitan Police have been losing the propaganda war fought by the left wing, aided and abetted by vacillating politicians, indifferent legislators, naive senior police officers, and ably assisted by judges and magistrates.

The left, he went on, had 'driven a wedge' between the police and the community, particularly in multi-ethnic areas:

> The subject I refer to is the new fad, the latest in word – racism – and the blanket catch-all smear which goes with it and can be thrown at anyone who fails to comply with left-wing points of view . . . local criminals [become] martyrs to be looked up to as defenders of the local ethnic community. The left's political representatives persuade senior police officers to agree to making the areas concerned or specific clubs and pubs effectively 'no go' areas.

Bonczoszek added that the time had come to stop paying lip service to 'quasi organisations' who claimed to represent ethnic minorities: 'Senior officers should deal with the ethnic criminal in the same way as the rest.' He concluded:

> I hope that we never again see weakness displayed towards the criminals within the ethnic community. I trust that our masters were not waiting for an outrage such as the Tottenham riot and the tragic death of a police officer to provide them with enough courage to act decisively and correctly, they having lost their grip on those renegade sections of society originally. But I have my doubts.

The November issue of *Police*, the official organ of the Police Federation, spelt out the difficulties facing Sir Kenneth still more explicitly. The previous edition, published before the riot, carried on the cover an old picture of a bobby carrying a cricket bat and stumps away from a gaggle of naughty Edwardian schoolboys, with the caption 'End of play'. Now the Federation cartoonist Jedd updated it: the same bobby had a rifle under his arm and was walking away from a tombstone inscribed 'Tottenham, a bloody good hiding, 6 Oct 1985'.

Most of the issue was devoted to Broadwater Farm and

Blakelock, beginning with a bitter editorial headed 'Scarmanised!' At Handsworth, Toxteth and Tottenham, it claimed, 'the police have followed a deliberate policy of avoiding confrontation at all costs, in the vain hope that peace, no matter how uneasy, could be maintained . . . yet there has been an orgy of destruction and violence'. The lesson for police commanders, it concluded, was that the post-Scarman initiatives of community policing and consultation amounted to a compromise with criminals:

> Compromise and the avoidance of confrontation only leads to disaster. This is the time to reassert the primacy of law. Senior officers must, from now on, do that which is right, rather than that which is expedient.

The main article, 'The Battle of Broadwater Farm', sought to explain why the police had been required to stand their ground, absorbing such heavy punishment: 'Now, in bewilderment and anger, the men demand to know why this happened.' In something of a journalistic coup, the magazine's editor Tony Judge revealed the existence of the contingency plan, adding:

> The contingency plan was ignored on the night of the riot. The failure of senior officers to appreciate fully the reality of the dangerous situation that had been developing on the estate in the days and weeks leading up to the riot, appears now to be the cardinal error from which all subsequent events flowed . . . Sir Kenneth's defence of his senior officers' decision not to send police against a cascade of missiles 'waiting to be hurled down' on them ignores the vital question – why were the rioters permitted to seize the high ground in the first place?

In the same issue, Sir Eldon Griffiths, the parliamentary spokesman for the Police Federation, contributed an article headed 'Community Policing Confuses the Force'. Its conclusion was:

> Community policing, in theory, is an unarguable public good. But it can only work where there is a comparatively settled and homogenous community. And such is not the case in our multicultural inner-city ghettoes . . . the police must be able

to respond to the challenge of violent crime and lawlessness with whatever lawful force is required to uphold the law as Parliament makes it . . . community policing has obscured this responsibility.

The vehemence of the opinions expressed in *Police* and *Police Review*, in every police station canteen, and by the Police Federation leaders, stunned the Scotland Yard hierarchy. These views presented a direct challenge to the authority of Sir Kenneth and his senior colleagues, while venting in public a picture of the Met as a rabble on the brink of mutiny.

The effect on the murder inquiry was direct and considerable. The future credibility of the Newman era seemed to hang in the balance, at the very moment when the commissioner's structural changes were getting under way. Even without this internal crisis, the pressure on Melvin and his team to get a result would have been great. Now, it was overwhelming.

Month after month, the internal dissent bubbled on. In December, *Police* published a series of reactions to its coverage of the previous month. DAC Richards was given half a column to say that the operation at Broadwater Farm was tailored to prevent disorder from breaking out in a wider area, and that 'storming the fortress' might have led to further fatal casualties – only to be rubbished again by the editor, in much the same terms as before.

Anonymous reactions from constables were also printed. One described 6 October as 'the biggest night of shame' in the history of the Met, and another remarked: 'No doubt those in authority will be displeased at your comments, and I would like you to know that I support you in your courageous attempt to lay blame on those who deserved it.' In January, the *Mail* published Sergeant Meynell's memo attacking Colin Couch, to be followed by the long row over DAC Richards' report, and its claims of lakes of petrol.

As Melvin and Gallagher moved to set up a computerised incident room at Southgate Police Station, the Met's collective need for arrests was profound.

There was another aspect to the police response to Keith Blakelock's death: an outpouring of great sadness, the enduring of a deeply emotional grief. He left a widow, Liz, and three children, who now had to cope not only with the shock of his passing but with the salacious attentions of the press.

Tom Williamson, now a chief superintendent, was then serving on DAC Richards' policy unit, based at City Road Police Station. It was well known he had a psychology degree and was active in the Christian Police Association: 'For weeks, quite senior officers used to telephone me, just to talk, to get things off their chests,' he says. 'Since that time, we have developed counselling for officers involved in traumatic incidents, but then there was nothing, and I suppose that was what I was being asked to do, counselling. We were supposed to be hard policemen, we weren't supposed to cry. That is one lesson we have now learnt.'

Intensifying the grief and anger within the service was an extraordinarily prevalent myth: that the rioters had 'almost severed' Blakelock's head. Within twenty-four hours of the murder, it was common gossip throughout the force, and was repeatedly emphasised in the following months to journalists. Eventually, a version of the story came to dominate the prosecution opening speech at the murder trial, which spoke of a plan to put the officer's head on a pole.

This was not a trivial point. As Williamson says, the peculiarly nightmarish perception of the crimes committed by the serial killer Dennis Nilsen stems from the way he dealt with the corpses of his thirteen victims, not just their number.

Keith Blakelock's injuries were horrific enough. There were fifty-four holes in his overalls, and the pathologist listed forty separate wounds caused by knives and other sharp instruments. Eight were to his head, dealt by a machete or a similar sword or axe-like weapon. As PC Roberts had seen when he tried to rescue him, there was a knife embedded in the back of his neck, and another six wounds to his face. There were fourteen stab or slash wounds in his back, and numerous cuts on his hands and forearms, sustained as he tried to protect himself, and in addition many bruises and abrasions caused by stamping and kicking all over his body. He also had one stab wound in the back of his right thigh.

The worst of all the wounds was a gaping hole across the right side of his head, where his jawbone had been smashed. The blow, in the words of the pathologist, echoed later by Mr Justice Hodgson in his summing up, had been dealt with such force '*almost as if* [my italics] to sever his head'. This was on any estimation a dreadful blow. But as the photographs taken at the autopsy make clear, it did not, in fact, come close to decapitating Keith Blakelock.

The attack on PC Blakelock was as brief as it was violent; it probably lasted no more than a few seconds. It happened in darkness, and most, if not all, of his killers were masked. The only statement to contain anything approaching a helpful description was Sergeant Pengelly's, with its snippet of information about the man with 'short, curly black hair, going grey'.

Police photographers took more than a thousand pictures on the night, but these depicted the scenes around the entrances to the estate at Willan Road and Adams Road, not Tangmere. More than thirty people who had seen Keith Blakelock die were ready and willing to talk to the police. Not one of them had information which got them any closer to identifying suspects.

Exacerbating the lack of initial leads were further disastrous errors made on the night of 6–7 October. As the news of Blakelock's death spread among the rioters, gradually the fighting died down; at the same time, Couch's prayer for rain was answered at last.

At that moment, Broadwater Farm contained a wealth of potential evidence. The wounds suffered by Blakelock must have sprayed blood over many of his attackers; their clothes would have been stained, or drenched. Other forensic evidence lay all around: objects or weapons with fingerprints, and all manner of other clues. 'We should have done two things,' says one experienced north London detective. 'We should have sealed the estate, so that when we finally moved in, the killers would still have been there. And we should have treated the forensics as if we had been dealing with a terrorist bomb: cordoned off the area, and sifted every particle with a fine-tooth comb. It was dealt with only as the scene of public disorder, not as the scene of many crimes.'

Some senior officers present, including Colin Couch, wanted to move on to the Farm in strength as early as 1 am, but they were overruled; the police did not enter the estate until four o'clock. All this time, the way into the rec to the north stayed open, and at the road entrances, people who did not live on Broadwater Farm, who might well have played a part in the riot, were allowed to leave without even giving their names.

'They were just allowed to wander off,' says a sergeant who was disgusted and amazed at this lack of regard for what might prove to be vital evidence. 'It was as if the senior officers were still treating this as some kind of community exercise, not the aftermath of the worst UK mainland riot this century.'

Not long after the police at last re-established the rule of law on Broadwater Farm, the council, with the agreement of the police, began a massive clear-up operation. The forensic evidence was shovelled and bulldozed and packaged and eventually removed. All the murder investigators had to go on were some footprints in the mud.

6

The Police Infallibility Principle

Graham Melvin was a stranger to Tottenham; he started his inquiry without local knowledge or informants. The lack of arrests on the night of 6 October and the shortage of forensic evidence left him with only one starting point: the suspicions of local officers. This, remember, was the era of Sir Kenneth Newman's much-vaunted system of 'targeting and surveillance'. It did not take long for Melvin to discover that as far as the Tottenham CID was concerned, anything wrong on Broadwater Farm could usually be ascribed to one man: Winston Silcott.

Even now, after the Court of Appeal's decisive quashing of his conviction for the Blakelock murder, police officers who served near the Farm in the early 1980s will tell anyone who wants to listen that Silcott was a very bad man indeed. In doing so, they betray an unlovely and highly dangerous trait which is common throughout the force. It amounts to a belief in police infallibility, at least when it comes to identifying guilty men.

Among most police officers it is an article of faith that if a person is acquitted of a serious crime, it means the court is at fault. The defendant perhaps walked because of a legal technicality (as if such things did not, in themselves, matter), or because he engaged a clever 'brief'. With few exceptions, the last thing policemen and women will consider is that he was innocent all along.

The same thinking is all too often applied to the inexact science of police intelligence. 'We *know* chummy is guilty,' the detective will say, 'we're just having trouble finding evidence to prove it in a court of law.' Sometimes, there will be very good grounds for that statement. It may, however, be founded on the merest supposition, or a single, unverified whisper from a malicious informant.

The police infallibility principle frequently extends beyond a case in which the officer has been personally involved, to cover any allegation made by a colleague. If detective sergeant so and so says Fred is a professional mugger, then mugger he is. Rarely will the recipient of such an opinion stop to ask for details of the grounds for suspicion. The result may be that the impression is gained of a powerful case in the making, needing only the finishing touches before Fred gets dealt a judicial *coup de grâce*. Fred may never have been convicted of a single offence, but as far as the police are concerned, he is a 'scrote'.

Even if an officer harbours doubt, the culture of the job warns him to keep it to himself. Policemen like certainties. When talking to third parties, such as journalists or magistrates, they will not hint at possible second thoughts. The police infallibility principle was at work when Delroy Lindo and Stafford Scott were first arrested for 'sus' in the 1970s. Against Winston Silcott, it was operating with a vengeance.

These are the words of a former senior officer in Tottenham. By his own admission, he never personally investigated Winston Silcott; the basis of what follows is therefore secondhand. Wisely, perhaps, he has declined to be named:

> Police aren't stupid. We know who the violent people are, who are the villains. Silcott was the biggest mafioso in Tottenham, everybody knew that. Anecdotally among my officers he was the one who was associated with what was going on. The view of the officers was that he was the ringleader. He was running the mugging gangs, paying them with drugs.

Part of this belief was based on a racist view of black youth which would be funny if it weren't so serious:

> It was his eyes, they were terrifying. People had never seen such frightening eyes. You probably know, it's part of West Indian

culture: you and I, we have eye contact when we are speaking, but with them, you don't look someone in the eye unless you're prepared to take them on.

In 1979 Silcott was convicted of wounding and went to prison for six months; in 1980, he was charged and acquitted of murder. His defence at the murder trial was strong. A first trial ended in a hung jury; in the second, the not guilty verdict was unanimous. The officer continues:

> Wounding, murder, that suggests a pattern, doesn't it? I don't think anyone gets arrested, interrogated, and then has their case gone through by the Crown lawyers and brought to trial without there being a strong probability that they're guilty.

Questioned more closely about the 'mugging and drugs' allegation, the officer admitted that he had been imprecise, and could not be certain of Silcott's exact underworld role. As to why he had never been charged, or even questioned about such offences, the police infallibility principle has an answer to everything: 'He was so influential he was able to terrify witnesses, so that we could never get the evidence.'

Intelligence, especially on the lips of Sir Kenneth Newman, is an impressive sounding word, conjuring in the mind (as Newman intended) visions of the fight against terrorism in Northern Ireland, where a combination of money, bravery and luck has from time to time paid big dividends. Possibly one thought in the commissioner's mind when he first started laying such heavy stress on targeting and surveillance in 1983 was that the existing, largely anecdotal basis of police suspect information left a lot to be desired.

Pre-Newman, the only organised intelligence department in the Metropolitan Police was the old C11 unit at Scotland Yard, which dealt mainly with big-time, professional criminals. Even then, says one detective, 'there was nothing very sophisticated about it. An awful lot of what they put out was just the result of what snouts said on the phone.'

Newman set up a development group to look at ways of emulating the RUC's approach in London, and by 1984 there were several area Intelligence and Surveillance Units, ISUs. The unit for north London was based at Caledonian Road, Islington. It was supposed to combine information from detectives and from the Special Patrol Group when it was not needed elsewhere, while each borough district had six uniformed PCs – not CID officers – whose main job was intelligence collection. In addition, there were the collators on each division.

It was not until later that information fed into this system was officially graded, from A1 (which would amount to something approaching hard evidence) to D4 (which would be no more than unverifiable gossip). Sir Kenneth's fledgling apparatus had no more evidence about Winston Silcott's criminality than the Tottenham CID. A detective who does not adhere to the infallibility principle admits: 'Taking it all together, it is true that if you're not very careful, you have got all the ingredients for mythology.'

Winston Silcott left borstal in the summer of 1978 and took a job in the same rag trade workshop as his mother. Like many young black men in north London, sometimes he carried a knife.

Nine months after his release, Silcott went with a cousin to a nightclub in Southgate. In Tottenham, he was a 'face', but Southgate was unfamiliar country. This carried risks: the circles in which Winston and his friends moved could be highly territorial.

His cousin went upstairs to a balcony overlooking the dance floor, and Silcott waited in the lobby area. According to evidence heard in court, a strange man pushed into him, and the two had a heated exchange of views. Later, the man and his friends came looking for Winston, still inside the club. He jabbed at Winston with a broken glass; Winston parried with a metal chair, cutting the man in the chest. In September 1979, he was convicted of wounding, and sentenced to six months' imprisonment.

He had been out less than a fortnight when some friends asked him to accompany them to a blues party in Alexandra Palace. Winston says he was reluctant, because this too was unfamiliar ground and the memory of his misadventure in Southgate was fresh in his mind. Nevertheless, he went.

At the party, he got talking to a girl, unaware that she was otherwise attached. Her boy friend threw a few sour glances and then, without warning, stood over Winston with a knife. He swung at him, and Winston produced a blade of his own. His friends held him back, but his assailant kept coming, slashing Winston across the face and cutting his hand. His friends released him and Winston also drew blood, then chased the man from the building. The fight ended when he hurled a roadmender's warning lamp at the man who had attacked him.

Soon afterwards, Winston and company departed. Driving back to Tottenham, they were stopped by police, who saw Winston's injuries and found his bloodstained knife. He was placed under arrest. He volunteered the information that he had been at the party in Alexandra Palace, and now the police disclosed that a man called Leonard Mackintosh – not the man who fought Winston – had been murdered outside the building. Next day Winston was charged with the killing.

He spent nearly a year on remand at Brixton Prison. The basis of the Crown's case was that he was the only person seen at the party with a knife. His attacker was called as a prosecution witness: it transpired that the blood on Winston's knife belonged to him, not Mackintosh. No one said they had seen Winston stab Mackintosh, who was unknown to him; in fact there were no witnesses to the stabbing at all.

To the police, Winston's acquittal by a jury meant only that he had 'got away with murder'. George, his brother, says: 'He wasn't exactly liked before. From that day on, as far as the police were concerned, he had to be done.' His picture was posted inside Tottenham Police Station with the caption 'active criminal'. From time to time, friends of his would be arrested. On several occasions, they were shown the photograph while they were in custody and asked what they knew of his activities. This was targeting in action.

But there was life for Winston Silcott outside the criminal justice system. In 1980, he and Delroy Lindo started a mobile disco, known as 'Galaxy Soul Shuffle Out Of This World Sound System'. It was a big, powerful set-up, endowed with thousands of watts of amplification: 'A pumpin' lickin' tune,' says Delroy. Often with George in tow as a roadie, they played private parties and big, outdoor festivals, among them an annual event on the Broadwater Farm rec. They specialised in pure soul music, of the style now known as 'rare groove', sometimes working in collaboration with emerging big names of the London black music scene: the disc jockey Rebel MC, and the ensemble which was later to achieve world superstar status, Soul-II-Soul. Winston himself nursed a growing reputation as a DJ.

Socially, he was beginning to set his sights beyond north London. Usually smart and stylishly dressed, he and his close friends abandoned the clubs of Tottenham or Enfield for the most fashionable West End haunts of the period: the Valbonne, or Gossips. Delroy Lindo met and fell in love with Sonia, a girl who worked at the headquarters of the Social Democratic Party. Her colleagues threw a party shortly before their marriage. The guests included the MPs Roy Jenkins and Shirley Williams, and Winston, Delroy's best man.

In 1982, Winston fathered a daughter, Latoya. He was a fond parent, and although he is estranged from the mother, the girl still visits him in prison.

Winston was a founder member of the Youth Association, and in 1983, with the help of a government grant, he and his partner Luther Wilson took a lease on one of the Association spin-offs, a greengrocery shop on the Tangmere deck, It never made much money, although the back of the shop proved an ideal place to store the sound system equipment. In October that year, he was fined £150 for possession of an offensive weapon – a flick knife used in the shop for cutting vegetables.

Winston and his family came to believe that he was the natural suspect for every crime committed in Tottenham, so often was he stopped or arrested. In 1981, police arrested him and took him back to the family home in handcuffs, accusing him of a burglary – which he vehemently denied. Bill, his father, asked what was going on and was assaulted by several officers. His formal complaint was not substantiated by the police who investigated it.

In 1983, when PC Betts was stabbed on Broadwater Farm, Winston was arrested and accused. The Crown dropped the case when it emerged that the police had relied on the statement, supposedly given freely, of the youth whose arrest had provoked the confrontation in the first place. The statement claimed he had seen Winston stab the officer, but it emerged he was in the back of a police van at the time of the incident and unable to see anything.

In the same year, Winston spent six weeks on remand for aggravated burglary, until the police came to the magistrates' court and dropped the matter. The only evidence against Winston was an identification made five months after the event.

His experiences during this period sharpened his political instincts. To the police, he became not only a wanted man but a troublemaker, one of Sir Kenneth Newman's activists who made allegations of harassment and infringement of civil liberties. Like Stafford Scott, he acted as a champion for youths in trouble with the police on Broadwater Farm, sometimes trying to find them legal representation and visiting the police station to insist they saw a solicitor.

In March 1984 he was charged with obstructing the police, convicted and fined £50. He and two others had been given a lift in a car whose driver, it transpired, was only sixteen. The police stopped the car and began to give the boy a hard time, using what Winston considered to be unnecessary force in dealing with the situation. He ran off into a nearby school and appealed for witnesses to come and watch what was happening. The incident ended with the arrest of all four occupants of the car 'on suspicion of burglary'. The obstruction charge arose from what the police claimed was Winston's attempt to prevent the arrest of the driver.

Sometimes Winston dressed in military fatigues and boots, to create an impression. He was attired thus when Princess Diana visited Broadwater Farm in the spring of 1985. In an incident later hyped by the *Sun* as threatening the life of HRH, Winston told her she should not have bothered coming without bringing some jobs for the Farm's unemployed with her. Afterwards, a senior officer from Tottenham Police Station telephoned the Youth Association, saying: 'Tell Silcott that this time, he's gone too far.'

Believers in the police infallibility principle will see the above as a portrait of a dangerous criminal who needed to be taken out of circulation. That, at any rate, was the view of one senior Tottenham officer: 'We were trying to remove a difficult individual from the community.' But there must be an alternative interpretation, which at least has the virtue of depending on a less twisted logic. The police were convinced of the existence of a growing snowball of evidence. But they never subjected it to the heat of factual scrutiny – which would have caused it to melt away.

Finally, in the autumn of 1984, the Tottenham police took another leaf from Sir Kenneth Newman's book and instituted twenty-four hour surveillance of Winston Silcott. For two months he was watched in secret; his telephone was probably tapped. The existence of this project, which was personally approved by Colin Couch, has not been previously disclosed; Winston and his family had no idea they were being observed.

The evidence revealed by the surveillance came to zero.

Even then, the infallibility principle has the last word. The Silcott surveillance failed to come up with evidence of his criminality, says the senior officer, because it was not operational long enough.

In the good old days of English criminal justice, there was no evidence so strong as a confession by the accused. Sir Derek Hodgson, the now retired high court judge who tried the Blakelock murder, recalls: 'When I started at the bar in the 1940s, it simply didn't enter one's head that confessions might be unreliable. As defence counsel, we didn't think of going into how they might have been obtained.'

From the invention of police detectives in the mid-nineteenth century, that is how things were done. Once the investigators had their 'cough', the case could satisfactorily be closed. The police infallibility principle was held sacred by all concerned with criminal justice. It did not occur to anyone that the conditions in which a suspect had been held might have induced him to make false admissions. There was also a greater tolerance of police methods. Because defenders shared the belief in the principle, they were sceptical about allegations of misconduct. Little attention was paid to the notion that there were some people so inherently vulnerable or suggestible that they needed protection in custody, not only from the police but from themselves.

It was not always thus. In his brilliant *Religion and the Decline of Magic* (Weidenfeld and Nicolson, 1971), Sir Keith Thomas shows how in the sixteenth and seventeenth centuries, people confessed under pressure to a crime that did not exist at all, namely organised black magic. It follows that hundreds of men and women convicted and executed as witches were not guilty. 'Loath they are to confess without torture,' James I stated in his *Daemonologie*; this in itself 'witnesseth their guilt'. The more reluctant the confession, the more conclusive the evidence. In an early application of the infallibility principle, Matthew Hopkins, the most successful of the witch hunters, explained that reluctance was evidence that a witch had been silenced by a confederate, or possessed by the Devil. Some suspects, Keith Thomas observes perceptively, might accuse themselves 'in the expectation of being more leniently treated'. In 1736, the Witchcraft Act was repealed, and prosecutions for black magic ceased to sully the English legal system.

By the time the police came to investigate Broadwater Farm, there was a wealth of more recent evidence to question the wisdom of relying too heavily on admissions under interrogation. In the 1970s, the case of Maxwell Confait, in which three juveniles were wrongly convicted of murder as a result of their admissions, had led, via a judicial inquiry and a Royal Commission, to the new PACE Act, with its wide provisions governing police custody and access to legal advice. In 1974, the Guildford Four had been convicted of the pub bombings after an investigation which relied entirely on interrogations. In 1985, the shattering collapse of the Crown's case lay in the future, but public pressure to reopen the case was mounting.

There was another, more recent case, which in some ways was a direct precursor of the Blakelock inquiry. In 1981, a white youth, Terry May, was knocked off his motorbike by a gang of black youths in Thornton Heath, south London, and found stabbed to death in a garden nearby. Amid a media furore, the police decided to make progress through arrests, more than three hundred in all; one night they picked up 140 young blacks at a nightclub and questioned all of them about the May murder.

A year later, fifteen went on trial at the Old Bailey. There was no identification or forensic evidence, only their confessions. The trial was marked by allegations that juveniles had been mistreated and denied access to advice. Nearly all the crucial admissions, it emerged, had been made while the suspect was effectively held incommunicado. Mr Justice Farquharson, who as Lord Justice

Farquharson was to hear the Blakelock appeals nearly a decade later, threw out seven of the fifteen cases at the end of the prosecution case.

At the end of an eight-week trial, the jury convicted no one of murder, leaving only one, Ronnie Pilgrim, to go down for eight years for manslaughter, although the judge had stressed in his summing-up that Pilgrim could not have stabbed Terry May, and could be convicted only as an accomplice.

The infallibility principle knows no embarrassment. There are still policemen in Thornton Heath who will tell you off the record that all fifteen were guilty.

7

A Climate of Fear

They came for Andrew Pyke at 10 am on 8 October, just thirty-six hours after Keith Blakelock's death. Andrew was fifteen and emotionally insecure. When the police arrived, tipped off that he had gone missing for a while around the time of the riot, he was in care, staying with Jenny Kent, a teacher. He attended the Moselle School for educationally subnormal children, which bordered Broadwater Farm. Not only was he illiterate, he could not even recognise the letters of the alphabet.

A few months before the Broadwater Farm investigation began, the north London CID had begun an experimental project designed to protect suspects whose mental state might lead them to make misleading statements to police. Mindful of the Confait case and its long aftermath, senior local detectives consulted Barry Irving, the director of the independent research body, the Police Foundation, who had been closely involved in the Confait case and the consequent Royal Commission. The scheme provided for experts from MIND and Mencap to be available on a twenty-four-hour basis to be called in when the police began to interrogate anyone who was of low intelligence or mentally ill. They were supposed to sit in on the interviews to ensure they were conducted fairly.

Many local CID men were drafted on to the inquiry and they should have been aware of the scheme's existence. But it was not employed with Pyke, nor with any of the many other mentally vulnerable suspects arrested in connection with the Tottenham riot.

Early in the murder trial nearly sixteen months later, Mr Justice Hodgson made a typically perceptive remark. This was a 'very unusual' case, he said, because the police were trying to do two things at once. Each time they interviewed someone, they were looking for evidence that he (almost always he) was involved, but also trying to find out what he knew about what had happened and who was responsible. The two roles, said the judge, had got 'totally mixed up'. The case of Andrew Pyke, at the very start of the inquiry, typified this confusion.

The last thing a detective does in a textbook murder inquiry is arrest the suspect. 'When it gets to the point of interrogation,' says a veteran detective superintendent, who leads a Met 'area major investigation pool' murder squad, 'I try to make sure that I already have two or three planks of evidence which would be enough to convict on their own. And I try to have one piece of information known only to me and the killer. That way, if I do get some crazy wanting to confess to something he hasn't done, I have some way of knowing.'

But when the Blakelock murder investigators began making arrests with Andrew Pyke, they had not a twig, much less a plank, of evidence. About Broadwater Farm and the murder of PC Blakelock, they seem to have known only two things. The first was that all the local police they approached for ideas believed that Winston Silcott was the obvious prime suspect. The second was that his nickname was 'Sticks'. In fact, this term was applied not only to Winston but to at least one other person who lived near Broadwater Farm, Delroy Palmer, whom Winston knew well; it was used commonly to describe any tall, lean man. As far as the police were concerned, it was authentic black community nomenclature for Winston Silcott alone.

In their first session with Pyke, in the afternoon following his arrest, they played it by the book. Two police officers, led by Detective Sergeant Kenneth van Thal, conducted the interview, with a solicitor and a social worker sitting in.

The PACE Act, though passed in 1984, was not to come into force until the beginning of 1986. But because the law transformed police procedures in many ways, throughout the autumn of 1985 the Met was operating a 'dry run', imposed by a special force order. All the new forms and bureaucratic changes were being practised. Like all the Farm case suspects, Pyke had a 'custody officer' responsible for his welfare and for setting down everything that happened to him. All interviews, as PACE required, were to be recorded contemporaneously – laboriously transcribed, word for word, as they were spoken.

In this first interview, Pyke admitted being at Broadwater Farm during the riot, and to throwing 'ten or more' bricks at the police. Asked about the murder, he said the first he knew of it was much later, when he saw the TV news. He said he had been at the riot with his friend Mark Pennant, and that Pennant had been armed with a knife.

After the interview, the police left Pyke alone in his cell for five hours. At 4.40 pm, he was given a meat pie, chips and an apple pie. At 7.45, van Thal and PC Colin Perry saw him again. This time, there were no solicitors or social workers. He was not cautioned that the interview might be used in evidence; it was apparently 'for information purposes'. It is, however, a very important document. But its existence was kept secret from Winston Silcott's lawyers until halfway through the murder trial. They forced its disclosure after realising the custody record revealed an interrogation had taken place of which they had no record. According to normal procedures, the Crown should have disclosed it months earlier, at the committal.

The transcript of the interrogation reveals a remarkable change in Pyke's account. Notwithstanding his denial earlier in the day to knowing anything about PC Blakelock's murder until he saw it on TV, he immediately, according to the record, began accusing the very man identified by the police as the most likely suspect. There are no independent witnesses who can state whether anything was said in the interview room before the record begins. It starts as follows:

Q: When we saw you this afternoon I don't think you were telling me the whole truth, were you?
A: No.

Q: What more do you know about Sunday night's trouble than you told us? Did you see the policeman getting killed?
A: No.
Q: Did you see anyone with a machete?
A: Yes.
Q: What time?
A: I don't know.
Q: Who did you see with a machete?
A: A guy called Styx [*sic*].
Q: What's his surname?
A: I don't know.
Q: How long have you known him?
A: Only a few days.

'Styx,' Pyke went on, was 'quite tall, muscly, about 6'2", curly hair, *no moustache or beard* [my italics].' In fact, Winston Silcott had both a beard and a moustache. Pyke described the machete to the police: 'When I first saw it, it was all shiny and then the next time, it had a bit of blood on it.'

The leading questions continued:

Q: Did you see some firemen and police run down some stairs before Styx came up?
A: Yeah.
Q: How many youths went down the stairs after the policemen?
A: I don't know, about sixty or less.
Q: If you saw the policemen and firemen run down you must have seen Styx and the others at the front run down . . .

Silcott, Pyke said, told him of Blakelock's death with the curious phrase 'see the blood of them'. His friend Mark Pennant, he claimed, also told him a policeman had been stabbed; 'He said he, Sticks and some other guys did it.'

Q: Where did he say he stabbed him?
A: On the stairs.
Q: Which part of his body?
A: I think he said in the stomach.

Q: Whereabouts in the stomach?
A: He didn't show me, he just said, 'I stabbed him in the stomach.'
Q: Andrew, are you telling us the truth?
A: Yes.

Had the officers been better briefed about the events of the night, it should have been clear this account was worthless. Blakelock, as we have seen, was not stabbed until he reached the grass, nearly a hundred yards from the stairs. He had no knife wounds to his stomach.

Leaving aside the provisions of PACE and the Met dry run, as a juvenile Pyke should have been handed into the care of the local authority, according to the provisions of the 1959 Children and Young Persons Act. He should not have been held overnight for two nights in the police station. At 10.17 pm on the second night, the custody officer wrote in the official record: 'I authorise detention . . . as likely to abscond.' However, the reasons on a form later given to the juvenile court for not releasing him or sending him to a local authority centre were: 'It was impracticable to do so' and 'he is so unruly a character as to make it inappropriate to do so'.

After his first night in a cell, Pyke was interviewed again three times. Adding few details, he modified his description of Silcott, remembering 'he's got a little beard and a moustache curling up'. He still seemed prone to confusion, saying initially that Silcott always wore a baseball cap, and had been on the night; later Pyke described him as bareheaded.

The inaccurate detail of Pennant's claiming to have stabbed Blakelock in the stomach gave the police a problem, if he was to be of use as a witness against Silcott. At the end of Pyke's detention they sought to put it right in an extraordinarily clumsy way. The police needed Pyke to give evidence only against Silcott, because by this time, the morning of Thursday, 10 October, Mark Pennant had been arrested on the basis of Pyke's allegations and had made a confession. The record states:

Q: Did Mark Pennant tell you he'd stabbed a policeman?

A: No.

Q: Didn't you say to an officer before that Mark Pennant stabbed a policeman in the stomach?

A: Yeah.

Q: Why did you say that?

A: I don't know.

Q: When you said that you were asked if you were telling the truth and you said yes. Were you telling the truth then or telling the truth now or neither?

A: Telling the truth now.

Q: So why did you say that about Mark?

A: I don't know.

Q: Don't say you don't know, you must have had a reason.

A: I don't know.

Q: Were you saying it because that was the sort of thing the police officers wanted to hear?

A: Yeah.

Pennant, Pyke added, sometimes got him into trouble, so giving him a malicious motive for making false claims about him: 'I wanted to get him into trouble.' But Sticks had never got him into trouble:

Q: Have you any reason to lie about him? [Silcott]
A: No.

When Pyke appeared in the witness box at Tottenham Magistrates' Court during the committal stage of the case, he tried to retract his whole story. The prosecution had to apply to make him a 'hostile witness', a course which never does much for the credibility of a person's testimony. When it came to the murder trial, he was nowhere to be found. Eventually, a warrant was issued for his arrest, and he was brought to the Old Bailey in handcuffs. There, he consulted a solicitor, who made it clear to the Crown that he was no more enthusiastic. Wisely, Roy Amlot decided not to call him as a witness.

The affair of Andrew Pyke reveals a lot about the approach being adopted in even the earliest stages of the Blakelock murder inquiry; and while he may have been induced to retract his allegations against Mark Pennant, that did not stop the police pursuing the hapless Pennant for his own confession, as the next link in the investigative chain.

Pyke's non-appearance in the witness box was the occasion for a significant statement in open court from Detective Chief Superintendent Graham Melvin. Echoing the line which 'Scotland Yard sources' were peddling to journalists to explain the general absence of material witnesses, Melvin said:

> My concern is that the climate of fear around this case is very real. Pyke left home not because he was frightened of the police, or of giving evidence, but because he was frightened of what might happen to him if he did.

Forget the shaky basis of Pyke's testimony, the shameful ducking and weaving to get the statement of an illiterate boy right: the problem was intimidation by the Broadwater Farm mafiosi. There could be no neater statement of the police infallibility principle at work.

Interviewed in 1987, Pyke told me he had never met Winston Silcott, although someone had once pointed him out. He said the police kept pushing Winston's name, until finally he started to say what he thought they wanted to hear.

Although he had admitted throwing ten rocks, which would have been more than enough to get him charged with the serious offence of affray, he was dealt with in the magistrates' court on the much lesser charge of threatening behaviour, and sentenced to two months' youth custody. Before the murder trial, Pyke was visited by two police officers, who saw him in the presence of Jenny Kent. They spoke of arranging a 'new identity' and asked him where he would like to live. It might even be possible, they said, to arrange a training place in a motorcycle workshop.

Mark Pennant was a lot less fortunate. Like his friend Pyke, he was a pupil at the Moselle School for educationally subnormal children. It had been damaged during the riot, and some of its equipment stolen. When Detective Constable Colin Lockwood came to arrest him at midday on 9 October, he was temporarily attached to another school nearby.

Pennant did not live on the Farm, or even in Tottenham, but

two miles away in Finsbury Park. He was born in England, but as an infant was sent to the West Indies to be brought up by a friend of his mother. When he returned to her aged nine, he faced severe educational difficulties. His first primary school headmaster noted his short memory span, and the fact that he was totally unable to read letters or numerals.

The one thing those who knew Mark Pennant agreed upon was his willing and helpful personality: he was cheerful, and tried hard to please. At the same time, he was vulnerable and naive. Seven years of special education for children with learning difficulties had had little impact on Pennant by the time of his arrest; despite his enthusiasm and excellent relationship with his teachers, he was still virtually illiterate. Olive Tunstall, the psychologist who was eventually to examine him for the purposes of the murder trial, commented that Pennant was 'polite and co-operative' and 'appeared to be trying to do his best'. But his mental capacity in most respects was equivalent to that of a seven-year-old. His disadvantage was so great, she concluded, that it was possible he had suffered brain damage. His IQ bordered on mental handicap, and his educational attainments were low even in relation to his intelligence. His memory was poor. The stress of being interviewed in the police station would have exacerbated his plight. 'Mark would have had to struggle hard during the police interviews to understand what was being said,' Dr Tunstall testified, 'to remember both what had been said in the interviews and the events about which he was questioned.' She added:

> It is highly conceivable that under those circumstances Mark would say things which he thought would bring to an end an intolerable situation regardless of the long-term consequences to himself . . . I would also say that Mark would be more likely to make a false confession than would a boy of average intelligence . . . to take an action which would solve his immediate difficulties and ignore or even entirely fail to foresee the future consequences.

As his interrogation began at Wood Green Police Station, Mark's illiteracy was of course obvious to the police, who also knew that he attended a special school. Yet not only did they fail to treat him with the caution which the example of the Confait case ought to have advised, they blatantly disregarded the existing legal protection for juveniles. The new code of practice which accompanied the PACE Act, which should have been observed as part of the 'dry run' of the new procedures, was explicit:

> It is important to bear in mind that, although juveniles or persons who are mentally ill or mentally handicapped are often capable of providing reliable evidence, they may, without knowing or wishing to do so, be particularly prone in certain circumstances to provide information which is unreliable, misleading or self-incriminating. Special care should therefore always be exercised in questioning such a person.

Pennant's arrest was a frightening and humiliating experience: he was taken in handcuffs through the school grounds to a waiting police car. Detective Constable Lockwood later told the murder trial that making the arrest at school was 'unavoidable'. The judge, however, remarked that it was difficult to escape the conclusion that the purpose was to prevent his mother finding out. On arrival at Wood Green he was told that his rights to consult a solicitor and have someone informed of his arrest were being withheld, on the grounds that this might 'interfere with the investigation'.

After four and a half hours spent locked in a cell, his interrogation began. His mother, according to the law, should have been asked to sit in. Instead, a teacher, John Priest, was present, who cannot be blamed for his lack of experience in attending police interviews as what the law calls 'an appropriate adult'. The police told him that the boy's mother had refused to attend. In fact, she had no idea of the whereabouts of her son, and had not been consulted at all. Before the interview began, Pennant repeatedly asked for her. The police now repeated in his presence the lie that she had refused to help him. It was a devastating blow to the boy; in Priest's words, he became 'very frightened and subdued'.

At the very beginning of the interrogation, the record suggests that Pennant failed to understand the words of the caution, read to every suspect: 'You are not obliged to say anything, but anything you do say may be put in writing and given in evidence.' Pennant seems not to have appreciated that he had the option of saying nothing, for when Lockwood asked him what he thought the caution meant, he replied: 'It means I tell the truth and it can be used against me in a court of law.'

In six interviews over the next two days, Pennant admitted to involvement in the Blakelock murder and, like Andrew Pyke, ascribed a significant role to 'Sticks'. But again, there were major discrepancies between his account and what had actually happened, which the police failed to pursue. In addition, long after his confession, they continued to pump him for information, trawling his feeble memory for the names of his friends and acquaintances, and their supposed part in the riot. Like Pyke, he should have been held overnight by the local authority, but again this provision of the Children and Young Persons Act was ignored.

His first description of the murder, halfway through the first interview, bore absolutely no relation to events, sounding more like a child's fantasy based on half-digested news reports and gossip:

> I was at the bottom of the stairs and I saw this policeman was running down the stairs and Sticks was after him with this other man. When they reached the bottom they caught him, I think he tripped and fell over, and when he tried to run they hit him and one of them stabbed him and then the other one hit him and did the same thing and he stabbed him. Then they saw me so I started to run. Then I bumped into Linda and she said to me can I walk her home and she said 'what way' and I said, towards the 123 bus stop, and then we started to run because we thought the man was after us.

Details in the second interview, conducted later that evening, were equally inaccurate, hopeful guesses:

Q: Did you see the firemen?
A: All I saw was the hose on the floor, and these boys picking it up and spraying it at the policemen.
Q: How many policemen did you see run down the stairs?
A: At first I saw one, but then when Sticks came back up I saw seven or eight . . .
Q: How many boys chased the police down the stairs?
A: Three.

Q: Three boys?

A: No, but there was only one running down with Sticks, running after them.

Q: We have information from other witnesses who say that the murdered policeman was surrounded by a large group of boys.

A: Not when I saw him he wasn't. There was only three, unless they came along after.

The police put it to him that he was lying, and that he had been part of the attacking mob. His distress and confusion leap from the record:

A: I don't really like killing people. That's one of the last things I would do.

Q: I haven't said you killed him, I'm saying that if you were that close you must have been part of the large group that surrounded him.

A: No. If I was, the other policemen that were coming down the other stairs, they would have seen me.

Q: How many policemen did you see being attacked on the ground?

A: One.

Q: By how many men?

A: Quite a few.

Q: You've said it was only three.

A: There was three on him. I know Sticks was one of them.

Q: How many other boys were as close to him as you were?

A: One.

Q: That makes four.

A: He was just standing there looking at him.

Throughout his interviews, Pennant continued to say that only one officer was attacked, and that he had not been stabbed, only 'cut' about the face. Like other details of his accounts, neither statement, as we have seen, was true.

Eventually, responding to the leading question 'was the policeman completely surrounded', Pennant agreed that there had been more than three attackers. Yet even then there were highly improbable touches. According to the eyewitness accounts of the surviving policemen, the fire officers and the residents who saw the killing from their flats, the mob dispersed. Pennant said that everyone returned to the deck at Tangmere where to cheers and applause Sticks displayed his machete and announced: 'This is bullman's blood.'

According to the police, Mark Pennant's first confession was not made in the interview room, where he had the limited protection of John Priest, and later his colleague Jenny Kent, but on the way back to the cells, to PC Perry alone. Their conversation supposedly began when Mark said: 'I'm afraid.' It continued, Perry claimed:

Q: Who are you afraid of?
A: Sticks. He told me not to say anything. I cut him.
Q: You cut the police officer?
A: Yes. I kicked him. Only twice.

Perhaps, remembering Dr Tunstall's opinion, this was Pennant incriminating himself in the hope of a short-term reward, such as being allowed to see his mother. But the police regarded it as a most significant development. The interview was immediately restarted, at 11.15 pm, in front of no less a person than Detective Chief Superintendent Melvin.

Pennant repeated his confession to cutting PC Blakelock, but said he intended only to 'beat him up'. Now, and in three further interrogations over the next thirty-six hours, the names started to flow: Mark Lambie and Craig Dunn, both of whom were arrested next day; Sammy Lee, Nicky Jacobs, Mark Maver and Danny Tripp, who were all picked up soon afterwards.

If at times the police seemed unsure whether Mark Pennant's value lay as a witness or as a suspect, by the end of his ordeal they had made their minds up. Five days after the killing, he became the first person to be charged with the murder of PC Blakelock. His immediate reaction summed up the monstrous absurdity of his position. He turned to Jenny Kent and said: 'Does this mean I have to come and live with you, Jenny?'

Already, in this first week of the inquiry, it was clear that Melvin, Gallagher and their superiors at Scotland Yard had made a fundamental decision about how to proceed.

The shortage of objective evidence meant that by definition the only people with information about the murder had probably played some part in the riot. This gave the police a simple choice: they could try to build bridges with the community and gather intelligence and witnesses by stealth; or they could rely almost entirely on arrests and lengthy interrogations. They chose the second course.

In case after case, suspects were held incommunicado, denied access to a solicitor, and refused permission to tell their families in which of the many north London police stations used for questioning they were being held. Twenty-five had been taken into custody by the end of the first week, another thirteen in week two; by 6 November, a month after the murder, the total stood at seventy-three. Eventually, as the investigation ground on into 1986, it was to reach 359. Only ninety-four were interviewed in the presence of a lawyer, and in some of these cases the important admissions had already been made when the solicitor was allowed in.

The Met's official statistics stated that only seventy-seven people were refused access to a solicitor by the police, of whom thirty-eight were not charged with an offence. However, of the 232 who supposedly signed a form to say they did not require a lawyer, some were unaware of what they were doing, others were later to claim they had been deceived. In none of the fifty-seven serious cases dependent on confessions which reached the Old Bailey had a lawyer been present when the admissions were made.

Under the old judges' rules, all those charged should normally have been brought before a court after a maximum of forty-eight hours. Sometimes this period was exceeded, and in at least thirty cases an appearance was made only for the police to apply for, and be granted, leave to question the suspect in custody for a further three days. The new rule laid down by PACE, and which should have been applied in the Met dry run, that no one can be detained for more than thirty-six hours, was honoured mainly in the breach.

The police did not observe any niceties in making their arrests. In numerous cases they began at dawn with the smashing of doors with sledgehammers and the entry of a squad of armed police. One woman described the police entry to her flat:

They said, 'It's your bastard's birthday tomorrow, isn't it?' I said, 'What do you mean by that?' and they said, 'It's your little bastard's birthday, open the door, we've got a warrant for your arrest.' When I opened the door the sledgehammer was coming back on the door. They grabbed me, they put me to spread out on the wall, and they searched me. All I had on was my tee shirt and my knickers . . . it's not affected me, it's my daughter, because she saw everything that happened and she was screaming, literally screaming when she saw, especially when the gun was at my head, you know, she was really, really screaming.

In evidence to the Gifford inquiry, Joanne Grey described the anxiety of those months. 'You would go to bed and just lie there,' she said, 'and you would think, are they going to come and kick my door, what's going to happen to my children? It was the horrible fear that you lived with day after day, knowing they could come and kick down your door and hold you for hours.'

There were many complaints about searches in which possessions were needlessly strewn about, furniture damaged and food – not a negligible matter for families subsisting on income support – deliberately spoilt. Throughout this period, the Farm had the feeling of being under occupation. On any given day, rows of white district support unit vans stood parked in The Avenue. The roster of officers patrolling the estate was ninety, an elevenfold increase in the pre-riot complement. For weeks on end, about 1,800 policemen were kept on standby in case of further disorder, and to assist with arrests. Regularly, the telephone junction boxes at Gloucester Road were seen being opened up and examined: lines, it seems certain, were being tapped.

At the same time, policy decisions of great importance were made by the Crown lawyers, who held regular conferences with the leading inquiry officers. At Handsworth, there were 408 arrests, and at Brixton 292; and at all three riots, the largest group of offences for which people were eventually charged was burglary or theft. One person was charged with murder in Handsworth, one with affray, and six with arson and explosives charges associated with the manufacture of petrol bombs and the firing of the Post

Office. In Brixton, one person was charged with rape, but as with the majority of Handsworth cases, the authorities decided to bring only summary charges for public order offences, which could be dealt with in the magistrates' court.

In Tottenham, the rioting had been more violent and intense. But those who admitted to no more than throwing a few stones were charged with affray, and faced an Old Bailey trial and a sentence of up to ten years. Those accused of participating in the attack on PC Blakelock's serial faced the still more serious charge of riot, for which the maximum penalty was life imprisonment. Eventually, seventy-two people were charged with affray, of whom thirteen were also accused of riot. Six of the latter group were charged with murder.

The police and prosecution were creating their own vicious circle. If anything was responsible for fostering, if not actually creating, a climate of fear on Broadwater Farm, it was the pincer action of the twin policies of flamboyant, heavy-handed arrests, detention incommunicado and rigorous interrogation, and charges of affray in response to the least admission. Some witnesses, horrified at Blakelock's ghastly death, might initially have been prepared to come forward, but they soon found reasons for remaining silent. Anyone who admitted being present near the killing, or during the riot at all, was running the risk of being charged with a very serious criminal offence. The supply of witnesses was always, perhaps, going to be circumscribed. But by moving directly to arrests and charges on such a scale, it was cut off entirely.

As a result, the Crown was left with a case based only on a confession in all but thirteen of the sixty-nine heard at the Old Bailey (three of the seventy-two charges were dropped at an earlier stage when the prosecution decided to offer no evidence). It took all the twisted logic of the police infallibility principle to blame this on the people of the estate.

Each arrest was made from the gleanings of the last. Andrew Pyke and Mark Pennant were but the first two links in a flimsy daisy chain. Suspects, particularly juvenile suspects, interrogated by highly motivated detectives in circumstances such as these, do not think how best to assist police inquires; they consider only how best to save their skins. All intelligence acquired in this way, even without the oppression apparent in the treatment of Mark Pennant, is liable to be tainted.

But the most serious charge that must be levelled against an investigation which becomes dependent on confessions is that the main perpetrators of the killing are likely to escape. The unreliable nature of much of the information being processed may simply never identify them. And in the Blakelock investigation, those charged with the worst crimes were not the tough, hardened criminals, able to withstand interrogation, but the youngest, the weakest, the most vulnerable and easily cracked.

The strategy adopted was conscious, approved by the highest levels of the Metropolitan police hierarchy. Interviewed on Channel 4's *Diverse Reports* in 1986, Deputy Assistant Commissioner Richards said:

> Evidence would be forthcoming as a result of lengthy and detailed interviews and that is the course that this particular investigation took. It was necessary to have people taken to the police station to conduct interviews and interrogations, in order to gain the evidence sufficient to bring this investigation to a successful conclusion . . . they have certainly seen armed officers. They have seen officers wielding sledgehammers. I understand their point of view but it has been necessary and we don't take these decisions easily, you may be assured of that.

Later he added:

> If we are seeking murderers and gunmen we will have to take what some people will see as dramatic action, reactive measures.

Colin Couch may have been regarded by some as a liberal before the riot, but interviewed in 1992 he showed no dissent from the inquiry methods: 'At the time it seemed right. A British bobby had been murdered; there was concern for the community of Tottenham.'

Ultimately we go back to Sir Kenneth Newman, and his bleak comparison of the methods which might be necessary to defeat terrorism and 'multi-ethnic' crime. Newman considered the people of his symbolic location 'rookeries' so alienated as to be outside the democratic scheme, meriting social control, not a say in how they were to be policed. Such a community, it must follow, could not be expected to assist inquiries; any information it had would have to be squeezed out the hard way.

The civil liberty sacrifices this entailed were brought home unmistakeably to solicitors who tried to protect their clients when they were arrested. Gabriel Black, who worked for a local firm, acted for more than twenty riot suspects, and found life extremely difficult. On one occasion, after a magistrate had remanded a youth back into police custody, Detective Inspector Dingle ordered Black's counsel out of the courtroom cells as she tried to snatch a few moments' consultation before the client disappeared back into the custodial maw.

'It was just complete chaos, like a madhouse', she says. 'We were inundated with calls for help from the families of arrested youths, and it was all we could do just to find out where they were. We were told repeatedly that this case was so overwhelmingly serious we would have to bite our tongues and accept whatever the police did. It was absolutely unique in my experience.'

In virtually every case, she was refused access until her client had made admissions: 'You were left making feeble representations by telephone to these very motivated, determined officers who seemed to be ready to stop at nothing because they had lost one of their own.' One juvenile she acted for was released without charge in Chingford, miles from home – without his shoes.

She acted for John Broomfield, arrested on 10 October after he had bragged to the *Daily Mirror* about his supposed role in the riot. After he had been held for forty-eight hours without appearing in court or Ms Black being granted access, she and Lord Gifford went to the High Court, seeking an injunction to compel the police to produce him. Contesting the action, Melvin came up with an argument which was to be heard often: that the risk to the investigation of allowing a solicitor to attend was too great, because 'wittingly or unwittingly' a lawyer might pass on information from the interview, and so enable other suspects to conceal evidence. Ms Black's application was rejected.

From then on, she says, 'the police knew they could do exactly as they liked. They just kept on churning out this witting/unwitting line.' On some occasions, the police even took the unprecedented step of trying to block a client's choice of solicitor, on the grounds that a firm might already be acting for one or more Broadwater Farm clients, so creating a 'conflict of interest'. There are circumstances where such a conflict is conceivable. But it is for the solicitor to judge, not the police.

Gabriel Black adds: 'The police frightened the living daylights out of everybody. That's why they were faced with the so-called wall of silence. People were simply terrified.'

Would an alternative approach have been more successful? One answer is to point out that it could scarcely have been less successful. Three wrongful convictions and no one now in jail for PC Blakelock's murder is not much of a result.

Another answer is provided by a former detective inspector, one of several north London CID men who had their doubts about the inquiry at the time. He says: 'Had it been done by the local CID, I suspect it would have been different. They dealt with it the way the Yard has traditionally dealt with such things, called into regional forces or local areas of London. I happen to think it's neither sensitive nor effective. It was a pre-scientific inquiry, it was all about how to get Winston Silcott convicted, not discovering who killed Keith Blakelock.'

A third response came from a senior Crown lawyer on the day after the 1991 appeals, who first asked the question of me and then answered it himself. He said only: 'Yes.'

8

Dragnet

Throughout the autumn and winter, the daisy chains of evidence grew and multiplied. One had its origins in the arrest of John Broomfield, who at one stage in his interviews was given a piece of paper on which he wrote eleven names. Among them was Engin Raghip, a youth of Turkish-Cypriot descent who ended up charged with murder. Another grew out of the lurid and shocking confession by Jason Hill, aged thirteen, who was arrested on 11 October because he had been seen taking sweets from the Tangmere shop. His conditions of detention were still more oppressive than those endured by Mark Pennant. Jason Hill, too, was charged with the killing. Another murder defendant was Mark Lambie, named by Hill and by Mark Pennant. Next came the turn of Winston Silcott, arrested on 12 October and charged the following day, a few hours after Hill. The sixth man accused, Mark Braithwaite, was not arrested until February. His daisy chain went back to Bernard Kinghorn, a youth facing trial for affray.

It all looked very impressive. But as the first affray trials got underway at the Old Bailey at the end of July 1986, there were signs, for those who wished to look, that the inquiry was founded on sand.

One sign was Howard Kerr. He was arrested at 7 am on 30 October when a squad of twenty officers, some of them armed, raided his family home. Howard was in bed, and he was man-handled half-naked, without shoes, into a waiting police van. 'Do not believe the stories about it being necessary to make arrests at dawn with guns because of the possible risk to the arresting officers,' says one former north London detective inspector. 'It is done for one reason alone: to soften them up for questioning.'

The police had a search warrant stating they wanted to look for stolen goods, but once Kerr, aged seventeen, was in custody, it became clear that the only subject which interested them was his possible role in the riot.

He fell into a familiar pattern. He attended a school for the educationally subnormal, and his reading age was seven. He was refused access to a solicitor, while Detective Constables Paul Biggerstaff and Brian Faulkner subjected him to interrogation over a period totalling nearly sixty hours. The officers' first question was to ask his whereabouts on the night of 6 October. Kerr said he was in Windsor, with his girl friend. He stuck to his story throughout the first interview; then, after some more time to think about it in the cells at Barnet Police Station, he began to crack.

Throughout his detention he wore only his T-shirt and pants. He was given no clean clothes and felt cold, miserable and alone. To all intents and purposes, he was in solitary confinement. During the interrogations, he told his solicitor Jim Nichol, one officer sat facing him, the other immediately behind, with his foot on his chair, his face by his ear.

Kerr's confession was long and copiously detailed, filling more than fifty sheets of paper, and included references to 'Sticks'. Kerr admitted throwing stones and petrol bombs at police, and described a bomb 'factory' where youths made Molotov cocktails during the riot and stacked them in crates. He said he watched the murder of PC Blakelock, and named more than twenty others as taking part in the rioting. Some were arrested soon afterwards, including a young man called Hassan Muller.

Jim Nichol tracked down Kerr's girl friend, Claire Speakman, and other witnesses who confirmed he had been in Windsor. Claire's mother, Margaret, said she drove Kerr to the station to catch the last train to London. His alibi was clinched when a night bus conductress was found who remembered him getting on her bus and cadging a free ride to Tottenham at 2 am, when the riot was over. She had even written the incident down on a spare ticket roll, as she had recorded everything mildly interesting on her bus for the previous ten years.

On 4 December, Nichol confronted a chief inspector on the Farm inquiry with the evidence of Kerr's alibi. The officer admitted it looked as if the case had 'fallen through', but he refused to drop the charges. He said he was worried lest the new Broadwater Farm Defence Campaign, an organisation formed to co-ordinate defence activity, lobby the press and support the families of the accused, 'seized on' the Howard Kerr fiasco.

Finally, at a remand hearing at Tottenham Magistrates' Court on 13 March, the prosecution was forced to withdraw the matter. Crown counsel Susannah Johnston argued that because the confession had been full of detail and signed by Kerr, there had been 'no choice but to proceed to this stage'. Stephen Irwin, counsel for Kerr, retorted that it was detailed because 'suggestions are made in interviews which are then taken up'.

The Kerr affair had a direct bearing on the Old Bailey trial of one of those arrested because of his confession, Hassan Muller. One of the earliest affray trials to be heard, it disclosed further alarming features of the police inquiry.

Muller, too, could barely read and, according to the evidence of psychologists, was unusually suggestible. He was seventeen at the time of his arrest on 4 November. He was held incommunicado for two and a half days. He signed his custody record to say he did not want a solicitor, but at his trial he said he thought he was signing for fingerprints and photographs to be taken. Later, according to his evidence, he asked for a lawyer, but a police officer told him: 'You're not fucking getting one.' In due course, he admitted throwing stones and petrol bombs at the police, and was charged with affray.

At the trial, the police at first claimed that before arresting him they had good evidence that he had thrown petrol bombs. Finally Detective Sergeant Rex Sargent was forced to admit that other than the statement of Howard Kerr, there was neither written nor eyewitness evidence which implicated Muller in the riot. Nevertheless, Judge Neil Dennison refused to allow defence counsel to call

Howard Kerr to give any details of the affair, saying it was 'not relevant' to Muller's case.

This was the first of fourteen cases which involved DS Sargent, and it was soon apparent that his substantial part in the inquiry – in all, he interrogated thirty-four different suspects – was going to be a grave embarrassment to the Met. In March 1986, between the inquiry and the trials, a black youth called Derek Pascall sued the Met and won £3,500 damages at Shoreditch County Court, after giving evidence that Sargent was present when another officer tortured him in order to force a confession. Pascall had admitted a number of burglaries, but at his trial he was able to show that some of them had never taken place. In his civil action, he said he had been held down by Sargent while the other officer beat him and burnt him with cigarettes, and Sargent had threatened to beat him about the genitals.

Muller said the way questions were written down and the way they had been asked was completely different: 'They kept saying, "We know you're involved," raising their voices and banging the table. They said, "You're lying." The only way to get them off me was to say I was throwing stones, that made them happy. They kept putting words to me, telling me what had happened. They said, "You can get out of this the easy way or the hard way." I thought it meant that if I didn't admit to things, they would take me down to the cell and give me a good beating . . . the whole bit about Broadwater Farm was made up. I was never in the Farm.'

David Mitchels, Muller's defence counsel, did not shrink from drawing parallels between the Derek Pascall affair and Muller's case when he put DS Sargent through his cross-examination:

Q: Did you have any evidence against him [Muller] when you started interviewing him? If he had sat still and declined to say anything at all, he would have been released without charge?
A: He would have had to have been, yes.
Q: So the confession was of great importance, the basis for charging him.
A: Yes.
Q: It was difficult because of the lack of evidence. It was

important to interrogate suspects in very great detail, and to keep going until you got what you wanted out of them.

A: Until we got the truth.

Q: Are you an officer who would not tolerate undue pressure on a defendant?

A: No, never.

Q: You've been in the force twenty-four years, but there's a dark cloud hanging over you.

A: Yes, a disciplinary inquiry has started.

Q: Because once you had dealings with a man called Derek Pascall.

Mitchels took Sargent through the details of the case and his part in it, then delivered the pay-off:

Q: I suggest that you were prepared to stand by and watch Pascall being beaten up, and come to court and lie about it. You're prepared to pressure people under interrogation and come here and lie about it.

A: No.

After a week-long trial, the jury took just forty minutes to reach a unanimous verdict that Muller was not guilty.

Notwithstanding the result of Derek Pascall's civil action, Sargent continued to deny that the youth had been ill-treated. But the strain on him as he was forced repeatedly to go over the details of the Pascall affair took its toll. One night, after the court had adjourned in another affray trial halfway through a particularly tough cross-examination by the barrister Patrick O'Connor, Sargent suffered a nervous breakdown. He was, the police said, too ill to give evidence at any of the eight trials outstanding in which he had played a part in the interrogation.

The last affray trial was not heard until October 1987, two years after PC Blakelock's death. The results of the contested hearings in themselves suggested that something had gone wrong. Twenty people pleaded guilty; but of those who protested their innocence, a clear majority was acquitted – twenty-four to nineteen. All these defendants had confessed their supposed guilt but now contested their admissions, often on grounds that they had been obtained by oppression. The proportion of acquittals was higher than the normal Old Bailey rate of about 50 per cent; twenty-four separate juries, each fresh to the facts, were troubled enough to throw confessions out, even in the intense atmosphere of all the Farm trials.

The judges imposed severe sentences. Simon McMinn, who was found to have thrown a few stones, was given a sentence of seven years in August 1986, which the Lord Chief Justice later reduced on appeal to four and a half years. Harsh sentences like McMinn's, which was typical, contrasted with the punishments awarded youths convicted of more serious crimes in Handsworth. There, two men who had set fire to the Post Office, so immolating its occupants, received sentences of five and four and a half years.

Some of the trials where the jury reached a not guilty verdict saw troubling allegations of police malpractice. James Roberts was acquitted in February 1987 of affray. His case was particularly unusual because he had gone to the police station voluntarily, worried after a search of his home where his mother was in poor health. On arrival at the police station, he was placed under arrest. He denied any part in the riot, but then, according to his evidence, became concerned that an accurate record of his words was not being kept.

He raised the matter with his interrogators, and then, he claimed, the atmosphere in the interview room changed dramatically. He stood up and said if they were going to fake his answers, he might as well go back to the cell. He refused to answer questions: the officers, he said, simply mimicked his voice in answering their own questions and fabricated the replies. Finally, he claimed, the interviewing officers lost their patience and pushed the table into his stomach while striking him around the face. He said he was terrified of a beating in the cells, and was dragged out of the room.

Roberts' account was partly supported by the police custody record, which included some details of the struggle. The interrogators claimed he had been trying to escape, but the record stated the struggle arose when he refused to leave the room. It added that he was held down in his seat, a point which the interviewing officers denied. He was acquitted of affray.

Alan Chance was another defendant acquitted on all charges. In his case, there were five separate counts, including riot, affray and arson. Like so many of those arrested, Chance, aged seventeen, was of low mental age and unusually suggestible.

He said in evidence that when he told the police he had spent the night of the riot at home with his girl friend, he had been slapped across the face and told not to lie. He was jabbed in the stomach, and finally, he said, he made up a confession because he thought it was what the police wanted to hear.

His psychological vulnerability and initial resistance did not, however, deter the police from attempting to make him a pros-ecution witness. He was held in police custody for three days after being charged, and at one stage Sargent and a colleague drove across north London for twenty minutes to see him – for the reason, they told the court, that they thought he could 'do with some exercise'. Mr Justice Hodgson poured scorn on this claim, asking the jury: 'Do you really believe that the sole purpose of two busy police officers investigating these matters in driving to Enfield Police Station was merely to give this seventeen-year-old some exercise? If you find it impossible to accept, then it does throw, you may think, some doubt on their credibility.'

The officers spent two hours alone with Chance. He was not interested in giving evidence for the prosecution. At his trial, it emerged that not only was there good evidence to discredit his admissions, he had an unusually strong alibi. He was cleared of all charges.

The efforts made by the police to add at least a few live witnesses to the confessions seem, in general, to have been clumsy and inept. In the case of Gary Potter, for example, a first trial ended with a hung jury, and a retrial was ordered. Here two youths who had already been convicted of other offences were called as prosecution witnesses. Simon Whyte, serving a three-year sentence for affray, told the court that he was giving evidence against Potter because police had told him that it was Potter who had 'grassed him up'. He said they had visited him in prison the week before the retrial, showed him some photos of Potter and told him to 'pick Potter out'.

The other new witness was Mark Palmer. He said the police had offered to 'forget' about photographs taken during the riot which depicted him and charge him only with threatening behaviour and possession of an offensive weapon. Palmer accepted and pleaded guilty to these charges at the magistrates' court. Palmer added that officers later visited him in prison, where he was serving time for an unrelated offence, and wrote out witness statements for him to sign, falsely identifying Potter at the scene of the disturbances.

Potter's second trial was notable for some remarkable evidence by Detective Superintendent Gallagher, the joint head of the investigation. Potter was one of those interrogated by Rex Sargent, and at one point Gallagher delivered a beautifully neat encapsulation of the police infallibility principle. Asked whether he thought Sargent had participated in the assault on Derek Pascall, Gallagher said: 'I have my doubts,' adding that Pascall had not made a written complaint, while Sargent had not been suspended from duty despite careful consideration by senior officers.

Cross-examined about denying access to a solicitor, he stuck at first to the same line used by Melvin, that lawyers might 'wittingly or unwittingly' disclose information which might lead to further evidence being concealed. Then he seemed to become exasperated, and expressed himself in forthright terms: 'Unfortunately some solicitors behave completely improperly . . . in the thirty years I have been in the police force the standard of ethics in the legal profession has dropped alarmingly.' Asked what he meant by this, he denied that he had been chiefly concerned lest Potter's 'brief' advise him to exercise his right of silence. The second trial of Gary Potter also ended with a hung jury, and he was discharged.

Paul Keys was one of the first affray defendants to appear at the Old Bailey, where he pleaded guilty in July 1986 and was sentenced to five years' imprisonment. He appeared for the prosecution in the trial of Nicky Jacobs, to whom belonged the dubious distinction of receiving the longest sentence for affray – eight years, subsequently cut to six on appeal. Keys gave evidence on the second day of the hearing, the police admitting that they had visited him in prison the night before. No statement by Keys had hitherto formed part of the prosecution case against Jacobs. At his subsequent appeal, Keys' sentence of five years was reduced to three.

In off the record conversations with journalists, the police ignored these unedifying examples and continued to blame the climate of fear for the shortage of witnesses, sometimes with the variant that this was now an organised climate, co-ordinated by the Broadwater Farm Defence Campaign. Anyone who worked with this organisation, which received council funding, knew that the suggestion that it had the power to send out hit squads to frighten witnesses was absurd. It was a thorn in the side of the police, no doubt, and strongly committed to remedying the injustice which its members saw unfolding before their eyes. Its staff worked hard, visiting families, trying to ensure that defendants had the best possible representation, and simply recording the course of events. But its weapons were the leaflet, the picket and the strident press release, not threats in the night.

As the start of the murder trial drew nearer, there was still little sign that the police investigators were questioning the quality of the information on which their cases were based.

In law, for obvious reasons, if someone being interrogated makes allegations about another person who is subsequently charged with a crime, the allegations are not admissible as evidence. If juries were to hear details of statements of this kind, the effect would be enormously prejudicial. Leaving aside the questions of suggestion or vulnerability, a man facing charges for a serious offence is very capable of lying in the hope of more lenient treatment. Only if the source is prepared to repeat the accusations in the witness box, where they may be tested by cross-examination, can they be put to the jury.

In all but one of the cases of the six charged with murder, the only evidence was confessions. At the same time, several of the murder defendants had made terrible allegations about each other to the police. Two of the juveniles, Mark Pennant and Jason Hill, had ascribed a particularly deadly role to Winston Silcott. In addition to the murder defendants, seven youths were charged not only with affray but with the more serious crime of riot, on the basis that they had joined in the attack on serial 502, and some had also accused

Silcott. The police knew all these allegations were inadmissible. But in speaking to journalists, they repeatedly emphasised the strength of this 'hidden evidence'.

The inadmissible pre-history to a confession could sometimes cast grave doubt upon it. Had the jury in Hassan Muller's trial known that he was in the dock only because of Howard Kerr, his acquittal would have been still more certain. Here a defendant confessed to doing exactly what the last stage in the daisy chain had described – but the dangers of trusting that earlier source remained hidden from the court.

The same applied to the numerous interrogation records which mentioned 'Sticks' or Winston Silcott. Reporters were told that here was a truly impressive body of evidence, if only the tiresome rules of legal procedure were not preventing it from reaching the jury! No doubt many police officers were convinced by this material. But like the mass of unfounded allegations which had convinced the Tottenham CID of Silcott's status as a major criminal before the riot, under the heat of close scrutiny it assumes the character of a snowball and melts away.

There were more than thirty different descriptions of Silcott offered by people undergoing interrogation, none of which matched the clothes which he was sure he had been wearing on 6 October – a red beret, red shirt, white trousers, black turtleneck sweater and suede shoes. When he signed on for bail for another offence at Tottenham Police Station at 7.15 on 6 October, according to a WPC, he was certainly dressed in this fashion. Andrew Pyke, the first person to accuse him, said he was dressed in a white jumper, green puffed-out jacket, and a mask made from a diagonally striped handkerchief tied over his mouth. Mark Pennant gave two different descriptions: the first had Sticks in a black zip-up jacket, blue trousers, and blue hat with signs on it; the second in a dark blue denim jacket and blue jeans.

Jason Hill had Silcott in a black leather pilot's jacket, jeans (stonewashed, light blue), a black balaclava, and white trainers. Perry Kelsey, however, one of those charged with riot after describing the killing in vivid detail, said he was wearing a green army cap, army jacket, camouflage trousers and boots. In a somewhat rococo touch, Kelsey described his carrying a 'long case, like a sword case', adding that he wore a pink glove on the hand holding the case, a black glove on the other. Raghip said he was in a dark jumper and trousers, with a black woolly hat. Carl Williams thought he wore a jogging top with a hood. As far as Bernard Kinghorn was concerned, he was dressed entirely in green.

The inconsistencies between the descriptions prove no more than what their authors' lawyers argued in court: that they were pure fantasy. Other details from the interview records point inexorably in the same direction. After two days being interrogated by Detective Inspector Dingle from 22 October, Junior Lee, eighteen, was eagerly accusing not only Silcott but Floyd Jarrett of having taken leading roles in the killing. He added the vivid phrase: 'It was like one of those survival programmes where sharks taste blood and go mad.'

As was to become clear, the police had no photographs of Silcott taken during the riot. Lee, who had never met Silcott, weakened his claims by wrongly identifying him from a series of pictures Dingle set before him.

Carl Williams provided one of the most dramatic descriptions of the killing. He said he saw Blakelock lying on his back, trying to protect himself with his hands, as Silcott, Mark Lambie and others attacked him:

> Q: Did you see anyone do anything to that officer other than kick him?
> A: I only saw one person chop him, that was Sticks.
> Q: Does it upset you to talk about it?
> A: Yeah.

He added that Silcott 'chopped his neck, it wasn't completely cut . . . it was a short, powerful chop, like a butcher cutting chops'.

Ignoring the fact that Williams, aged twenty, was held and interrogated for no less than four days, there was the clearest internal evidence that his confessions and allegations were untrue. The person who gave the order to attack PC Blakelock, he claimed, was none other than Dolly Kiffin. After the killing, he went on, Silcott stood chatting to her holding his machete on the deck of Tangmere, Miss Dolly announcing in a high voice that she and Silcott were going inside for a meeting and would be back shortly. Dolly Kiffin was not on Broadwater Farm, but at a fast-food restaurant a mile away.

Towards the end of his interviews, Williams claimed Silcott had been wearing pink washing-up gloves. There was a police photograph which did show a man so attired, and for a time the police seem to have thought it depicted Winston Silcott. The same photograph was shown to Silcott during his own interview. As the officers soon came to recognise, it was of someone entirely different.

Perry Kelsey was another youth charged with riot who seems to have slipped into fantasy. His account had Sticks and others coming back up the stairs on to the deck shouting 'we got a bullman', adding that he 'couldn't look at him because his reputation is enough to scare everyone'. His story was also spoilt by the allegation that Dolly Kiffin had joined the celebrations immediately after the murder, talking to the killers on the Tangmere deck. People stood chatting to her, drinking beer and saying 'things like, a life for a life', he said.

The inadmissible material against Winston Silcott gives us a picture of the police infallibility principle run wild. From the moment the police arrested Andrew Pyke, the inquiry seemed to be tailored principally to one end: to prove Silcott was the man with the machete, the monstrous ringleader of the killing of PC Blakelock.

As time went on, the contradictions grew more and more acute, yet every sign that the investigation might be off course was dismissed, if it was considered at all. That a man could make very serious allegations against Silcott but then identify him wrongly from photographs was not a trivial matter. That the police could take seriously confessions in which key details were woefully misplaced, such as the 'order' to attack PC Blakelock by Dolly Kiffin, is suggestive, at best, of tunnel vision. The more 'evidence' the investigators had about Silcott's involvement, the less was its value in court. The investigation was gathering the momentum of a lumbering juggernaut, and not one officer, apparently, was prepared to raise queries or to stand in its way.

9

'Put his head on a pole'

The old part of the Central Criminal Court is a place where the majesty of the law survives. In the Old Bailey's larger, post-war wing, the courtrooms are characterless, with soft carpets and pine furniture. But here, beneath the great dome of the central landing, the style is Marshall Hall, not *LA Law*. As the courts open for the daily business, heels click and echo on the marble floors, and clerks stagger beneath the weight of documents. Barristers in horsehair wigs do not, for once, seem anachronistic.

Court number two, the favoured venue for terrorism trials, heightens the impression of awe. Dark wood panels rise to stone, gloomily illuminated by a grubby skylight. The dock is massive, dominating half the room, high-walled, with solid metal bars facing the bench. In front are rows of pews for counsel, and a tiny box for the press. The public gallery, built like a Victorian theatre circle, is invisible to the jury.

The trial of the six accused of Keith Blakelock's murder began on Wednesday, 14 January 1987, but before Roy Amlot could begin his opening speech, there were frustrating delays. More than seventy potential jurors crowded into court on the first day to hear Mr Justice Hodgson warn that the trial would last two months or more. No sooner had the twelve been chosen than defence counsel began a long series of arguments about the admissibility of evidence, with the jury sent out. Then one juror recognised Courtenay Griffiths,

The police absorbing heavy punishment at the height of the
Broadwater Farm riot, 6 October 1985.

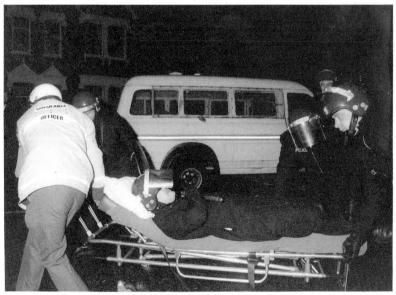
An injured police officer is wheeled to an ambulance.

PC Keith Blakelock.

A relaxed-looking Winston Silcott chatting to policemen outside his shop on the Tangmere deck on the morning after the murder of PC Blakelock.

After the riot.

Bill Silcott in tears on the day after his son's conviction,
20 March 1987.

Sharon Raghip and her six-year-old son, Don, at home during
the years of waiting.

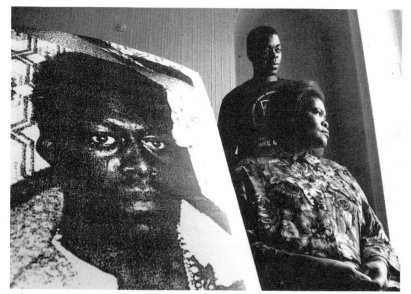

The campaigning continues: Winston Silcott's mother, Mary, and his brother, George.

Andrew Hall, Silcott's solicitor, with Mary and George, after students at the LSE elected Winston Silcott their honorary president, 1989.

Mark Braithwaite and Engin Raghip are swept in tumult from
the Court of Appeal after being given their freedom,
27 November 1991.

Engin and Sharon Raghip arriving at the Court of Appeal for the final judgement, 5 December 1991.

Sir Kenneth Newman.

Detective Chief Superintendent Graham Melvin leaves Bow Street Magistrates' Court, facing charges of perjury and conspiracy to pervert the course of justice, January 1992.

junior counsel for Mark Lambie, as a friend of a friend, and the process had to begin again, this time with a record panel of four hundred. It was not for a full week, on 21 January, that Amlot at last got underway.

There was nothing flowery or flamboyant about Amlot's delivery. A slim, tall man, his pale face had the look of a youth preserved by underindulgence. He eschewed barristers' gestures; not for Amlot the hitching up of the gown or disbelieving tug on the braces during cross-examination. Yet his courtroom presence was considerable. It derived, above all, from an overwhelming sense of control. Amlot's voice was seldom raised, and could even, at first hearing, seem colourless. But he rarely stumbled and he did not indulge in long-winded circumlocutions. Years of prosecuting the most serious criminal cases had made him relentless. His long fingers and cold, clear eyes suggested he might, in another life, have been a surgeon.

Outside the courtroom, the seven days of waiting had cranked up the feverish emotions surrounding the trial several notches. By 9.30 on the morning of 21 January, an hour before the proceedings were due to start, the little press enclave had overflowed, and forty or fifty journalists packed the oak benches on either side of the dock.

The start of Amlot's opening was calm and low-key: 'On Sunday, 6 October 1985, a severe riot disrupted Tottenham. The focal point was the Broadwater Farm estate, a large council estate known locally as the Farm.'

With meticulous clarity, he rapidly summarised the death of Mrs Jarrett, the outbreak of the fighting, and Colin Couch's decision to send Keith Blakelock's serial into Tangmere. The silence in court as he described the prelude to the killing was absolute: 'A large crowd of youths started to appear at the head of the stairway opposite the one the police had come up. Most of them were masked. They came streaming in from below the building and another part of the estate. Word had obviously gone round and some people heard a bell ringing, which may well have been some kind of signal. Sensing danger Sergeant Pengelly shouted out more than once: "All we are doing is protecting the firemen. Let them do their job." Nevertheless a brick was thrown, which heralded a terrible attack.'

One of the rioters, Amlot said, shouted to the officers: 'This is the Farm. You must be mad. You'll never get out of here alive.'

Of the onslaught against PC Blakelock, Amlot said: 'The attack on that lone officer was brutal and without pity. He had no chance. It is clear they were intending to murder him.'

After describing Blakelock's injuries, Amlot turned to the case against each of the six. Silcott, Braithwaite and Raghip sat in the massive dock, dressed in suits, impassive. Occasionally Mark Braithwaite revealed the flash of a gold tooth; Silcott's head was shaved. The three juveniles, Pennant, Hill and Lambie, sat at a table in front of the barristers' pews with social workers, often lolling in their seats, looking bored.

Amlot summarised Mark Pennant's interviews, concealing references to Silcott by speaking simply of 'a man'. Before opening the case, he and defence counsel had held a long discussion about how best to prevent the jury from finding out what one defendant had said about another. These allegations, as we saw in the previous chapter, were inadmissible as evidence.

Barbara Mills QC, for Silcott, had been particularly concerned that if only the names of co-defendants were hidden when the jury came to consider the records of interrogation, they would quickly work out what was going on. Mr Justice Hodgson therefore made an innovative and unusual ruling. In the interviews put before the jury, *every* name was to be concealed by a letter of the alphabet, whether or not they were involved in the trial. Silcott, for example, became N. There were so many names that the alphabet was used more than twice over, with a ZZ, and a DDD. Before the jury could actually be given copies of the interview documents, someone had to go through all of them, painting over the names with correcting fluid and substituting the agreed letters.

The second defendant charged was Mark Lambie. Interviewed in the presence of his father, he made no admissions to being near the attack on PC Blakelock. But there was a witness, Amlot said, who saw Lambie taking part in the killing, working his way through the mob around the body until he could land a blow.

Next came Jason Hill. At first, he told the police he had only watched the riot, and taken a few sweets from the Tangmere supermarket. But in the second session with his interrogators,

Amlot said, he began to open up. He admitted watching the murder, and saw Blakelock kicked, and his helmet ripped off. In his interview, Hill had said: 'A machete hit him on the side of the head. I looked away because I felt sick. They were trying to chop his head off. They said they were going to put it on a pole and plant it in the grass in front of the police.' With one sentence, Amlot had rekindled the dark talk of Blakelock's head being 'nearly severed'. The point was not lost on the listening press corps.

In Hill's last interview, Amlot went on, the key parts were not written down contemporaneously because the suspect became too emotional: 'He said it was like a horror movie, that the officer was hacked to pieces. He said you had to do what this certain person said, that friends said they'd seen too much and two masked men were sent over to where he and his friend were standing. The sword was forced into his hand and he was forced to make his mark. The man said after he'd done this "You're cool, what have you seen here, nothing." After this Jason was let go.'

That 'certain person', as every reporter knew, was Winston Silcott, to whom Amlot now came. He was arrested, he said, on 12 October, and interrogated at Paddington Green Police Station. This, as some members of the jury may have known, was the high-security station used for questioning IRA and other terrorist suspects. In four interviews on the 12th and the following day, Amlot told the jury, Silcott said nothing. Then came the fifth session, when he was questioned by Detective Chief Superintendent Graham Melvin. The interview was crucial. It may have been brief and ambiguous, but it lay at the heart of the trial. Amlot read the important passages to the jury in full:

Q: I believe that you were with others standing over PC Blakelock when he was on the ground. You had either a machete or something like a sword with which you struck the officer.
A: Who told you that?
Q: I am not prepared to tell you who described your part in the murder of the officer. Suffice it to say, that I've been told you played an active part in murdering him.
A: They're only kids. No one's going to believe them. You say they say that. How do I know? I don't go with kids.

Q: What makes you think that the people I'm referring to who have witnessed your part in the murder are young people?

A: You have only had kids in here so far, haven't you?

Q: If only one person had told me of your part in the crime I would not be so confident in my belief that you were the ringleader that night. When there is more than one person saying the same thing the facts become clear.

At this point, Amlot said, the interrogation record stated that Silcott 'looked out of the window, stood up, went back to his chair and then said, with tears in his eyes, "You cunts." He then leaned back in his chair and said, "Jesus, Jesus." The record continued:

Q: Did you murder PC Blakelock?

A: You ain't got enough evidence. Those kids will never go to court. You wait and see. No one else will talk to you. You can't keep me away from them.

Q: What do you mean by that?

A: I ain't saying no more. You've got a big surprise coming. You will probably be out of a job.

Q: Are you saying that any witness is in danger from you?

A: Just take me down and charge me. I ain't saying no more. You ain't got no evidence.

Q: Apart from the murder, it is important to recover the firearms and weapons that were used that night. Can you tell me where they might be?

A: You're too slow, man, they gone.

Q: Mr Silcott, in order to save further life it is essential we find those weapons. Can you help me?

A: No, fuck you, you find them.

Q: Mr Silcott, I firmly believe that you were the ringleader in the attack upon the officer. You had a weapon. You used it on the officer and caused other people to stab and cut that officer.

A: They won't give evidence against me.

Q: I have further reason to believe that it was your intention to sever the officer's head and to parade it on a pole through the estate within sight of the other police officers on duty that night. Do you deny that?

A: I'm not saying anything more. I won't answer any more questions. You can't force me, man.

Silcott, Amlot said, was then charged with murder, and replied: 'They won't give evidence against me.'

After that, the rest of Amlot's opening was an anticlimax. Raghip, he said, had been arrested next, and in his fifth interview he told the police he had carried a broom handle with which he would have hit the officer had he been able to 'get in'.

Braithwaite was not arrested until 4 February. His key admission came in his fourth interview, when he said: 'All I want to say is that I hit him with a bar twice whilst he was on the ground. Others were stabbing and kicking. There were about ten around him. I was not the first or the last to kick him. The PC was covering his face and rolling on the ground.' Later, he repeated this confession, Amlot said, but denied he had hit Blakelock, saying his victim was another officer.

The indictment was read: all six were charged with murder, riot and affray, and Lambie also with throwing petrol bombs.

Early that first day, as the jury left before a short break, Mr Justice Hodgson warned: 'There'll be lots of public interest in this case. Your relatives and your friends will want to talk about it. Resist the temptation, speak to no one about it.' These were wise words. But nothing could have prepared the judge for the newspapers next day.

All carried prominent reports on their front pages. The shocking image of the plan to put Blakelock's head on a pole dominated the coverage, including my own, published in the *Guardian*. But the *Sun* went rather further. For some weeks, one of the Old Bailey news agencies had been offering national newspapers a photograph of Winston Silcott, taken by a police photographer, and apparently leaked. Now, it took up half the paper's front page, under the headline: 'FACE OF MAN IN RIOT PC MURDER CHARGE'.

The accompanying text, by the *Sun*'s Old Bailey reporter James Lewthwaite, began: 'This is the first picture of Winston "Sticks" Silcott, who police believe wielded a machete in the horrific murder of bobby Keith Blakelock.' In a case where identification, or the lack of it, was certain to be a substantial issue, a more serious contempt of court could hardly be imagined. The *Sun*, which the previous year had happily published a picture of the victim of the terrible Ealing vicarage rape, had spat in the face of the legal process. It had utterly disregarded the principle that material of this kind should not be published while a case remains *sub judice*.

Mr Justice Hodgson's rage was barely suppressed in court next day. He condemned the paper in the strongest terms, and took the rare step of ordering an immediate reference to the Attorney-General, with a view to prosecution. But the damage was done. Silcott's solicitor, Andrew Hall, says: 'There could have been no clearer way of telling the jury that whatever the evidence, Silcott was the man they had to convict. It had an incalculable prejudicial effect, and although the judge obviously directed them to ignore it, I am sure it coloured the way they viewed the case from that moment on.'

Stafford Scott and his friends felt the same way. 'I think once we saw that front page, we all knew we were going to be waving Winston goodbye.' No action was ever taken against the *Sun*.

Defence and prosecution counsel agreed that there was no need for the jury to be given copies of the photographs of PC Blakelock's body, lest they suffer unnecessary distress. But in the next few days, the evidence called by Roy Amlot about the murder left little to the imagination. After hearing the testimony of the firemen, the surviving police officers and the residents who saw the attack from their windows, the jury knew that this had been a killing of appalling brutality. But none of this evidence got the court any nearer to the guilt or innocence of the accused.

For the first few days, the press benches stayed crowded. PC Coombes made headlines with his evidence that the mob around Blakelock looked like 'vultures' pecking at his prostrate form. On 28 January, another stir was caused by the evidence of PC Robin Clarke, a member of serial 502, who in a written statement read to the court said Blakelock died unnecessarily: had another serial been left to guard the foot of the stairs leading to the Tangmere deck, he would not have been killed.

But gradually, news editors and reporters lost interest. Amlot did not reach the first real substance of the trial until 30 January, nine days after his opening and sixteen days after the proceedings commenced. As he turned to Detective Constable Lockwood and asked him to give evidence of his interviews with Mark Pennant, there were only three reporters left in court: Colin Randall of the *Daily Telegraph*, a representative of the Press Association news agency, and myself. With the occasional addition of one of the specialist Old Bailey agencies, that was how things stayed until the closing days of the trial.

Pennant was defended by Michael West QC, and in cross-examining Lockwood he made straight for the questions of Pennant's vulnerability, and the confusion shown by the police as to whether he was a suspect or a witness. He was a fifteen-year-old with the mental age of a seven-year-old, West told Lockwood, 'a lemon to be squeezed until the pips were dry'. At the time of the interview, Lockwood said, 'I was unaware of any mental handicap.' He claimed he did not know Pennant was a pupil at a special school.

Why had the judges' rules defining the different ways of treating suspects and witnesses not been followed? West demanded to know. 'I can't answer that,' Lockwood replied.

West suggested a reason why he had no solicitor present, or his parents: 'Mr Melvin came to the scene and said he was not to have a solicitor at any time, and that his parents were not to be let in.'

Lockwood nodded and agreed: 'The decision was made by the senior officer.'

On 3 February, Detective Chief Superintendent Melvin entered the witness box for the first time. West questioned him closely about his refusal of a solicitor, and he repeated the argument first heard in the High Court seventeen months before: 'In this wholly exceptional case, there was great pressure on solicitors and their friends which might interfere with the course of justice . . . there were many outstanding witnesses, suspects and evidence. I believed that the presence of a solicitor would allow those suspects, either wittingly or unwittingly, to be informed.'

West suggested that the real reason was that without a solicitor, an educationally subnormal child might be more likely to confess. Melvin vehemently denied this.

The most poignant moment of the case came shortly afterwards when Jenny Kent, Pennant's teacher, took the stand. She described how he had asked if being charged with murder meant he would be coming to live with her, and said she felt shocked to her core: 'I felt like turning round and saying, he didn't murder anyone!' Not until then, she said, did the seriousness of his plight begin to sink in.

The next defendant dealt with by Amlot was Mark Lambie. His case, in the context of the Broadwater Farm inquiry, was highly unusual. Lambie's interviews, by Detective Inspector Dingle, had been conducted with impeccable fairness, in the presence of both his father and a solicitor, Brian Raymond. Lambie was of normal intelligence for his age, fourteen at the time of his arrest. As the court now heard, Dingle made rigorous efforts to ensure that Lambie knew what was going on and understood the caution before proceeding. He took him through it stage by stage, asking what school he attended, and whether he was of average academic ability. All this, of course, was in sharp contrast to the cursory efforts made with Mark Pennant.

Lambie did admit playing a minor role in the disturbances, but the foundation of the Crown's case against him was a witness, Jason Cobham, aged seventeen at the time of the riot. Examined by Amlot on 9 February, he said he saw Lambie shouting 'out of my way' as he forced a path through the centre of the crowd around PC Blakelock. He heard someone shouting 'we got a pig down' and recognised Lambie by his clothes: training shoes, jeans and a dark jacket. He had been 'fairly roughed up, agitated', and yelled at the others to let him through two or three times. 'He got into the crowd, but as the crowd was moving so much I lost sight of him,' Cobham said.

Michael Mansfield began to cross-examine Cobham quietly, skirting round the main issues, establishing a few apparently unimportant facts.

His advocacy was the opposite of the cold and passionless approach employed by Roy Amlot. Amlot's appeal was to the common sense of the jury, his method an attempt to make the charges laid by the state appear to coincide with reason. Mansfield was driven by anger, and tried to show that injustice mattered. At his best, his speeches and cross-examinations had a visceral political impact, as dissections in microcosm of a system he thought in gravest need of reform.

In court, Amlot and Mansfield regarded each other with visible disdain. There was no barristers' camaraderie linking prosecution and defence in the PC Blakelock murder trial. Unlike after some big cases, there was no cosy dinner with the judge and counsel for both sides when it was all over.

But committed as he was, Mansfield had not earned his huge and growing reputation by being politically correct. His success was the embodiment of the old barrister's adage, 'Never ask a question unless you know the answer.' His victories were built on careful research and preparation. Before the Blakelock trial, Mansfield and his junior, Courtenay Griffiths, had spent weeks in a room at the Old Bailey reserved by the Director of Public Prosecutions, trawling through piles of printouts from the HOLMES computer – used and unused interview records, a mine of valuable information, available for inspection by any defence counsel.

As Mansfield knew from his sifting of the police interview records, Cobham's friends before the riot had included Simon McMinn and his brother Vernon, and Paul Parker. On the night of the riot, did he go to Broadwater Farm with the McMinns and Parker? Mansfield asked. Cobham denied it, then wavered, and changed his mind. Mansfield quickly pressed his advantage: 'Now that's the first time you've told the truth.'

As Mansfield's cross-examination proceeded, Cobham admitted he had been at the riot armed with a stick but had not told the police, explaining his omission: 'What with the pressure from the police, I must have forgotten.' It had been his first time in a cell, he said, and it was 'extremely worrying'. But he had done no more than throw a few stones.

Vernon and Simon McMinn had thrown a few stones, Mansfield reminded him, and Simon had been convicted of affray and sentenced to seven years' imprisonment. Now Cobham made his first really damaging admission. He might, he said, 'have been the most active' during the riot, measured against the McMinns and Paul Parker. However, he had not been charged with affray, but only with stealing a bottle of Cherryade and threatening behaviour, for which Tottenham Magistrates' Court had fined him £200.

Was it possible, Mansfield went on, that he had not been at Tangmere at all? Cobham denied this, but then agreed he had had a 'lot of help' from the police since his arrest. They had fixed him up with a flat, on which they paid the rent, and had given him money to buy groceries. Twice, they had helped arrange a job: 'Once I actually went to the interview while they waited for me.' Had the police brought him to the Old Bailey? Yes, Jason said, DC Lockwood was his 'minder'. The cross-examination continued:

Q: This help from the police – when will it all end?
A: I don't really know.
Q: Do you think it depends on your coming here today and sticking at least to the bit about Blakelock's death?
A: No.
Q: Would they be happy if you went back on it?
A: I haven't got a clue.

After the lunch adjournment, the defeat of Jason Cobham turned into a rout. He admitted telling lies: a statement he made before Paul Parker's trial had been 'dotted with lies'. He had not wanted, he agreed, to give evidence in the Blakelock case: 'If I couldn't be here I wouldn't, but I have to be here.'

He admitted he had seriously played down his own role in the riot: 'I was caught up in the stupidity of it all.' Mansfield asked if it was true he had set fire to a car: 'I think I might have done.'

In his first interview he made no mention of the events at Tangmere, and had not named Mark Lambie. Then, at 2.05 pm, he had been seen by DC Lockwood who told him he might be charged with murder. 'I was frightened out of my wits,' he said. Yet still he denied making a deal in return for giving evidence: 'I thought I'd co-operate because it would make things easier for me.'

Questioned in detail about the attack on serial 502, it emerged that Cobham had not seen the firemen, nor their hoses, nor a second policeman fall, nor knives going up and down, nor any machetes. He had not seen where the police came from, nor any officer being dragged off. Mansfield said: 'What you had to do, I suggest, is that because you knew where the death was supposed to have occurred, you made things up to fit in.' At the magistrates' court committal,

Cobham had said he watched the attack for five or ten minutes. Now, he said it lasted only two minutes: 'I've not really any idea how long I was there.'

Before the trial, Cobham had written a letter to Vernon McMinn in jail. It said: 'I want to simply say this mess I'm in is mainly to help you and Simon. I didn't want to face bird. Don't worry about paying me back. You one are the cool one left and I would not dream of charging you.' In another letter, he referred to his job as a tyre fitter: 'I forgot to say they got me a job as a kwik-fit fitter. Teaching me the dance and the words of the song.' This, he insisted, referred to a television advertisement, not coaching for his evidence.

Next day, Mansfield added a few final touches. Cobham said he had accused another youth, Gary Potter, falsely, but couldn't remember why. He had agreed to give evidence because he 'wanted out' of a prison sentence. The police had claimed he had a two-foot machete; he had been 'really sweating', it was an 'horrific situation'.

It is impossible not to feel pity for Jason Cobham, who probably saw nothing of the attack on serial 502. His collapse under cross-examination was the collapse of the Crown's case against Mark Lambie, as Amlot recognised. He stood up as Mansfield finished and quietly withdrew the charges of murder and riot. Cobham's miserable performance was another illustration of the shortcomings of the police inquiry. Evidence rooted in fear and desperation was always liable to have its weaknesses exposed.

Immediately after Cobham had been dealt with, I asked one of the senior inquiry detectives, a Serious Crime Squad member who attended much of the trial, what he thought. He said: 'The coloureds make notoriously bad witnesses.' He added:

All the coloureds carry knives, and an officer in a London station doesn't have to look at statistics to know that they do most of the muggings. So it's the coloureds who get stopped – but then they call it racial harassment. But the anger in the force now is such that if there is another riot, you might find some of these coloured youths happen to jump off the balconies. The police know what happened, who led the riot and the murder, but we can't prove it. Justice isn't being done. The public deserve better.

10

Suffer Little Children

Halfway through the trial, things were not going well for Roy Amlot and the prosecution. Lambie had been lost, and it appeared that Mr Justice Hodgson might well rule Pennant's interviews inadmissible, on the grounds that he had been subjected to oppression. The police began to cover themselves for a possible disaster, letting it be known that they were braced for all six defendants to 'walk'. But in the case of Jason Hill, there was further trouble in store.

Hill was thirteen, and small for his age. He had not reached puberty. He lived in the Stapleford block on Broadwater Farm. He and his younger brother were both seen looting the shop at Tangmere, and this was reported to the police. On 13 October, they came to the flat and arrested not only the boys but their parents, finding stolen goods from the shop worth about £100.

Hill was taken to Leyton Police Station and locked in a cell, alone, for eight hours. He asked for a solicitor, Melvin refused to allow access. Before the start of the trial proper, before the jury was sworn in, Hill's lawyers held a *voir dire* in front of the judge, a pre-trial review of the evidence, accompanied by a legal submission asking him to rule Hill's confessions inadmissible. In this *voir dire* hearing, Melvin used the familiar argument that a lawyer might wittingly or unwittingly leak valuable information. The submissions were rejected.

Towards the end of the first afternoon of Hill's detention, a social worker called Joe Heatley arrived at the police station to sit in on his interviews as an 'appropriate adult'. By the end of a four-hour interrogation, Hill had admitted stealing, saying with authentic gusto that he 'just had to nick the big Dairy Milk bars, because I just love them'. He should, according to the judges' rules which prevailed until the PACE Act came into force on 1 January 1986, have been charged with theft then, and brought before a magistrate. Under the rules, there was now a *prima facie* case against him for the offence for which he had been arrested, and there was no reason to question or detain him any longer.

Heatley asked if he was to be transferred to the local authority overnight. No such arrangements had been made, and he was kept in the police station.

Next day, a Saturday, Heatley returned, expecting to be allowed to sit in on the resumed interrogation. One of the two officers dealing with Hill was a young PC called Perry Cockram who, by the time of the trial, had been promoted to detective constable.

Cockram told the court that before interviewing Jason Hill again, he had something of an altercation with Joe Heatley, during which the social worker said he had been told by his local authority bosses to 'instruct' Hill not to answer questions. Later Heatley told a very different story. He said he had wanted simply to advise the boy that he had the right of silence, and that he should be very careful about what he said, because he was being asked about very serious matters. This would have been quite proper for an 'appropriate adult' attending the interrogation of a juvenile; in fact, it was exactly how the law defined his role.

In any event, Heatley was turned out on his ear. Cross-examined by Hill's counsel, Bruce Laughland QC, Cockram made clear his opinion of Heatley. The council, he said, had a 'policy of non-cooperation' with the police. As far as he was concerned, Heatley was 'obstructing the course of justice'. The appropriate adult invited to attend the rest of Hill's interviews in Heatley's place was Hyacinth Moody, of the Haringey Community Relations Council police liaison committee.

In the four-hour interview that followed that morning, Laughland established that Hill was asked only one question about stealing from the shop – the ostensible reason for which he was being held. Rapidly, the interrogation moved on to more dangerous territory.

Hill said he had been on the Tangmere deck when the police appeared and saw 'five or six people' follow them downstairs. He stood on the last step and watched as the mob 'chopped him [Blakelock] up'. The officer had slipped in the mud; one black man, a stranger, hit him twice on the leg with a machete. In the interview Hill went on to name Silcott, Lambie and others among the attackers, and then made his dramatic claim that the rioters intended to sever the officer's head and plant it on a pole.

There was internal evidence that Hill might not have witnessed what he claimed to have seen. He said he had seen Nicky Jacobs repeatedly slashing at Blakelock's chest, cutting away his uniform; there were, as we have seen, no knife wounds to this part of the body. In a later exchange Hill's confusion during the interrogation seems clear:

Q: Did you see any police try and rescue the policeman on the ground?
A: No. Probably, I might have.
Q: Look, did you see a policeman try to save his colleague?
A: I ran off.
Q: This policeman would have been in the same area as the policeman being stabbed. So you would have seen him, surely.
A: No, I ran off.

And soon afterwards:

Q: You must have seen who ended up with the policeman's helmet.
A: No I didn't.
Q: You saw it being cut from his head though.
A: It was kept on the floor, weren't it?

This, at the very end of the interview, seems to have provoked an all too rare note of scepticism from the police: 'I think we've come to a stage where you are obviously telling lies about the sequence of events,' said PC Higgs. Alas, he failed to draw the obvious conclusion that Hill was making it up, suggesting instead: 'It would appear you have become vague in order to protect certain persons involved in the murder of PC Blakelock.'

After this interview, Hill was at last charged with burglary. The reason, Laughland suggested, was that under the PACE Act, and the force order which imposed its provisions in the dry run, a suspect must be charged or brought before a court after thirty-six hours. This time was running out. Once he had been charged, he certainly should not have been questioned again without going before a court. But next morning, the interrogation resumed.

PC Cockram began with intense questioning about the supposed role of 'Sticks' in the killing, Hill providing the officers with elaborate details such as the colour and shape of an ornamental scabbard Silcott was supposed to be wearing on his belt. Suddenly, at about 10.45 am, two hours into the interview, the police stopped keeping a contemporaneous record. The reason, Cockram said in court, was that 'there was a marked change, and he became very emotional'.

Cockram said he could not recall what question had provoked this change in Hill. Laughland suggested that the reason was a sharp change in the method of interrogation: instead of the measured pace dictated by the contemporaneous recording, with one officer doing nothing but writing, they suddenly came at Hill together, rapidly firing off questions in turn. This the officers denied. But in his ruling ten days later, Mr Justice Hodgson supported the defence view: 'There then followed precisely that which contemporaneously recorded interviews . . . are aimed at preventing. From conducting a contemporaneous interview, the officers suddenly started asking questions in turn.' The reason for the officers' vagueness as to what provoked Hill's outburst, the judge said, 'seems to me to be all too obvious'.

More than an hour's worth of interrogation was not written up until the afternoon, when Cockram and his colleague PC Higgs compared their recollections and wrote out a record. This, Cockram said, they did in Mrs Moody's office, so that where necessary they could consult her. At 11.58, contemporaneous recording began again, and Hill was asked to repeat what he had said during his breakdown. There followed the most lurid and shocking evidence given throughout all the long series of Broadwater Farm trials. As it was read to the jury for the first time, with letters substituted for the names, it made a deep and visible impression.

Hill, the record stated, described a ritual murder, which sounds more like a chapter from the novel *Lord of the Flies* than a realistic account of the killing of Keith Blakelock:

Q: Was anybody giving orders over the body?
A: Sticks.
Q: What did you hear him say?
A: Drag him into the flats.
Q: Why were you taken over to the body?
A: 'Cos we'd seen too much.
Q: What did you do when you were standing by the body?
A: I was looking away just telling them to let us go.
Q: Were you given a weapon?
A: Yeah.
Q: What sort?
A: The sword.
Q: Who gave you it?
A: Sticks.
Q: What were you expected to do with it?
A: Hit him with it.
Q: You were told to?
A: Yeah, but I wouldn't at first. Then I was forced to.
Q: Who by?
A: Sticks, Lambie and Jacobs said just do it or we'll do it to you.
Q: What did you do with the sword?
A: The first time I was made to do it I went over another cut, but the second time I made my own mark.

His first cut, Hill said, was to Blakelock's leg, just below the knee. No such wound was recorded in the autopsy report. The interrogation continued:

Q: Why did you have to slash the policeman the second time?
A: Because Sticks told me I had to make my own mark.

Q: Can you remember what Sticks said to you?
A: After the second time, he said, 'you cool guy' and passed the
sword to Craig to do the same.

Hill's second mark was to Keith Blakelock's chest, and he
described it very vividly:

> [The sword] was harder to lift than a knife. I'm not entirely sure
> which part of the policeman's chest I cut because it was covered
> in blood. The policeman was flat on his back. I cut him on the
> middle of the chest.

PC Cockram, it seems, had no idea where Keith Blakelock was
wounded. The interview continued:

Q: What else did Sticks say?
A: He said I was cool, 'What have you just seen here?' I said,
'Nothing.' He said, 'Well, you can go.'

At 7.25 the same evening, Hill was interviewed again, this time
by DC Lockwood. At last his solicitor, Jill Bendix, had been
allowed in. Hill said immediately: 'I don't know how to say this
but the last police officers really put some pressure on me, and
they really made me say things I didn't do. What I said last time
was a complete lie and fantasy story . . . the police officer said that
if I told him everything that I did he would let me home. So I made
up everything I said in the last statement. He was pressurising me
and he made me say I was at the murder and I didn't know about
the murder until the next day.'

Hill said PC Higgs visited him in the cell before the morning
interview and told him: 'Now I want the truth. I want no fucking
about. You know all the main men up there and who made the
petrol bombs and where they are stored.'

The end of this last interview contained a section headed 'points
you have raised which we have not been able to get down'. Here,
Hill said he had slept poorly because of the fierce heating in the
cells: 'It's so hot in there you can't breathe.' He had been really
sweating, but despite asking for water frequently he was refused.
As for Mrs Moody, 'she just used to sit there if I said something,
whatever I said, for example "I want got home and watch the telly."

She would ramble on about PC Keith Blakelock, that man that died, saying, "He can't go home and watch the telly."'

Laughland's cross-examination of Cockram now revealed the astonishing fact that Hill's clothes were removed for forensic examination just after he was charged with burglary on the second evening. No replacements were provided, and he was left to spend his second night in a cell, isolated from his family or anyone who knew him, wearing only his underpants and a blanket. He was still dressed in this way when he was questioned on the Sunday morning, but by now the blanket was stained with flecks of his own vomit. 'This was happening in England, wasn't it?' Laughland asked. 'Rioting, thank God, is a rare occurrence in England,' Cockram replied. Was the officer shocked that a boy aged thirteen might be locked up half-naked in a cell? 'No, sir.'

Earlier, in the *voir dire*, Laughland had questioned Cockram about the failure to provide Hill with replacement clothing. Cockram gave inconsistent replies. He said he thought that Hill's family would be bringing clothes to the police station, but he also stated that he had not been aware that they had been released from custody.

In the second interview, and for the early part of the third, Hill was not asked about his own supposed involvement in the riot, only about others'; nor was he told he was being questioned on suspicion of murdering PC Blakelock. Why was this so? Laughland asked.

A: I have my own individual interviewing technique, and I like to establish a rapport when I start to ask questions.
Q: How long does it take your interviewing technique to bear fruit?
A: How long is a piece of string, sir.

Next to give evidence was Hyacinth Moody. Examined by Amlot, she told the court that Hill's admissions were like a horror movie, that every time he closed his eyes, he saw the policeman being chopped up. She had made notes of the salient parts of the interviews, she said, but unfortunately she had lost them.

As Laughland began to cross-examine her, she soon adopted a combative attitude. Laughland tried to establish what she knew of the role of an appropriate adult, and what she could do to advise Hill. She suddenly exploded: 'You don't expect me to go through the whole thing, do you, unless you want to give me a Collins type dictionary!'

Mr Justice Hodgson intervened: 'We would get on a lot quicker if you weren't so suspicious of counsel.'

She said: 'He's trying to discredit me, Your Honour, and I don't like it one little bit!'

The cross-examination went on:

Q: Suppose you had gone along to the police station and found there a thirteen-year-old boy, who had been locked in a cell for nine hours, refused access to a solicitor, refused the possibility of communicating with the outside world and not told he was suspected of a serious crime like murder. Would that come in your view under the category of harassment?

A: Depends what degree of harassment you mean.

Q: [repeats the same question]

A: I fail to answer that question, it is hypothetical. I do not think I have to come here and answer questions about all these suppositions. I'm not here to be harassed by you. You're wasting my time, sir.

Persevering, Laughland discovered that Mrs Moody knew Hill had no solicitor, but had not known his request for one had been refused by the police. Her own role, it emerged, she considered was to 'observe', not to advise Hill in his interviews.

Q: What advice did you give him when you first met him?

A: After his rights were read to him I think I said that the officers were not going to do him any harm, just speak the truth and that's all.

Q: Didn't it cross your mind that all this was going on a bit long for a thirteen-year-old?

A: When you're talking in the room the time goes quickly. It was a very, very good atmosphere.

Q: Did you suggest they stop?

A: Have I got the right to go into a police station and tell them to stop questioning?

Judge: Put it another way: did you think you didn't?

A: Yes.

Later Laughland asked whether she had not been concerned about Hill's lack of clothing. She said she did ask why he was half-naked, but was told no clothes were available.

Q: Wouldn't he have been at a disadvantage?
A: No, I'm not a psychiatrist. Oh, it's not the usual practice, to see a young man in a blanket etc., and then I heard his clothes had been taken. It was a large blanket and he was wrapped in it.
Q: [repeats question]
A: I'm not a psychiatrist. How would I know? If you strip me now it wouldn't prevent me talking. It wouldn't encourage me to talk less or more, no.

Mrs Moody risked becoming the only comic turn of the Blakelock murder trial. Bruce Laughland belonged to the aristocratic school of advocacy. His questions were placed with the skill of an oar dipped silently in still water, but they broke over Mrs Moody in cold, drenching waves.

In an attempt to establish her lack of independence of the police, he asked her about her meetings with Colin Couch and DAC Richards before the riot. Why were these questions being asked? she demanded to know. What business had counsel to probe in this direction? The judge tried to restrain her, but she retorted: 'I thought this was a democratic society!' Laughland went on:

Q: Do you find it flattering to mix with senior officers?
A: I refuse to answer, because that is a personal question. He is a man, and I am a woman.

She denied the police had made their notes in her presence, saying: 'The notes were not prepared in my office. I'm not collaborating with the police, that would be illegal!'

Here was a significant discrepancy between the evidence of PC Cockram and that of Mrs Moody. Another followed. The police, Laughland said, had insisted she made no notes of her own. If so, she replied, that was a 'diabolical lie'. She had lost them, having hidden them away because they were 'confidential'.

A week later, at the very end of the prosecution case, the jury was sent out while Laughland made a series of new submissions about the case of Jason Hill, arguing that all his interviews, the only evidence against him, should be ruled inadmissible. Much of the argument had been put before, at the end of the *voir dire*.

Mr Justice Hodgson's ruling of 24 February was something of a legal landmark. He began with a few words about Detective Chief Superintendent Melvin. He understood, he said, the pressure the police were under, and the difficulties of finding witnesses. He accepted that Melvin wished to conduct the investigation with fairness and absolute propriety. However: 'I regret that I have to find that, in the case of Jason Hill, there were improprieties, and serious ones. Three, I consider very serious.' Responsibility for one, the refusal of a solicitor, had to rest with Melvin alone: 'He forgot that Jason Hill was a child . . . I have, to an extent, to criticise him personally, I regret.'

Only in exceptional cases could a judge allow a second submission on the admissibility of evidence when a first had failed. Mr Justice Hodgson said he had made his first ruling without knowing many of the facts of the case, and as they began to emerge, the thought that he might not be able to throw Jason's interviews out had given him 'sleepless nights'. But the circumstances were so exceptional that he could, after all, rule them out of court.

There was no justification, the judge said, for refusing Jason Hill a solicitor; Melvin had accepted there was no evidence that the lawyer instructed by the family 'was, to use an unhappy phrase, bent'. Hill should, at an early stage, have been told the reason for his arrest; and he certainly should have been charged at the end of the first evening of interviews: 'That he was not was a plain breach of legal principle (d) in the preamble to the judges' rules.'

Mr Heatley, the judge recalled, had asked if Hill was to be taken into local authority care overnight: 'That he was not, was a plain breach of the Children and Young Persons Act 1969, now in more stringent terms section 38 of the Police and Criminal Evidence Act.' On the following day, 'no effort at all was made to transfer him into the care of the local authority, in even more flagrant breach of the Act'.

It was wrong, Mr Justice Hodgson went on, that Joe Heatley was asked to leave, so depriving Hill of the advice and protection to which he was entitled. Mrs Moody was an 'admirably public-spirited lady', but she had little idea of what her function was as an appropriate adult.

Hill had been charged with the burglary that second evening because of the new thirty-six-hour rule; not to have done so then 'would have had inconvenient consequences for the police'. Amlot, the judge said, had submitted that the reason why Hill had not been charged the previous day was that this would have prevented further interrogation, 'and so, for the time being, it ought to have done'. As to the further questioning on the Sunday after he had been charged, this should not have happened: 'I have no idea who authorised it. I do not think it was Mr Melvin.'

The judge found Cockram's explanations why the boy had been left half-naked for so long 'less than candid'. Years earlier, he had sat in a case where he found the questioning in such circumstances of an adult was oppressive. He had personally directed the chief constable of the police force concerned to see that it never happened again: 'My observations would have been far more emphatic had I been dealing with a thirteen-year-old.' Moreover, a paragraph of PACE, which had effectively been in force through the dry run, stated that if a suspect's clothing had to be removed, clean, decent replacements should be provided. Mrs Moody had 'proved her inadequacy' by allowing the final interview to proceed with Hill wrapped only in a blanket.

Mr Justice Hodgson said that in considering the conflict between the police and Mrs Moody's accounts as to where they made their notes of the non-contemporaneous interview record, he believed her statement that they had not used her office. 'And it does prompt the question why the two police officers should have given the evidence they did.' The day before, Hill's claims were becoming more and more fantastic. As to the content of the final dramatic confession: 'The end result was an account which, on the *voir dire*, seemed improbable, but not impossible, but which now I have heard and spent many hours collating the evidence of what happened, seems to me to be simply impossible. The ritualistic nature of the account, to me, shouts: "Fantasy!"'

Three very serious improprieties, amounting to oppression, had been committed: locking Hill in a cell instead of transferring him to local authority care; interviewing him in his underpants; and the pursuit of a confession when he started breaking down. He should have been calmed and allowed to recover his composure. Here was an exercise of authority which was 'burdensome, harsh and wrongful, and unjust'.

There was, the judge added, 'one final matter of importance'. This was that the officers seemed to have very little idea of the facts of the case. Had they been more fully informed, they might have been in a better position to realise when Hill drifted into fantasy. Given the dangers shown by the Confait case, it was vital to bear in mind the possibility that young or vulnerable suspects might make things up: 'I do not think these officers had these things in mind at all.'

The judge said: 'When one has a confession made by a child of which there is no confirmation at all, it is vitally important to check the accuracy of the confession to see whether it accords with the known facts. Time and again Jason Hill gave the police warning signs that he was straying into make-believe but, through no fault of theirs, the signs were not noticed. And when, even to their limited knowledge, what he was saying was plainly inaccurate, they put it down to deliberate lying.'

This ruling could scarcely have been more critical of the way the police treated Jason Hill. But again the infallibility principle held firm. As the court adjourned, one of the senior detectives told me in the lobby: 'This isn't reality. That isn't reality in there.'

Jason Hill did not give evidence at the trial, but in the summer of 1991 he described his experiences to me. The Blakelock case, he says, played havoc with his education and his sanity: 'It really fucked me up. I had to see a psychiatrist. I had constant nightmares: for six months after my release I couldn't go for a walk down the street because I felt terrified. No school would have me, so now I'm a bleeding glazier. I've got a shit job because there's nothing I can do without qualifications. All I want to do is get married, get a little house, have a couple of kids. But what chance do I have?'

He had never met Winston Silcott, although he knew him vaguely by sight. But when the police first came to get him from his cell, before the interviews began, 'they said to me, did I know a geezer called Winston, then Mark Pennant. In the interviews, they pushed Winston's name more than the others, they just kept on, did I know him, did I see him in the riot.'

Between the recorded interrogations, he says, he was questioned 'unofficially' in the cells several times. Soon, 'I lost track of time. I didn't know where I was, no one knew where I was. All I could see was when it was light outside.' When his clothes were removed, 'all I had was the pants and the blanket, nothing on my feet on the bare floor. There was nowhere to wash, nowhere to brush my teeth. They tried to stop me sleeping, the lights kept flashing on and off. I'll never forget it, it was like sitting in an oven with the door shut.'

In the Sunday interview, Jason says, 'the police kept pushing me really hard, telling me, "Go on, admit it, you had a stab." They threatened to keep me there for two weeks, told me I'd never see my family. Anyone would have broken down. I was hungry, I was tired, they told me that if I told them what they wanted, they'd let me go home. Once I started to break down they just kept coming, saying, "It was Sticks, wasn't it? Sticks was there." If I said no, they'd keep on. I just had to say yes to keep them off my back. They could have told me Prince Charles and I would have said it was him.'

Jason spent sixteen months in youth custody in Suffolk, awaiting trial: 'It was horrible, I used to cry myself to sleep every night. Sometimes visits from my mum would be kept down to only five minutes. I was only a boy; I could take a lot more now. I'd never been arrested before. All I'd done was taken a few cans of drink and some chocolate from the shop. Well, everyone was doing it, it was one big laugh.'

Barbara, Jason's mother, shudders as she remembers his appearance at Tottenham Magistrates' Court: 'He looked terrible. His skin was yellow, his hair was standing up, and he had dried vomit on his chest. He was unrecognisable as he came up the stairs in a paper boiler suit and a blanket, with no shoes. As I sat down he got hold of my hand and said, "Mum, they're trying to say I killed the policeman but I never." It leaves you with a constant fear: if they ever pull him, next time they put him in a cell he won't come out. He'll be one of those who bangs his head.

'Instead of going about the investigation properly, saying never mind if it takes twenty years, we'll get the right people, they said "we'll have you, you and you". Three innocent men were put in prison because they couldn't do their jobs properly.'

As a result of the judge's criticisms of Graham Melvin, the Police Complaints Authority launched an inquiry. It took more than three years before Melvin faced four charges at a disciplinary tribunal in the summer of 1990. He was represented by a qualified barrister policeman, Chief Inspector Jack Wadd, who spent several days attempting to argue that the tribunal should not proceed because natural justice had been abused by the long delay. This approach failed, and Melvin was found guilty of one charge relating to denying Jason Hill a solicitor. However, he appealed to the Home Secretary, and the tribunal finding was overturned in January 1991. At the time of writing, Jason Hill is waiting for an action to come to court, in which he is suing the police for wrongful arrest, false imprisonment and malicious prosecution.

The case of Jason Hill represented the nadir for the prosecution in the Blakelock trial. It was shocking, and in many ways it exemplified, in more extreme form, defects in the police inquiry method which were only too evident elsewhere, not least their lack of 'quality control' of the information coming in. But the story told by Jason was so outlandish, and so much at variance with other known facts, that it seems astonishing that no one noticed. Until she was cross-examined, the deficiencies of Mrs Moody were not obvious. But the Crown lawyers who endorsed the decision to charge Jason with murder, and who toiled on with the case through the committal and beyond, would have known of his breakdown, and of his detention in a cell for two nights. They would have seen from the record that he was not treated as a murder suspect until almost the end, and that he was not brought before a court after being charged with theft until he had been interviewed again.

PC Blakelock was not wounded in the chest, and the attack, swift, brutal and cloaked by darkness, did not allow any 'orders' to be given over the body, nor any fetching of juveniles from the shadows and thrusting of weapons into their hands. Under our system, the job of the prosecution lawyers is only to decide whether a winnable case exists: problems such as these are for judge and jury. But the case of Jason Hill must raise the matter of whether this is adequate, and of whether what is needed is a prosecuting authority with the power to ask many more questions.

11

Not Enough Evidence

The jury did not hear Mr Justice Hodgson's ruling in the case of Jason Hill. When they were led back into court after a somewhat lengthy absence, it was to hear him say only that he had now heard legal arguments and in consequence was directing them to enter a verdict of not guilty. The press could not report the ruling until the end of the trial. The copies of Hill's interviews were removed from the jurors' bundles of documents. But the impression of his vivid account, with its baseless claim that the rioters had planned to put PC Blakelock's head on a pole, must, to some extent, have stayed.

They had not heard the judge dismiss the lurid account of 'N' forcing a sword into Jason's hand as fantasy. They must have wondered who this N might be; it will not have escaped their notice that the same person, according to Mark Pennant, had held a machete aloft and exclaimed: 'This is bullman's blood.' For the time being, moreover, they still had their copies of Pennant's interrogation. Eventually, the judge would dismiss the case against Pennant in terms almost as strong as his ruling on Jason Hill. But for reasons best known to himself, Michael West, Pennant's counsel, had decided not to make a submission until the very end of the trial, after the defence had made its case, instead of taking the more normal course of doing so at half time.

After the days of gripping cross-examination of the witnesses called against Lambie and Hill, the prosecution case against Silcott was brief. It consisted of Detective Chief Superintendent Melvin reading his interview record in the witness box, and in all took no more than half an hour.

There was, of course, no other evidence against Silcott. Apart from stating in the fourth of the interviews that he had been with his girl friend on the night of the riot, he said nothing remotely of significance until the fifth and final interview, which Amlot had read in his opening speech. The jury was not allowed to keep a copy of Silcott's interrogation record, because he had not signed it.

In 1991 the Court of Appeal heard evidence that the last interview was fabricated, and Silcott's conviction was quashed. But at the trial, Barbara Mills QC, now the Director of Public Prosecutions, Silcott's counsel, made no attempt to challenge the accuracy of the police record. Her cross-examination was even briefer than Melvin's evidence in chief. She did no more than get him to confirm that no blood had been found on clothes and shoes taken from Silcott's house, that none of his shoes matched the prints found in the Broadwater Farm mud, and that none of the thousand police photographs was of Silcott. There were sound reasons for this approach.

Defending Winston Silcott was no easy task, however scant the evidence against him. In January 1986, a year before the Blakelock trial, he had been convicted at the Old Bailey of murdering a man called Anthony Smith, which created a considerable difficulty for his defence in the Broadwater Farm case.

In English law, if a defendant accuses a prosecution witness of lying, or of some other sin which casts a stain on his character, it is normal for the Crown to be able to tell the jury about the previous character of the defendant. Silcott could have gone into the witness box and made allegations about the way the interrogation was recorded. But Barbara Mills and Andrew Hall, Silcott's solicitor, believed there would then be a very high risk that the jury would learn that Silcott was already a murderer. The consequences, it goes without saying, would have been disastrous.

Interviewed in 1992, Sir Derek Hodgson said he would not have allowed Silcott's previous murder conviction to go before the jury: 'The prejudicial effect would have been enormous, devastating. I don't think any judge would have allowed it. Its prejudicial impact would have far outstripped any probative value it might have had.' Mrs Mills did not ask what his attitude would have been. However, in most criminal trials, the question of raising previous convictions has to wait till the defendant is in the witness box. Judges will not rule until they hear what allegations are made. It renders the job of defence counsel, says one experienced barrister, like 'a game of poker'.

Even if Silcott's previous murder conviction had not been disclosed, attacking the veracity of Melvin and Dingle would probably have been of little help. 'At the end of the day,' says Andrew Hall, 'it would have been his word, a lone black defendant accused of being the ringleader of PC Blakelock's murder, against that of two very senior police officers, Melvin and Dingle, highly experienced members of the Serious Crime Squad. In the context of this case, and in the atmosphere of the time, we did not think he stood much of a chance. It seemed likely to do him only harm.' Engin Raghip did later challenge many details of his interview records, but he was clearly not believed.

At the same time, the defence was labouring against the fact that a large part of the case against Silcott was subterranean; hidden, or rather partly hidden, from the jury.

The crucial phrases in Silcott's fifth interview all appeared to link back to the statements of Pennant and Hill: 'All you've had in here is kids . . . those kids will never go to court . . . you can't keep me away from them.' Pennant and Hill were among the initial links in Silcott's daisy chain, and had made terrifying allegations against him. Pennant, in his sudden confession on the way back to his cell, had said he was frightened of Sticks, while Hill said he had forced him to cut the body and then say nothing of what he had seen. But as things stood, there was no way for the defence to explore the relationship of the juveniles' statements with the fifth Silcott interview. They could do little but hope against hope that the jury would not realise the connection.

Several of those charged with riot had, as we have seen, also made claims against Silcott, on an equally flimsy basis. Again, there was no easy way to explore this. There was the matter of the photograph which the police initially believed to be of Silcott, the man in the pink washing-up gloves. Whoever it depicted, he was very different in appearance to Winston Silcott. He had much lighter skin, and longish hair, as opposed to Silcott's close crop. The prosecution never tendered it in evidence, although they showed it to the defence. The fact that at least one of those who made serious allegations against Silcott, Carl Williams, thought it was a picture of Silcott never emerged.

Originally, the seven charged with riot had all been on the same indictment as the murder defendants. Until a 'practice directions' hearings in the autumn of 1986, all thirteen were supposed to be tried together. Silcott's lawyers had applied at that stage to have him tried alone, which would have eliminated the prejudicial, subterranean evidence once and for all. The arrangement eventually adopted was the most Mr Justice Hodgson was prepared to allow.

The decision to separate Silcott and the murder defendants from the riot cases and the judge's innovative move to conceal names with letters at least reduced the scope for prejudicial backwash. But they did not eliminate it.

Even presenting an alibi was fraught with problems. On the evening of 6 October Silcott signed on at Tottenham Police Station, a mile from the Farm, for his bail in the Anthony Smith murder case. His girl friend had driven him there from a friend's home in another part of London, and waited outside in her car. Silcott was kept waiting for a few minutes. He began to become impatient, and looked at the clock on the wall. It said the time was 7.10 pm. According to some of the statements taken from defendants in the riot trials, he was supposed to have spent the preceding hour making inflammatory speeches at the Youth Association meeting, and then to have led the first attacks on police. In any event, by 7.10 the road entrances to the estate were already sealed with burning cars and rapidly growing lines of police. However, even to have adduced evidence of this apparently simple matter would have involved challenging the police head on, with all that that implied. A statement from a WPC served on Silcott's defence after he was charged claimed he had signed on an hour earlier, at 6.10. Silcott did not remember seeing any female officers at the police station, and the signature on her statement seemed to be different from that recorded against his name in the bail book.

The original version of this vital document would have settled the matter. But for reasons which were never explained, it had been 'lost', the police claimed, although a photocopy survived. Here, the timing was so smudged as to be illegible. That left Silcott with only his word and that of his girl friend. But spouses and lovers rarely make convincing alibi witnesses: it is too easy for the prosecution to suggest that their attachment to the accused has coloured their evidence.

Ultimately, defending Silcott presented a dreadful dilemma. Behind Melvin's thirty minutes in the witness box was a dark mass of secret, untested evidence. One course would have been to blow the whole case open, calling all the material, from the murder case juveniles to the statements made by the riot defendants and the missing bail book; and then to seek to demolish the whole rickety structure piece by piece.

But in the pre-Guildford Four climate of 1987, the risks would have been colossal. Mr Justice Hodgson might have kept Silcott's murder conviction hidden had he simply queried Melvin's interview record, but a wide-ranging attack on many fronts might have made it much more difficult. There is nothing more dangerous than calling evidence only to knock it down. It is a strategy in which a single slip, or an unconvincing witness, can lead to disaster. In these circumstances, Andrew Hall, Mrs Mills and her junior, Ed Rees, concluded that their only course was to keep the lowest possible profile, while attempting to argue before the judge and jury that the fifth interview could not possibly amount to proof beyond reasonable doubt.

Mrs Mills tried valiantly to do this three times: in a pre-trial *voir dire*, in a submission at the end of the prosecution case, and in her closing speech to the jury. Both her submissions to the judge took the same tack: that there was no case to answer, and that it would be dangerous to allow the matter to go to the jury.

The prosecution was arguing that the record of interview five showed Silcott 'accepting' or 'adopting' the allegation of murder, and threatening witnesses to boot. Melvin had said to him: 'I believe you were with Mark Lambie, Nicky Jacobs and others standing over PC Blakelock when he was on the ground. You had either a machete or a sword with which you struck the officer.' Silcott's response was to say that only kids had been into the police station thus far, and that no one would believe them. This, Mrs Mills argued, could not be construed as anything more than passing a comment on Melvin's allegation, rather than accepting its truth.

Another problem, she said, was that Melvin had said in the interview he had witnesses, and Silcott had implicitly threatened them, while the jury knew that one witness (Andrew Pyke) had been due at court but had failed to appear. Overall, she said, 'it is a case in which Your Lordship should take the responsibility on yourself, rather than leave it to the jury, because of the risk that the jury may feel, because of the extraordinary pressures, "the police say he is the ringleader, we cannot acquit him".' Mr Justice Hodgson complimented her on the quality of her submissions, but disagreed; Silcott's guilt was a matter for the jury.

There was also a subterranean element to the case against Engin Raghip.

The second youngest of six children, Engin was born in Britain ten years after his parents emigrated from Cyprus to north London in 1956. His father worked for many years in a battery factory, until an industrial accident cost him the fingers of one hand, for which he received £800 compensation.

Raghip's education was not a success. He changed schools with weary frequency, and learnt little at any of them. Like so many of those arrested in the Broadwater Farm inquiry, he was still illiterate when he left school at the age of fifteen. Before his arrest in connection with the riot, he had been convicted twice for taking and driving away cars, and once for burglary. But for the previous two and a half years, he had been on the straight and narrow. During that time he was living with his common-law wife Sharon Daly, who was determined to see he stayed away from trouble. In 1985, aged nineteen, Raghip was alternating spells of unemployment with work as a mechanic in a garage owned by a cousin; then, as now, cars and motor sport were a consuming interest.

The couple met when they were both thirteen, when Sharon's sister Linda married Engin's brother Djemal, commonly known as Jimmy. Sharon and Engin had a two-year-old boy, Don, and lived in a flat at Wood Green, though they were often to be found at the Raghip family home in Palmers Green. As for Broadwater Farm, Engin says he had only been there once or twice in his life, taken there by a cousin.

He went there on 6 October. He had spent the afternoon with John Lacey, a close friend who grew up with the Dalys. Driving towards Wood Green, they noticed the police activity, a lot of rushing vans and blue flashing lights. They stopped at a Kentucky Fried Chicken restaurant and heard that trouble was brewing at the Farm. They decided to take a look. They were forced to park in Dunmore Road, ten minutes' walk away, because of the police cordons.

When they arrived some time after 7 pm, cars were still alight at the entrances. They saw Colin Couch talking to the leaders from the West Indian Centre at Gloucester Road and discussed what to do. John tried to dissuade Raghip from entering, but curiosity prevailed. They walked past Colin Couch, who made no attempt to stop them. 'I suppose if we'd been black men, it would have been different,' Engin says now.

They watched the rioting at Adams Road for a while, and met another friend of Raghip, John Broomfield. Then Raghip and Broomfield went off together, Lacey remembers. After twenty minutes, he left to see if Raghip was waiting at his car. There was no one there, so he went back on to the Farm to look for him there. Their paths must have crossed, for at one stage Raghip and Broomfield also left the estate, via the Gloucester Road entrance, to see if Lacey was at the car. In the end, Lacey got bored and drove off. Raghip later said in evidence he left the Farm by 9.45 because he had to get home.

Broomfield, whose solicitor, it will be recalled, went to the High Court in a vain attempt to get access, was arrested on 23 October, after boasting to the *Daily Mirror* of his supposed part in the riot. That, perhaps, was suggestive of a lack of judgement, or even instability. 'He was always bonkers, a psychopath,' Engin Raghip says now.

Since the events of 1985, Broomfield has been convicted of an unrelated murder and is serving a life sentence. At the time of the Blakelock inquiry this lay in the future. But there was evidence that his interrogation seriously affected the balance of his mind. On his second night in custody, he tried to commit suicide.

Before this, Broomfield, who was charged with riot and affray, told the police he had been with Raghip during the evening, and described the attack on PC Blakelock. Broomfield's interview record states:

> Q: Did Engin go into the crowd around the policeman?
> A: He tried to.
> Q: What did Engin do?
> A: He was with Junior. They tried to get in but there was too many people.

Raghip's account to the police of the same event uses almost the same words:

> A: I got there and there was so many people around him trying to get in.
> Q: Go on.
> A: There was so many people round him. I tried to get in but I couldn't.

The police, Raghip says now, had Broomfield's statement in front of them as they questioned him. But like the 'dark' evidence in the Silcott case, the relationship between the two interview records was never examined.

There were other close similarities between the two men's interviews:

> Q: Did you see Engin either running or at the crowd with a weapon?
> A: All he had was a little stick.
> Q: What sort of stick?
> A: Looked like a little short broom handle.

Raghip's crucial admission came when he had been in custody for three days, and like Broomfield held incommunicado. The interview record states:

Q: You have had some time to think now, is there anything more you remembered since we last spoke?
A: Yes, I didn't tell you all the truth before.
Q: What more do you want to tell?
A: I had a weapon when I was running towards the policeman, a broom handle.

Other parts of Broomfield's interviews suggested, at the least, a degree of unreliability. He was insistent, for example, that only one policeman was attacked outside Tangmere. He said he had no watch, yet gave exact timings for events throughout the evening. In general, he gave an account which displayed a remarkable ability to analyse and recall a confused and rapid series of events, including the exact order in which PC Blakelock's various assailants attacked him.

Engin Raghip was arrested on 24 October. Not realising he and Sharon lived in their own flat at Wood Green, a detachment of armed police turned up before 7 am at his mother's house in Palmers Green. She was happy to put them right but insisted they first come in for tea and biscuits. This they did, guns and all. Engin's brother Jimmy happened to be present and at once set off for Engin's flat at Wood Green, where he witnessed his arrest. Before Engin was driven away in the police car, Jimmy yelled at him: 'I'll get you a fucking brief.'

Jimmy telephoned Martin Harvey from the local firm Derek Attridge and Co. Like so many solicitors, Harvey was refused access to his client.

The prosecution case against Raghip took longer than that against Silcott, but its essence was the same: there were his interrogation records, and nothing else. Detective Sergeant van Thal and Detective Inspector John Kennedy interviewed him no fewer than ten times in all, spread over four days.

At first he admitted throwing a few stones at police, and seeing Broomfield. In his second interview, he said he had seen a policeman being attacked. During his third interrogation, on the evening of the 24th, which was not signed, he supposedly described a conversation about the killing in which Silcott took part. He said Silcott had a hammer with a hook on one side.

After the fifth session, thirty-six hours after his arrest, Raghip was charged with affray. He was immediately interviewed again, and now for the first time described the attack on PC Blakelock: 'It was like you see in a film, a helpless man with dogs on him. It was just like that, it was really quick.' This interview was not signed, and a few minutes after its conclusion, Raghip vomited. A doctor was called, who diagnosed a fever and viral infection but pronounced Raghip still fit to be detained.

Next morning he appeared in the magistrates' court, only to be remanded in police custody once more. The seventh interview contained more detail about the Blakelock attack, and included the vivid sentence: 'You should have heard the noises coming from him, it was like a continuous "ah" sound from him as he was attacked, it was like he was being really hurt.' DI Kennedy told the court that few statements had made such a deep impression on him as this.

At last, in interview eight, some sixty hours after his arrest, Raghip allegedly volunteered the fact that he had a broomstick, and would have used it against Blakelock had he been able 'to get in'. Had he done, 'I might have kicked him or hit him with the broom handle. But I wouldn't have done no more. I feel like shit just talking about it.'

Raghip was held for another two days, and finally released, still charged only with affray, on bail. Six weeks later the police came to his house and asked him to attend the police station because one of the Crown lawyers wished to ask him a question. There he was charged with the murder of PC Blakelock. There was no evidence that he landed a single blow on Keith Blakelock's body; at one stage in the absence of the jury, Mr Justice Hodgson was moved to remark that the case against him sounded more like 'attempted common assault' than murder. But the law of common purpose, and the wafer-thin evidence of his intent to harm Blakelock contained in his statement that he would have kicked him, had convinced the prosecuting authorities to charge him with the killing.

Raghip was defended by John Morris QC, a Labour MP and the shadow Attorney-General. In general terms, Morris put it to the police who interrogated Engin Raghip that they had not recorded the interviews accurately; that there had been threats and other conversations which were never written down; and that some of the comments attributed to him had been suggested by the police. Time and again, Morris simply put to Kennedy that an answer was not properly recorded, or had been suggested to Raghip; the officer would deny it, and Morris would move on to the next question in the interview record. It did not appear as if Kennedy was deeply worried. Sometimes he said no more than: 'As written, sir,' or 'Totally wrong, sir.'

Raghip had told his lawyers he had been threatened and made his confessions because he was frightened out of his wits. Morris did not make the most dramatic use of these claims. On occasion he gave away what chance there may have been to make headway by swallowing up the question in an admission that Raghip could not be exact about when the threats occurred:

Q: We are now on interview seven, Officer, and Mr Raghip, doing his best now to recollect when he heard this suggestion, and he cannot be absolutely certain as to when it was, but in all probability it was somewhere around this time, thought you said: 'It will be very hard for you if you don't tell us what we want to know.'
A: No, I never said that. Are you on page 1454?
Q: I am on page 1456. Mr Raghip was not making a note. Those are my instructions. I would put it at a precise point in time if I could.
A: Absolutely, sir.
Q: You say it was never put as he recalls?
A: If it had been said, it would have been recorded.
Q: And Mr van Thal said 'We will lick shit out of you'?
A: Sorry?
Q: And Mr van Thal said 'We will lick shit out of you'?
A: That was never said by anybody.
Q: Still at page 1456, still in that interview. I cannot put to you specific suggestions as regards the earlier part because Mr Raghip cannot remember the questions being put or the answers being given.

A: I see, sir.

This was not the way to break down a member of the Scotland
Yard Serious Crime Squad. In his summing up, the judge gently
poured scorn on the allegation that there was anything wrong about
Raghip's interviews, or that his admissions were the product of
suggestion by the police.

In a *voir dire* before the evidence against Raghip was adduced,
Morris did, however, establish disquieting details about the failure
to provide him with a solicitor. He was never told by the police
that Martin Harvey had telephoned, and the officers claimed he
had not asked for representation. This Raghip strongly contested,
maintaining that he asked for a lawyer before each and every
interview.

Stuart Miller, who was duty solicitor at Tottenham Magistrates'
Court on 26 October when Raghip was charged with affray, saw
him before his appearance and agreed to represent him. He did not
know of Jimmy's telephone call to Derek Attridge and Co., and
later, when a member of that firm arrived, Achilles Achillea, he
agreed to let Miller handle the case for the time being. Miller gave
evidence in the *voir dire* that when the police asked for Raghip to
be remanded in their custody again, he asked the magistrate to
stipulate that there should be a solicitor present in any further
interrogations. Later, Achillea told me: 'When we saw him, he
was in a real state. He was completely confused, saying things
like he hadn't been interviewed by the police at all. I don't think
he knew what day of the week it was. It was clear he badly needed
to be represented at any future interrogation.'

Miller told the court: 'The magistrate agreed with the observa-
tion I made. He felt it was right that Mr Raghip had the benefit
of a solicitor.' He saw his client in the cells again and gave him his
business card. Raghip's mother and Sharon were there, and after
Miller had explained to him what his rights were, they told him
insistently to ensure he had a solicitor in future police interviews.
Raghip gave evidence about what happened next:

Q: Did you want to be represented?
A: Yes.

Q: And was that in accord with what you had been telling the police in earlier interviews?
A: Yes.
Q: Did you at any stage withdraw or change your mind that you did not want a solicitor?
A: No.

Morris produced Raghip's custody record, revealing it had two crosses on the top left-hand corner:

Q: Who put those crosses there? Was it you or someone else?
A: It was the police officer who gave them to me to sign.
Q: Were you given a copy of your rights?
A: No.
Q: How was it pointed out to you to sign that?
A: It was marked with a cross, and he said, 'Sign here and sign there.'
Q: Before you left for the magistrates' court, do you recall any conversation that Mr Kennedy was involved with before you left the station?
A: Yes, sir.
Q: What was that?
A: 'Make sure he doesn't see a brief.'
Q: After you had got back from the magistrates' court, what was your state of mind regarding a solicitor?
A: I wanted a solicitor at all times.

Raghip had signed away his right to a solicitor; his signature on the custody record purported to confirm he had no wish for legal advice. The police, in their evidence, said he had done this voluntarily, knowing exactly what was entailed. In the last of his eight interviews, the record contained the question: 'It is right that you have not asked for a solicitor to be present at your interviews?' Raghip supposedly replied: 'I don't want a solicitor, what's the point till I go to court.'

His *voir dire* evidence continued:

Q: Now those words are recorded. Are they right or not?
A: No, they're not right.
Q: Were they said at all?

A: I can't remember them being said.

Q: Did you at any stage say after your return from court 'I don't want a solicitor, what's the point until I go to court'?

A: No.

Cross-examined by Amlot, Raghip said: 'I signed everything they gave me . . . because I was scared. I would have signed anything.'

At the end of the *voir dire*, Morris made a submission that in view of Raghip's treatment, his interviews, like those of Jason Hill, should be ruled inadmissible. Like Laughland, he was relying partly on section 76 of the new PACE Act, which placed an onus on the Crown to prove there had been no oppression, and that nothing said or done during an interrogation might have rendered it unreliable.

Morris argued that the length of Raghip's detention, the denial of a solicitor and the length of his interviews, in all 14 hours and 31 minutes, amounted to oppression. But Mr Justice Hodgson was unsympathetic: 'It was a good deal less than the interviews, and the length of them, that the children [Lambie and Hill] were subjected to.'

Morris cited Raghip's illiteracy. But as so often, the judge went straight to the real issue: 'He does not read very well, but the really important thing in all these matters is his suggestibility.' Alas for Engin Raghip, the court heard nothing whatsoever about whether he was unusually suggestible or not. There were, as we shall see, reasons for this which exonerate his lawyers, at least in this respect. But it was an omission which was to cost him six years in prison for a crime he did not commit.

12

Lying or Completely Mistaken

As with the others accused of PC Blakelock's murder, there was a strange and worrying background to the case of Mark Braithwaite, the last arrested and the last to be dealt with in court. Once again, it never surfaced at the trial.

Braithwaite, eighteen at the time of the riot, was not from the Farm, or even from Tottenham. His family lived five miles away in Islington, close to central London. His only connection with the estate was through his girl friend, Jackie, an older woman who had borne him a child. His life revolved around music, as a rapper and a disc jockey. Jazzie B, later internationally famous as the lead singer of Soul-II-Soul, was a friend. Two weeks before his arrest on 4 February 1986, Braithwaite was interviewed for a job as a youth worker. He passed, but by the time his prospective employer telephoned his mother, Patsie, with the news, he had been in custody for several days.

Throughout the autumn of 1985, Melvin and his team knew nothing of Mark Braithwaite. Not one of the two hundred or so people arrested by the end of the year had mentioned his name in connection with the riot. But on 16 January, they arrested and began to interrogate Bernard Kinghorn, who was quite emphatic. He had seen a man he knew by sight, though not to talk to, stab PC Blakelock repeatedly with a long kitchen knife – Mark Braithwaite.

Kinghorn was eventually jailed for four and a half years for affray and a series of theft, deception and fraud charges. In the weeks before the murder trial, the police visited him in prison at least once in an attempt to get him to give evidence against Braithwaite. At one stage, they seem to have been close to securing his services, and Kinghorn told his solicitor he was toying with the idea of appearing as a witness. The lawyer, Martin Harvey, had to withdraw from his case because he was already defending Engin Raghip, and if Kinghorn gave evidence in the murder trial, this would have created a conflict of interest. But Kinghorn changed his mind and declined to appear against Braithwaite. Three years later, he told BBC television that his allegations against Braithwaite had been false all along.

As far as the police were concerned, here were the 'climate of fear' and the demons of the Broadwater Farm Defence Campaign operating with a vengeance. As the case against Braithwaite, *sans* Kinghorn, unfolded, one of the most senior officers on the inquiry gave me this remarkable statement:

> We'll never find the truth as long it's being stifled by those who prevent us from investigating it. For all we know, some of those responsible for PC Blakelock's murder are on the Defence Committee. You would have thought that for Kinghorn, the opportunity to reduce his sentence ought to have been an incentive. But that's not enough: there was a real fear of not being alive to enjoy the freedom that might be made available to him. He told us he was a Tottenham boy and he wanted to be able to walk down Tottenham High Road without being in fear of his life. This was a greater problem than the Krays and Richardsons.
>
> The judge doesn't seem to see that interrogation is a reasonable means of obtaining evidence. The acquittals of Hill and Lambie are a tremendous blow to morale, a slap in the face. Perhaps the judge thinks we have got to change our entire system, but we've got to have some means of rooting out the evil in our society or we haven't got a society.

This was all too typical of the kind of apocalyptic comments being made to journalists as the case neared its end. The police were covering themselves in the event of a failure to return any convictions, and the fall-back plan was to blame everything on the judge. Once again, the principle of police infallibility was busily at work. But behind the vision of Kinghorn the intimidated witness lay an account of the murder still more fantastic than Jason Hill's. If Kinghorn had given evidence, it is difficult to see how he could have done anything but help Mark Braithwaite.

Kinghorn was interrogated without a solicitor present for three days. In his very first interview he denied having anything to do with the riot. A few hours later, in his second interrogation session, he gave Detective Sergeant van Thal an account of the killing. A few police officers and firemen were approaching Tangmere, not fleeing from it, he said. Two policemen fell over, and one got up and ran away. Two rioters approached the other officer and attacked him. One of them hit the officer with a blunt instrument, the other was Braithwaite with his kitchen knife. Kinghorn was insistent: there were only two people involved in the attack, and no crowd. How long did Braithwaite and the other man keep up their assault? van Thal asked. 'About fifteen minutes,' Kinghorn replied. He saw no one else attacked, he added.

Later details were still more at variance with everything known about the killing. The police had no riot shields, Kinghorn said, and one of the two who fell – not the one who was attacked – had an ordinary flat cap, not a riot helmet. The attack victim's helmet was removed and donned by Mark Braithwaite. Kinghorn was pressed about the numbers involved repeatedly. There might, he said, have been as many as six involved in the first charge. On day three, van Thal's patience snapped:

Q: Are you giving us a false story to cover up for anyone?
A: If I wanted to cover up for anyone or was lying I would have kept to my first story. Look what happens when you try to help police.
Q: I believe that many things you have told us are true and that you have remembered correctly but the main events you are describing are wrong. You've described certain events at Tangmere when you say you saw a policeman attacked by Mark Braithwaite. Yet you have not seen a large and very noisy crowd

of people attacking a police officer in front of Tangmere where you were standing . . . you could not have failed to see the crowd to which I was referring . . . that leaves me with two alternatives: either you are lying or completely mistaken about the main events you have described.

A: I'm not lying. Why would I say [things] for no reason?

Q: If you are right virtually everyone else we have spoken to are [sic] wrong.

A: Well, I'm not lying.

Even if Kinghorn had given a more convincing account in court, these interview records would have been disclosed to Mark Braithwaite's defence. 'Lying or completely mistaken': Rock Tansey QC, counsel for Mark Braithwaite, could not have put it better.

Mark Braithwaite was arrested in a minicab. The officers spreadeagled him across the roof of the car, forcing his hands behind his back at gunpoint, and told him he was being arrested on suspicion of murdering PC Blakelock. 'Murder, what murder?' he yelled. Kinghorn's interview alone was responsible for the arrest; three weeks later, the police had no additional information pointing to Braithwaite's involvement. Once again, Roy Amlot had nothing to offer the jury but Braithwaite's interview records.

Braithwaite was interrogated at Enfield Police Station by Detective Sergeant Dermot McDermott, with Detective Constable Colin Biggar acting as scribe. On Melvin's instructions he was denied a solicitor and interviewed eight times over two days; then another four times on the third day, when a solicitor was present throughout. In these later, accompanied sessions, he gave no replies at all.

The interrogation followed a similar pattern to that of Raghip. At first Braithwaite denied being anywhere near Broadwater Farm, saying he knew what had happened only from the TV news. The second interview, which began very shortly after he was taken back to the cells at his own request, included the admission that he had been on the estate but only 'had a look' at the disturbances. By interview four, on the afternoon of the second day, he was confessing to throwing a few stones and, by the fifth session, to being present at Tangmere while insisting he played no part in the murder.

The important admissions came in interview six, again carried out after a short period back in the cells at his request. He began: 'All I want to say is that I hit him with a bar . . . the young policeman.' He said he hit him in the chest and leg, while others set about him with knives. 'I never saw no one with no machete,' he said.

Q: Did anyone else attack the policeman that you hit?
A: Yes, a number of people.
Q: Did you see what they did?
A: Some was stabbing and some were kicking him.
Q: Did you see where they stabbed him?
A: On his legs.
Q: What sort of iron bar did you have?
A: I don't know.
Q: Where did you get it from?
A: It was on the floor, there was a number of things on the floor.
Q: What colour was it?
A: I don't know.
Q: Was it heavy?
A: I can't remember . . .
Q: Mark, this is very important, and I want you to tell the truth. Did you see the policeman get up?
A: No, I had walked off.

This was somewhat vague, and it does not accord with the established facts about the murder: there were no wounds on PC Blakelock's legs or chest compatible with blows from an iron bar. It was enough, however, to convict Mark Braithwaite of murder.

In a seventh interview shortly afterwards, Braithwaite insisted that the officer he hit was not PC Blakelock but one of his colleagues. He did see another officer attacked who had a moustache, like PC Blakelock, but this was not the man he hit, who was blond and cleanshaven.

By the time of Braithwaite's arrest the PACE Act was fully in force. Section 58, supported by new codes of practice for the police, stated that a suspect under interrogation had an absolute right to a solicitor. It could be overidden only on the authority of an officer of superintendent rank or above. The Act allowed this only when allowing access to a solicitor would:

(a) lead to interference with or harm to evidence connected with serious arrestable offences or interference with or physical injury to other persons, or (b) will lead to the alerting of other persons suspected of having committed such an offence but not yet arrested for it, or (c) will hinder the recovery of any property obtained as a result of such an offence.

Should an officer decide to deny access on any of these grounds, the burden of proof that he was right to do so would lie with the Crown in any trial.

Rock Tansey cross-examined Detective Chief Superintendent Melvin at length about his decision to deny a solicitor access to Mark Braithwaite. Once again, he trotted out the line that solicitors might, wittingly or unwittingly, leak information which might lead to evidence being concealed, or suspects alerted as to the course the inquiry was taking. Could Melvin really suggest that if he asked a lawyer not to pass on any messages, he would not comply? Tansey asked. Oh yes he could, Melvin replied:

Over the past four months of the investigation there were incidents which cropped up which led me to believe that the integrity of some firms of solicitors left a lot to be desired . . . [some were party to] a conspiracy to pervert the course of justice.

Melvin said that some firms had called claiming to represent people who had already instructed other firms:

My belief was that there was a possibility that they were being advised by persons who had an interest in what the suspects were actually saying. I had a firm who tried to blackmail me over the release of a person's property, otherwise they would not agree to the release of Keith Blakelock's body for burial. There was an incident where a solicitor . . . instructed a defendant to make allegations of assault when that person had given a full and frank confession.

Tansey asked: could any of these allegations be made against Braithwaite's solicitors, Marcus Barnett? 'I am not sure,' Melvin replied. Tansey went through it point by point. The firm had nothing to do with any alleged conspiracy to pervert the course of justice, Melvin agreed, and had not tried any blackmail. It had not made any false allegations of assault:

Q: Your reasons in this case were absolutely bogus. You allowed solicitors to be kept out to enable you to put pressure on him to extract a confession.

A: No I did not.

Q: It was very much public knowledge that in February last year the police were still continuing their inquiries.

A: Yes.

Q: And all parties to the murder would know the police were still looking for them – so how would a solicitor make any difference?

A: Well, they were on the alert, but it follows steps should be taken to ensure the police knew who they were.

Q: Did you really think you would find forensic evidence 120 days after the crime?

A: I would suggest at the scene of the crime forensic evidence might be found after 120 days . . .

Q: You kept everybody out because you wanted to break him.

A: No, sir.

Q: And keeping a solicitor out without good reason is a serious misuse of your power. Would you agree?

A: Without good reason, yes.

Q: I suggest that in this case you had no good reason, and you bent the rules.

A: I didn't bend the rules.

Four and a half years later, it emerged at the Court of Appeal that there had been a disagreement between Tansey and his junior,

Steven Kamlish. Kamlish had urged Tansey to capitalise on the disclosures of this cross-examination with a submission to the judge, asking him to rule the Braithwaite interviews inadmissible because of the apparent breaches of PACE. Tansey was not to be blamed for failing to ask the judge to do this: PACE was still relatively new legislation.

Less than nine months after the end of the Blakelock trial, Mr Justice Hodgson sat in the Court of Appeal in the case of a man called Samuel, and delivered a ruling which set a legal precedent of great importance. Samuel had been convicted of armed robbery and sentenced to ten years' imprisonment at Birmingham Crown Court. He was refused access to a solicitor, and in the last of several interviews confessed. The senior police officer in the case had given evidence remarkably similar to Melvin's to justify his decision: 'It was my opinion that the presence of a solicitor could be detrimental to the inquiry, and there was the likelihood of that solicitor inadvertently passing on information to the friends and relatives of the accused . . . thus enabling those persons to escape apprehension or to dispose of the firearms used in the robbery or dispose of the stolen property.'

In an unmistakeable reference to the Blakelock trial, Mr Justice Hodgson said that 'the experience of some members of this court . . . is that the practice adopted in this case is becoming more and more usual. Officers' "reasonable belief" is more and more being based upon the "inadvertent" or "unwitting" conduct of a solicitor.'

The judge proceeded to dispose of the police proposition in withering terms. Perhaps, he said, this had happened in the past. However, 'solicitors are intelligent, professional people', while suspects were often not very clever. The idea that lawyers might unwittingly pass on these messages 'seems to contemplate a degree of intelligence and sophistication in persons detained, and perhaps a naivete and lack of common sense in solicitors, which we doubt often occurs'. For the police to advance such an argument, they would have to be able to be specific about the person detained: perhaps he would be some kind of criminal mastermind or gang leader.

Mr Justice Hodgson's ruling went on:

Any officer attempting to justify his decision to delay the exercise of this fundamental right of a citizen will, in our judgement, be unable to do so save by reference to specific circumstances including evidence as to the person detained or the actual solicitor sought to be consulted.

In Samuel's case, he concluded, there was a 'sinister side' to the decision. He had already been in custody for twenty-four hours, and 'time was running out' before PACE would compel the police to bring him to court. The decision to refuse access 'was very probably motivated by a desire to have one last chance of interviewing the appellant in the absence of a solicitor'. This, of course, was virtually the argument Tansey put to Melvin about Mark Braithwaite.

In 1992 I asked Sir Derek Hodgson what his response would have been to a submission on similar lines for Braithwaite. 'I like to think I would have ruled that his interviews were inadmissible if it had been argued in front of me,' he says. Should he have taken steps to exclude the interviews, even without a submission? 'It's not for me to do the job of defence counsel, the job of a defence silk. But I'm ninety per cent sure I'd have had the courage to rule out Braithwaite's interviews.'

The evidence called by the defence on behalf of the four still left in the dock charged with PC Blakelock's murder took much less time than the prosecution: less than a week in all.

On behalf of Pennant, Michael West called Dr Tunstall, and revealed the extent of his suggestibility and low intelligence, and another psychologist, Dr Roscoe, who gave evidence about how vulnerable people come to make unreliable confessions. Engin Raghip called his brother Jimmy and sister-in-law Linda as alibi witnesses to attest to the fact that he had been home soon after 10 pm on 6 October, having walked the half-hour distance from Broadwater Farm. Raghip also went into the box himself and gave evidence of his allegations about the recording of his interviews, and his insistent requests for a solicitor.

As Morris took him through his interviews again, they reached the point where Raghip had spoken of Blakelock making a 'continuous "ah" sound'. The next question in the record was: 'Did you see the man you call Sticks around the crowd where the police officer was,' to which Engin had replied, 'No, I didn't.' The interview continued with a discussion about whether Raghip had seen Silcott or another man. Under the procedure adopted at the beginning of the trial, this meant Morris asking a series of questions about N and ZZ. Then Amlot rose to his feet and asked for the jury to go out, because he wished to raise a point of law.

There was a collective intake of breath. What Amlot planned to do was to lift the veil which had protected Silcott under the letter N: to put it to Raghip when it came to cross-examining him that N was Sticks, or Silcott. This, the rules of evidence stated, he was perfectly entitled to do.

The judge told him: 'It has always been obvious that in cross-examination you can ask him what you like.' Mrs Mills tried swiftly to intervene, visibly upset: 'The jury know the same initial is the same throughout all the interviews. The moment the veil drops they know who it is. I urge you not to make a stupid decision . . . it is very prejudicial evidence.'

It was particularly so, she went on, because Raghip had already told the court that he did not know Silcott or any of the other defendants. The name was there in the interview record not because he had mentioned Sticks but because it had been put to him by the police. Copies of Pennant's interviews, in which N was described with his bloody machete leading the attack on Blakelock, were still with the jury, although by now the court knew of his extreme vulnerability.

Mrs Mills went on: 'What I am querying is whether it is necessary in the case of Raghip for my learned friend to lift this veil. He has plenty of material to query these interviews. What he is doing is lifting the veil to show that N is Sticks.' Hill's interviews had gone, but the jury could hardly forget them, and they still had their notes. 'At this late stage, is it fair that the Crown try to lift the veil? My learned friend on behalf of Mr Raghip has not sought to damage Mr Silcott's case. The damage to Mr Silcott's case is overriding.'

With what sounded like genuine regret, Mr Justice Hodgson said there was nothing, in law, he could do. The most he could allow was to remove Pennant's interviews from the jury's bundles of documents, since it now looked likely he would dismiss them as inadmissible evidence: 'I am not going to stop Mr Amlot asking any question he wishes to ask. I really cannot. I know I do not have the power to do so.'

Next day, 4 March, Amlot's cross-examination began. Soon, he reached a point where he read from Raghip's third, unsigned interview. Raghip was describing a conversation – which he now denied had ever taken place – on a wall near the Moselle School. Speaking slowly, with deliberation and clarity, Amlot read from the interrogation record:

Q: 'They were just boasting about it and after that it broke up. The kids came out with the stuff from the school and N . . .' – that is Sticks, is it not?
A: Yeah.
Q: Silcott?
A: Yeah.
Q: ' . . . and this bloke took this stuff off the kids.' Did you say that?
A: Yes.
Q: 'A girl, a half-caste girl, who was with Sticks's mate, sat next to the stuff from the school.' Did you say that?
A: They put it to me . . .
Q: Did you tell them about Silcott?
A: No, I heard his name being mentioned at the police station.
Q: Did you tell them about the school?
A: Yes, I made it up . . .
Q: Did you say this: 'People were looking after the stuff and Sticks came along with a hammer with one side a hammer and the other side a hook. I don't know what you would use it for'? Did you say that?
A: No . . . I never said it was Sticks, [it came from] the po-lice.

Amlot carried on: 'Next interview, page 1426 in our bundle. Did they start off with Mr Kennedy saying, "Last night you mentioned a man called N" – that is Sticks – "can you describe him?"' The record had continued with a description of Silcott supposedly given by Raghip to the police: had he actually been dressed in this way?

Amlot asked. Raghip replied: 'I don't know. I didn't see him. What's written there I just made up. That's untrue.'

In law, as the judge had made clear, Amlot's tactic was unimpeachable. But no matter how well the jury was directed, their memories of N thrusting the sword into Jason Hill's hand, and of Pennant saying how frightened he was of him, cannot fail to have been stirred.

The only value that naming Silcott could have to the Crown's case against Raghip was to show that he had, in an allegedly contemporaneous interview, named a person accused of playing a leading role in the riot. But as we have seen, Raghip denied he had. Moreover, he had supposedly described Silcott not killing PC Blakelock but in much less noxious activity. Mrs Mills was surely right: the prejudicial effect to Silcott far outweighed any benefit to the prosecution case against Raghip.

The impact of lifting the veil seemed almost palpable. It was redoubled by N's name having lain concealed for so long. For weeks, the jury had wondered who this dreadful person could be, and now they saw him in front of them in the dock. Silcott's lawyers still believe that Mr Justice Hodgson should have stopped Amlot's cross-examination: having taken such pains to prevent prejudice for so long, he could, says Andrew Hall, have used his general discretion or powers granted by section 78 of PACE to keep the veil in place.

The whole subterranean background to the case now lumbered into view. The admissible evidence against Silcott was not, on any reckoning, copious. In plain words, lifting the veil helped ensure his conviction. Although it was legally right, the law must be changed. As it stands, it stains the reputation of English criminal justice.

Mark Braithwaite also had an alibi. He said he had spent the night of the riot at the home of Joan Daley, a friend of his girl friend Jackie. He had not told the police when he was interviewed, he told the court, because he had left a substantial quantity of cannabis – eight ounces – in her flat, and he was worried that a search would find it and get her into serious trouble.

Braithwaite gave evidence himself, making a series of claims about the conduct of the interviews. He had suffered from a headache at the very beginning, and had to see a doctor; he had found it stiflingly hot and oppressive in the cell. He suffered from claustrophobia, he said, and this was recorded in his custody record.

The details of the riot, he said, he had gleaned from gossip and news coverage. What was the attitude of the officers? Tansey asked him. 'They started pressurising and pressurising – I had to answer things over and over until I gave the right answer,' he said. Both McDermott and Biggar made threats and became aggressive, he told the court; had they continued to be reasonable, he would have told the truth, that he was not involved in the riot. He added: 'I hadn't had anything to eat. I was locked in. When I gave that sort of answer he calmed down and started talking reasonably so I thought that was it.'

Q: So when you said, 'Yes, throwing a few stones' – what did you think would happen?
A: I thought he would charge me and let me go.
Q: Did you think it was a serious admission you were making?
A: I hadn't done it so to me it wasn't a serious admission.
Q: When the interview finished, what did you say to the officer?
A: That I wanted to go home. The officer said I was not exactly telling him the truth and he had more questions to ask me.
Q: How were you feeling by this time?
A: I had been talking to the officer on an empty belly for hours and hours. I kept saying I was hungry. I felt terrible in the cells. I couldn't breathe so I asked to speak to the officers again.
Q: What was the officer saying then?
A: Mr McDermott was talking to me, saying I had a weapon – a machete or a knife. So I said, 'What are you talking about?' I hadn't heard that a bar had been used, so I said I had a bar.
Q: Did you give the answers set out in the interview where you talk about hitting a young officer with an iron bar on his side and his leg? Was there any truth in that?
A: I had to make it up. It was mixing things I had heard about that night.

Q: By doing this, what did you think would happen to you?
A: I thought to myself that they would let me go.
Q: In your final interview, is it true that you had buzzed for the police from your cell and asked to speak to them again?
A: Yes, because I wanted to go home.
Q: What did they say to that?
A: They said they still had a few more questions to ask. They were asking me about other people. They wanted names. Like names of people in this trial now. I said to them I don't know them.
Q: What did the police officer say?
A: He said me and certain other people were together and that I and others killed the officer. He said he had a witness statement from a geezer who'd known me for three years.
Q: Did he say anything else?
A: That by the time I came out my son wouldn't want to know me.
Q: Then what?
A: He said if I made a witness statement we could work something out. He had the statements on the table, the blank sheets. He wanted names.
Q: What did you say?
A: I said I don't know any names.

When Ray Barnett, Braithwaite's solicitor, was at last allowed access, Braithwaite complained of severe stomach cramps and vomited. He had already suffered diarrhoea. He saw two doctors and next day was taken to Barnet General Hospital where he had an anal examination. The doctor said he would like to keep Braithwaite in overnight for more tests, as he believed he was suffering from gastritis. The police refused. He was brought back to Barnet Police Station and charged with murder that afternoon.

Steven Kamlish, Tansey's junior, recalled DC Biggar, and put it to him that more should have been done about Braithwaite's claustrophobia. There was, he suggested, a larger room available where he could have been held: 'You know claustrophobia makes people panic?'

'I'm not medically qualified,' the officer replied.

On the custody record, Kamlish said, it stated that when Braithwaite complained of his headache, he had told his interrogators that he was happy to carry on and had signed the notes to that effect. Yet no signature appeared on the notes, nor any inquiry from the officers as to his willingness to continue. 'I can only assume Sergeant McDermott was going to ask him that and it wasn't done,' Biggar said. This, Kamlish suggested, was 'a deliberate attempt to make things look proper and fair when in fact they were not'. It raised the possibility that the notes were not a complete, contemporaneous record of what happened. Braithwaite had also claimed he was not properly cautioned.

Biggar admitted that Braithwaite, a man complaining of claustrophobia, ate nothing between his arrest and the end of his confessions nearly thirty hours later.

Before the trial moved into its final phase, there remained only to deal with Mark Pennant. As had by now been expected for some time, Mr Justice Hodgson ruled his interviews inadmissible in unequivocal language.

He should not, the judge said, have been arrested at school. He went on:

> I have no doubt whatsoever that there was no justification for withholding this youth access to a solicitor . . . the idea that this youth might have passed coded messages, or, indeed, messages in clear, via his solicitor, does not seem to me to hold water. One would have thought that by now the dangers of interviewing a juvenile in the absence of legal advice were too well known to require my repetition. In my judgement, the number of times when refusal to allow access to a solicitor by a juvenile is justified are so few as to be non-existent. To tell him that he was not to have anyone informed of his whereabouts was, in my judgement, an almost greater impropriety.

As with Jason Hill, the Children and Young Persons Act 'appears either to have been totally forgotten, or ignored'. There was nothing to prevent his being transferred overnight to local authority care, 'indeed, as it was known he was to be arrested, arrangements could and should have been made in advance'. His detention in a police cell was 'not only improper but unlawful'.

Mr Justice Hodgson expressed his shock that the police told Pennant that his mother was unwilling to attend his interviews, when at that very moment they had not even called on her in order to search her house: 'What the effect upon him was, when he learnt that his mother was unwilling to be with him, it hardly needs a psychologist to say.' So little attempt was made to ensure that Pennant understood the caution that with his meagre memory and intellectual equipment it seemed probable that he forgot completely that he had the option of remaining silent.

The report by Dr Roscoe had said that untrue confessions were especially likely when an accused person was subject to lengthy questioning in unfamiliar surroundings, was frightened, eager to please, immature or mentally handicapped to some degree. In the judge's view, 'all, or almost all, those factors were present in the case of Pennant. In the face of the unchallenged expert evidence it seems to me to be impossible that I should rule other than that the evidence of these interviews is inadmissible.'

And as with Hill again, large parts of Pennant's confession seemed to be fantasy; there was no mention of Coombes, or the rescue efforts led by Sergeant Pengelly, an event so dramatic that no one who was really there could have failed to notice it:

> The police did not make much effort to check the actual detail of Pennant's supposed part in the attack upon PC Blakelock, being far more concerned to get information about others involved. I think that if anyone had questioned him closely about the detail of his confession, on the assumption that they wanted to confirm its accuracy, they would soon have discovered that it was far from accurate.

As with the ruling on Jason Hill, the judge's remarks about Pennant's interrogation records were made in the absence of the jury. He gave his ruling less than a week after Amlot had lifted the veil over Silcott. The jury's knowledge that the key figure in Mark Pennant's confession was Winston Silcott must have weighed more heavily than the fact that they were formally asked, with no explanation, to find Pennant not guilty.

13

'A very vicious and a very evil man'

As the long trial drew to its close, the Fleet Street pack was gathering. As counsel began a week of closing speeches to the jury, day by day the numbers of reporters increased. Often they were to be seen at lunchtimes in the wine bar across the road from the Old Bailey, or in a pub round the corner, drinking with the police. Some took a serious and dispassionate interest in the case. Others, from certain tabloids, made an open display of bigotry and racial prejudice, swapping stories about 'evil' black men who had come up for trial at the Bailey in the past. Silcott, one well-known crime specialist told me, was sadly typical of his kind.

Among journalists from broadsheet, 'quality' papers, too, the assiduous public relations campaign run by the police had done its work. There was wide agreement that the evidence against Silcott was remarkably thin, and the prosecution would be fortunate to get a conviction. But briefed thoroughly about the Smith case and other details of the police version of Silcott's past life, few among the press corps doubted his guilt.

The closing speeches by Morris and Tansey went over the now familiar ground of their clients' allegations of oppression, the denial of legal advice and the claim that their admissions did not amount to murder: Braithwaite had allegedly hit a different officer, and Raghip had hit no one at all.

The closing speech by Roy Amlot was once more a model of

cold, portentous clarity. 'The whole world knows this is a very important trial,' he began. The attack on PC Blakelock and serial 502 was an act of 'barbarism, which we hope will never be repeated'. He went on: 'That sort of anarchy, however brief, sends a chill of fear and concern through thinking people and makes your task the more important. It imposes on you the task of doing justice according to the law.'

At first, he devoted considerable time to an attempt to dispose of Mansfield's arguments about the outbreak of the riot once and for all. Lambie, though now acquitted of murder, was still facing a charge of riot, and his defence – preposterous as it seemed to Amlot – was that he had acted on the night of 6 October in self-defence against an unwarranted incursion on to Broadwater Farm by the police. The personal antipathy between the two barristers surfaced again. The rioters knew that the Police Complaints Authority was to conduct an inquiry into Mrs Jarrett's death, Amlot reminded the jury: 'Mr Mansfield may sneer but the PCA are an independent authority with a civilian deputy.'

Amlot defended the methods of the police inquiry:

Mr Melvin and his officers have been heavily criticised but they faced a formidable task. The administration alone was incredible – 359 arrested and 159 charged, not counting these defendants. They had to cope with a total lack of public support in the area and there was also a special police order from 1 July in operation, a dry run of PACE . . . lawyers had not got to grips with PACE yet, let alone the police. I take into account the many criticisms of the officers from all quarters but at the end of the day every single word of the interviews was recorded at the time by the interviewing officers and read over, except in the case of Winston Silcott who made it clear he would not sign anything . . . except in Raghip's case, not a word of the interviews has been challenged.

The police, Amlot said, had only one effective weapon: the fact that those being interviewed could not be sure who had talked about them and who had not: 'The use of that weapon by the police was legitimate and effective.' The extent of admissions might, he said, be related to what people thought others in custody had said about them.

As an explanation of why, for example, Raghip had gone no further than his confession to having a broom handle, this was ingenious. Yet it also implicitly referred to the mass of subterranean evidence which we have examined at length and found substantially wanting.

But it was when he turned to Silcott that Amlot's speech reached its most significant stage. Pausing occasionally to comment, Amlot read through the fifth interview a final time, speaking at dictation speed: 'They're . . . only . . . kids . . . No one's . . . going . . . to . . . believe . . . them . . . You . . . say . . . they . . . say . . . that . . . How . . . do . . . I . . . know . . . ? I . . . don't . . . go . . . with . . . kids . . .' The jurors picked up the hint and wrote down the text of the interview. They had, as we have seen, no copy because Silcott had not signed it.

'In other words,' Amlot said, 'Melvin is alleging Silcott was the ringleader that night. None of this is challenged and Melvin notices his conduct: "Silcott . . . stood . . . up . . . looked . . . out . . . of . . . the . . . window . . . returned . . . to . . . his . . . chair . . . and . . . sat . . . down . . . He said . . . you . . . cunts . . . you cunts . . . He . . . leant . . . back . . . in . . . his . . . chair . . . and . . . with . . . tears . . . in . . . his . . . eyes . . . his . . . arms . . . above . . . his . . . head . . . he . . . said . . . Jesus, Jesus . . ."'

Silcott's actions, Amlot argued, amounted to the adoption of a guilty posture, while his words contained nothing approaching a simple denial of what was being said. Somehow he knew that 50 per cent of those the police had interviewed by this stage were juveniles, while he appeared to know something of the disposal of weapons – 'Fuck . . . you . . . you . . . find . . . them.' Amlot urged the jury: 'Look at the whole and ask yourself if he is either by his answers or his conduct supporting the allegations made to Mr Melvin.'

Mrs Mills did her best to put the opposing view. Silcott's replies, she suggested, may have come from deep frustration. As far as the remarks about kids went, the juveniles originally charged with murder were no longer in the case. And what did Silcott's replies really amount to? Was he not simply mystified as to the basis for Melvin's belief? Then he is accused of being the ringleader and moves to the window, and has his small outburst. 'How can that be seen as acceptance? Members of the jury, that behaviour is consistent with feeling the most ultimate frustration, despair and anger.'

Overall, she said, 'Winston Silcott's responses are those of a desperate man wrongly accused. He was trying to say to the officers, "You've got it wrong." He ends by saying,"You ain't got no evidence," and I will say the same to you: there is no evidence.' The prosecution could not even allege exactly what Silcott had done: 'Is it fair to ask you to try and spell out what he did when they cannot? Unless you can say what Winston Silcott did, you cannot convict.'

She concluded: 'That's all I've got to say. Everyone is aware how terrifying the events of that night were. There can only be one more dreadful thing added to the events of that night, and that would be the conviction of an innocent man.'

It may be that Mrs Mills's eloquence cause serious alarm at Scotland Yard, or perhaps the police were merely looking for an insurance policy. In any event, there now took place one of the murkiest events in this whole story. On Sunday, 15 March, as Mr Justice Hodgson prepared his summing up, the *Sunday Express* led its front page with the headline: 'FLASHPOINT TOTTENHAM'. Sub-heads proclaimed a 'terror alert as Blakelock murder trial nears end', with claims that guns had been stolen, milk bottles were missing, that youths had been seen with 'deadly bags' of nails and that (bizarrely) there had been a run on washers sold in hardware shops. The article by Andrew Alderson began:

A mass of lethal weapons is being stockpiled in London ready for a riot to coincide with the end of the Police Constable Blakelock murder trial. Senior police officers have met community leaders in Tottenham over the past two days in an attempt to avert a clash. Among the schemes they know about is one to 'take out' Tottenham police station by burning . . . the murder trial into the death of PC Blakelock during the Broadwater Farm estate riot in 1985 is expected to finish at the end of this week. Unrest is feared, whatever the outcome.

According to Mr Alderson, *Sunday Express* inquiries had revealed that 'sophisticated walkie talkie equipment' had been found in a raid on a pirate radio station: 'It is believed this may have been an intended centre for the riot, keeping leaders constantly in contact.' Some shotgun cartridges had been stolen in January, milk bottles had not been returned and 'garages in the district report a big increase in sales of petrol cans and fuel to black youths'. As to the washers sold by hardware shops, these could be 'shotgun ammunition' or missiles.

A leading article described this story as 'a profoundly disturbing report', adding: 'It is beyond doubt that a criminal conspiracy is bent on promoting arson, looting and murder.'

In fact, it was very far beyond doubt. No riot was being prepared. That did not stop it being followed up by the rest of the national press, and by the broadcasting organisations. The *Sunday Times* and the *Sunday Telegraph* both managed to carry versions in their later editions, helped by statements from Scotland Yard's press office confirming that Deputy Assistant Commissioner Douglas Cree was meeting community leaders 'to express certain fears and seek their support in ensuring peace and calm prevailed in the area'. That much may have been true; it was very far from evidence of a 'criminal conspiracy'. A Tory councillor, Andrew Mitchell, was stupid enough to declare that 'it's getting close to IRA terrorism'.

There was further coverage of Tottenham's *grande peur* on the Monday. It was left to a *Guardian* leader writer to draw the obvious conclusion. The story might, he suggested, have emerged because there really was a riot in the offing, and someone hoped that by giving it publicity it might be averted. However, 'it may also be because the entire tale is pretty much a fantasy, [and] someone is trying to use the press to influence the outcome of the trial'.

The *Guardian* was right. Years later, after I made a programme for the Channel 4 series *Hard News* about press coverage of the Blakelock case and the way it had prejudiced the trial, a senior Scotland Yard press officer took me aside and admitted that it had been he who was the source of the story. He had been acting, he said, on the basis of information made available to him both from the Specialist Operations department, which included the Serious Crime Squad, and from officers in north London. Washers, milk bottles, CB radios notwithstanding, the last thing the people of the Farm were planning as the trial approached its end was another riot.

Like the *Sun* picture of Silcott eight weeks earlier, the story roused Mr Justice Hodgson to fury. There had been 'a huge coverage' of the case at the weekend, he told the jury, 'some of it extremely reprehensible'. He was confident they would put all media reporting out of their minds. But however clear his directions, the thought had been planted: that there was a direct, conspiratorial link between the men in the dock and further mayhem on the streets of Tottenham.

The summing up was fair, lucid and sensible as everything else uttered by Mr Justice Hodgson during the trial. There were several ingredients in the brewing miscarriage of justice in the Blakelock murder case; Mr Justice Hodgson was not one of them. No judge, as Amlot had said at one point, with what in a lesser man might have been construed as regret, could have made more strenuous efforts to exclude prejudicial evidence. His efforts to lower the temperature of the trial and to conduct it in a proper atmosphere of forensic detachment could not have been greater. For the defendants and their lawyers, one of the biggest problems in the years to come was that his rulings on matters of law and summing up of the evidence left so few openings for grounds of appeal.

The only evidence which could be considered in reaching a verdict, the judge reminded the jury, was the contents of the interview records. Nothing that might have been said by one defendant about another must be taken into account. The judge went on to give a full account of 5 and 6 October, up to and including Blakelock's death.

The law of murder when more than one person was involved was complicated, he said. Anyone who aided and abetted the offence was also guilty. If he was a 'principal', one of those who actually landed a blow, then to be guilty of murder he had to have had the intent of killing or causing 'really serious harm'. If he was guilty as an aider and abettor, a secondary party, then he had to have intended that those he was aiding and abetting should kill or cause really serious injury. 'It is the intention which is the all-important factor,' he said. As far as Blakelock was concerned, a defendant would be guilty of murder if he used a lethal weapon, such as a knife, on him, or if he helped the attackers, intending at least serious injury, and knowing that other people there had lethal weapons.

But if someone attacked the officer intending only 'some harm' or encouraged the others knowing they would cause some harm, then manslaughter would be the appropriate verdict. This, it seemed, might be particularly applicable to the case of Engin Raghip. He had no lethal weapon and landed no blow; asked whether he wanted to kill the officer he had answered, 'No way.'

Turning to the individual cases, Mr Justice Hodgson dealt first with Silcott. If a police officer was interrogating someone, they might put an accusation, which on its own had no weight. It would become important only if the accused 'accepted' it, through words, demeanour or action. Equally, 'mere denial' might not render the accusation worthless: 'He may deny the accusation in such a manner and under such circumstances as may lead you to disbelieve him.' The 'stage directions' in Silcott's interview record, the description of his trip to the window and the tears in his eyes, were, it would appear, crucial in evaluating what the police claimed he had said. In deciding the case, the jury must remember there was no forensic evidence or photographs, despite a thousand taken on the night.

Silcott's fifth interview was again read out, now by the judge. Counsel for either side had put very different interpretations upon it, he said: 'Whichever way you look at them is entirely a matter for you,' he told the jury, reminding them that the burden of proof was with the prosecution.

In no sense was this a direction to convict Winston Silcott. Mr Justice Hodgson was not only fair but right in law. Yet the jury was being asked to perform an impossible task: to guess the meaning of gestures written in a police record, and to use the interview and nothing else to make a psychological assessment of Silcott's alleged replies: acceptance of guilt or angry frustration.

Raghip, Mr Justice Hodgson reminded the jury, had challenged his interviews in many respects, yet his account seemed to accord in high degree to what had happened. At one stage, he had said he had seen an officer attacked at Griffin Road, on the opposite side of the estate, but not at Tangmere. Did his interviews really sound like a description of that? the judge asked. As to the crucial admissions about hearing the 'ah' sound and the broom handle, Raghip had claimed the police suggested them to him. If this were true, the judge said, it meant the police must have said something like, 'I expect you heard noises coming from him when he was being attacked which were like a continuous "ah" sound.' This, the judge said, 'is something which the system of contemporaneous recording is aimed at preventing'. No doubt the jury would remember that at the end of each interview a uniformed officer had been brought in to read the record, and that Raghip had not dissented while this was done. But the jury must remember there was no evidence of his hitting PC Blakelock: 'You could not find him guilty of murder as principal . . . if you are not satisfied that you are sure that he is guilty as an aider and abettor to murder, you would then of course go on to consider, after looking at manslaughter, whether you were sure there was a riot, and whether you were sure that Raghip took part in it.' The jury here were being asked to look at the technical definition of the riot charge as the law then defined it: it required effectively a conspiracy, a 'joint enterprise', as opposed to less organised disorder represented by the charge of affray. This, it seemed, was a clear suggestion that to convict Raghip of murder would be inappropriate.

Neither Braithwaite's alibi, nor his allegations about the conduct of his interviews, seem to have convinced Mr Justice Hodgson. But he stressed that PC Blakelock had sustained no leg injuries consistent with blows from an iron bar, though Braithwaite said he had hit a policeman on the leg, adding: 'You would then have to ask yourselves what may be a much more difficult question, and that is whether, from the interviews, from what he confessed to, you can be sure it was PC Blakelock whom he hit with the bar . . . if you are not sure it was Blakelock whom he struck, then obviously you will find him not guilty of murder.'

The jury stayed out for three nerve-wracking days. For two months we had looked at them, mute in their box: seven men and five women. There was only one Afro-Caribbean, a woman. The foreman was an executive from a leading industrial company. Throughout the long proceedings they had followed the case with close attention, and many had taken copious notes. Now their time had come.

Twice they were taken to stay in an hotel. Once they came back and asked for all the originals of Raghip's interviews. The judge had made it clear he wanted the verdicts all at once, not piecemeal. The press was at fever pitch. Primed by off-the-record conversations with the police to cope with acquittals, at least one tabloid reporter spent a lot of time in the basement Old Bailey press room, obsessively telephoning policemen, lawyers and anyone else he could think of for 'dirt' on Mr Justice Hodgson.

At long last, at nearly five o'clock on Thursday, 19 March, the word went out: the jury was ready to return.

They shuffled back into the box like shell-shocked refugees, strain etched on their faces. Three of the women were weeping; some of the men seemed to be shaking. The three men were brought up into the dock for a last time. After the seemingly endless evidence, wrangling and legal discussion of the previous two months, there was a terrible swiftness about what followed. How did the jury find them? Guilty, guilty, guilty.

Silcott looked up at his brother, George, in the public gallery with a despairing smile: he had suspected what would happen. Their previous convictions were read out and the whole court now knew that a year and two months earlier, Winston Silcott had been convicted of the murder of Anthony Smith. Sentencing took almost no time at all. 'Silcott, you are both a very vicious and a very evil man,' Mr Justice Hodgson said. He would go to prison for life, with a recommendation he serve a minimum of thirty years. Raghip and Braithwaite were also jailed for life, but the judge neither commented nor made any recommendation.

The black woman juror fainted and had to be revived. Raghip shouted: 'You've made a big mistake, I didn't do it!' The three were led from view, down into the basement cells. From the public gallery, there was suddenly a great wailing as the men's families absorbed the verdicts; a sound of anguish and terrible grief. One woman was dragged away by police. Then the court was cleared.

That was the end of the PC Blakelock murder trial.

Detective Chief Superintendent Graham Melvin returned to Scotland Yard that night to a hero's welcome. As he entered an office where some of his colleagues had gathered, they stood up and applauded.

In the press next day, there was one small voice urging caution – another editorial in the *Guardian*. The police, it said, had acted with indecent haste in getting someone in the dock for the killing, and had made the lack of evidence worse by the way they handled interrogations. With some prescience, it added: 'Shades of the Birmingham bombings there. We haven't heard the last of these cases, either.'

That was also my view. I was certain that the three were victims of a terrible miscarriage of justice, and as far as I could I tried to reflect this in my own news coverage for the *Guardian* that day and in the following weeks and months. But even within the paper, there were some who pointed to the unanimous jury verdict, and to Silcott's previous conviction. Doubters were swimming against a strong tide.

The tabloids knew no restraint. Ignoring the weakness of the evidence against Silcott entirely, they focused on his alleged 'ringleader' role, portraying him as a beast or monster. The racist subtext was barely hidden. 'Victim of the savages' was the headline the *Sun* used over a piece about PC Blakelock and his family; while the *Star* printed a two-page spread with an artist's impression of the murder, captioned: 'Hooded animals out for blood.' The piece began: 'The series of chilling pictures on the right show the beasts of Broadwater Farm moving in for the kill. They are led by an animal called Winston Silcott.' No need for accuracy here: 'Silcott and his pack of savages, some wearing sinister hoods, ambushed PC Blakelock on a first-floor walkway.'

The *Sun* front page reproduced the same picture of Silcott, with the headline: '30 years and he smiled.' The story started: 'Machete monster Winston Silcott was jailed for 30 years yesterday for hacking PC Keith Blakelock to death . . . and he simply smiled.' The paper promised to tell readers 'the savage's secret' on pages 2, 3, 4, 6, 16 and 17. The *Star* had the headline 'Smile of evil' and the *Mirror* 'Smile of hate'. The *Express* called Winston 'the butcher of Broadwater Farm' and described him as 'a six foot two inch black man with protuberant staring eyes [who] ruled Broadwater Farm with a brutal reign of terror'. The *Standard* headline read simply: 'This evil monster', the main text quoting Mark Pennant's inadmissible interviews as 'fact': 'It was also said that he [Silcott] had held up a bloodstained knife and said: "This is bullman's blood."'

The bestial imagery showed again in a *Mail* article describing Dolly Kiffin's reaction to the verdicts: 'A noise that made the young cops turn and walk back through a valley of long cold shadows . . . then the noise became like the scream of a jet and the cops walked faster through the midday darkness covering half of Broadwater Farm. Now no words could be understood. A huge man was on guard next to Dolly Kiffin. His hair was piled into a tea cosy on his head.' Broadwater Farm: the white man's grave.

Most newspapers took police briefings about Silcott at face value. 'If the jury had known one tenth of Silcott's appalling record, they might have had some understanding of the depth and extent of the terror he exercised over the people of Tottenham,' the *Mail* reported. The allegation that Silcott stabbed PC Graham Betts on the Farm in 1983 was trotted out, unquestioned, together with bits of cod sociology: 'There is no obvious reason why Silcott should have developed a violent grudge against society.'

Judge Lymbery, who had granted Silcott bail in the Smith case, came in for withering criticism. The usual 'rent a quote' Tory MPs demanded his resignation, together with the return of the death penalty. There was talk of amending the Bail Act to prevent men charged with murder being released.

On the day after the verdicts, the Broadwater Farm Defence Campaign held a press conference on the estate. Stafford Scott angrily accused journalists of helping to frame Silcott and the others, and failing to make the least attempt at investigating what had really gone on: 'Why do you always believe black men need a leader? Did you all really believe there was going to be a riot here after the verdicts? Are we being set up all over again? We don't want war, we don't want confrontation. We want justice, we want parity. Like our brothers and sisters in the South African townships, we shall not stop fighting; we shall not stop defending ourselves; we shall not lay down. We have the right to live and we are going to use it.'

Another speaker denounced the riot scare stories: 'None of you are naive. You talk of washers being brought on to the Farm. They talk about bottles being brought on to the Farm. But nothing is produced, laid out for the press. And you fell for it.'

Floyd Jarrett said: 'I went to school with Winston Silcott, I know him well. It's like they have killed my mother all over again, what they have done to them.'

When Winston's father began to speak, the anger was for a moment replaced by deep sadness. Speaking slowly, choking back tears, he said: 'I am the father of Winston Silcott, whom you have tried to crucify like Christ was crucified. It's not right, it's not right. Silcott is innocent of this crime. It's not right in the sight of God. I will be the next one. Winston is innocent.'

14

No Lurking Doubt

Until some three hours before the jury came back, Sharon Raghip was sure her husband would be acquitted. 'I had faith in British justice, it was as simple as that. Despite everything that had happened, I didn't think anyone could find Engin guilty. Then it clicked. They wanted Winston so badly, and Engin was going down with him.' Engin also had faith: 'I was naive. I didn't do it, and I thought the jury would believe my defence.'

It was the same for Mark Braithwaite: 'When the jury reached their verdict, everything closed in. I couldn't believe this was happening. The press were looking at us like we were animals, paraded in the zoo.'

On remand in Brixton Prison, one of the most notorious of Victorian jails with the highest suicide rate in the country, all three had already suffered. 'It was disgusting,' says Mark, 'the place was oppressive, the screws' attitude was appalling. The fact that we were charged with the murder of a policeman made it much more difficult. As we left for court each morning they would shout: "HMP against the cop killers."' Sometimes there was racist abuse – 'They called us black bastard and the various terms that can be used.' On Valentine's Day in the middle of the trial, his girl friend sent a card. By the time it reached Mark, it had been defaced with a picture of a gallows, and a message saying Mark was a cop killer and deserved to die. He asked the wing officer how the card had come to be in this state and was told: 'It must have been posted like this.'

Throughout the months on remand, Mark says, 'we swallowed all this because Engin and I, at least, had the belief that we would be acquitted'.

After conviction, there seemed to be no way out. Life sentence prisoners are at the mercy of the system. Most of the decisions which affect them – where they stay, on what regime, and when they might in due course be released – are made in secret, by officials whose remit knows no scrutiny, and no right of appeal.

Mr Justice Hodgson had given clear hints in his summing up to the jury that murder convictions might not be justified for Mark Braithwaite and Engin Raghip, and it was striking that he made no comment on their characters and actions as he passed the only sentence available in law, life imprisonment. In communication with the Home Office after the end of the trial, he made his views plain.

The length of a life sentence is governed primarily by the 'tariff', a term set by the judge in consultation with the Lord Chief Justice and then ratified by the Home Secretary to mark the punitive element of the sentence. Once it has expired, the only criterion for continued imprisonment is possible danger to the public.

Home Office sources have confirmed to me that at the close of the Blakelock murder case, Mr Justice Hodgson recommended terms for Braithwaite and Raghip which would normally be thought astonishingly low for the killers of a policeman: just eight years each. In a letter to Douglas Hurd, the Home Secretary, the judge gave reasons for setting such relatively low limits. Braithwaite, on the evidence of his confession, could not be guilty of murdering Blakelock, but appeared to have hit another officer, possibly PC Coombes. Raghip might in law have been part of the joint enterprise of the murder, but he had not landed a blow, while according to his confession he had not intended to kill the officer, only to kick him.

In 1988, Mark and Engin discovered what Hurd thought of the judge's recommendations: he simply disregarded them. Each received a letter from the Home Office stating that their cases would not be considered by local review committees of the Parole

Board until 2002, and they must expect to serve a minimum of twenty years.

There is, of course, no legal recourse by which a prisoner may challenge the tariff set.

The public vilification of Winston Silcott and his portrayal as a beast or monster led to gratuitous acts of cruelty. Five times, while he was at his first prison after conviction, Wormwood Scrubs, his mother brought him a radio: five times, by the time it reached Winston, the radio was smashed. After eighteen months he was transferred to Albany on the Isle of Wight, a long and difficult journey for his parents to make from Tottenham. There, he was constantly challenged, threatened and provoked by prison staff. He became depressed and withdrawn.

Repeatedly, he tried to get work in the prison carpentry shop but was made to work on a sewing machine. When he downed tools one day he was put in the punishment block, where he began a hunger strike. For weeks, there ensued a cat and mouse game in which he would serve a spell 'on the block', go back to normal accommodation, and then get another punishment sentence when he again refused to sew, leading to another hunger strike.

Eventually Adam Sampson, a probation officer from Tottenham, went to see him during a period when he was refusing food in the punishment block. He was concerned about Winston's condition, and raised the matter with the probation service office at the prison. He was given instructions not to mention it on any account to Winston's family, or the Broadwater Farm Defence Campaign. Sampson felt this was unreasonable, and on his return to Haringey raised it with his superiors. They repeated the instructions. Sampson promptly telephoned Winston's mother and the campaign, and left the probation service soon afterwards to become the highly effective deputy director of the Prison Reform Trust.

Mark Braithwaite was moved to Chelmsford after his conviction, 'one of the most depressing prisons in the country'. He was never beaten up, he says, 'but there were occasions when they came near. The door had shut; the media said we were vicious monsters. I felt alone, and I felt frightened.' After two months, he was moved to Aylesbury youth custody centre, which was physically more comfortable but worse in terms of harassment. 'One officer used to go on and on at me, telling me I'd never get out, that I was a black bastard. They thought that if they could suppress me, they could suppress anyone. I was under the spotlight because of what I was supposed to have done. If I committed some small offence they'd give me ten days down the block. Someone else would have got three for the same thing.'

Mark applied for a place on an accountancy course. The governor allowed him out of the segregation wing to attend an interview and he was given a place. But a short while before the course was due to begin, he was moved to Wormwood Scrubs, so it came to nothing. Unknown to anyone at the murder trial, he had been virtually illiterate when he was arrested but while on remand he taught himself to read with a dictionary and an Ed McBain thriller lent by a cell mate. By the time Mark reached the Scrubs, he was reading voraciously – 'not fiction, but fact, especially business'.

One of the more exquisite features of the criminal justice system is that after the expiry of the tariff, one of the most common grounds for continuing to hold a lifer is that he still protests his innocence. If a killer has not 'come to terms' with the crime, the Home Office argument goes, then it is 'impossible to assess the risk to the public'. This lesson was not lost on Engin: 'I soon knew from talking to other prisoners that they'd never let me go while I said I hadn't done it. They can keep you as long as they like and tell you nothing. Sometimes I didn't feel up to much. I just used to go behind my cell door, soaking it up, feeling sorry for myself. But I wasn't going to give them the satisfaction of getting me down off no rope. I had to keep going.'

Delroy Lindo had started the first Winston Silcott campaign within a few days of his being charged with the murder and discovered at once that this was not an easy cause to champion. He and George, Winston's brother, organised pickets of the magistrates' courts where Winston came up for remand. But it was so difficult to generate sympathy that they resorted to graffiti expeditions in the middle of the night, desperate to get the message across somehow.

After the trial, the Broadwater Farm Defence Campaign remained in existence. A few months later, it published a report by two American jurists, Judge Margaret Burnham of Boston and Professor Lennox Hinds of Rutgers University, New York. They had attended part of the hearing, read many of the statements and interview records, and talked to defence lawyers. Their report was severely critical of the police inquiry, focusing particularly on the denial of legal advice. The assumption that witnesses could not be found without resorting to mass arrests was a 'slur on the Broadwater Farm community'. Winston Silcott's conviction on the basis of such slender evidence 'offends the fundamental sense of justice'. The report was barely noticed by most of the media. A few months later, a further report by Lord Gifford's inquiry team, and another by Amnesty International, which both came to similar conclusions, met the same fate.

The bleakest moment of the Blakelock story came in November 1988, with the three men's first appeal hearing. Raghip had changed his lawyers: his solicitor now was Gareth Peirce, a veteran of political cases including the Guildford Four and the Birmingham Six, while as counsel she briefed Mike Mansfield. Braithwaite was represented by Steven Kamlish alone in court, who had inherited his grounds of appeal from Tansey. Technically, it was not a proper appeal but only an application for leave to appeal in front of a full bench of three judges. They were led by the Lord Chief Justice, Lord Lane, who a few months earlier had dismissed the second appeal by the six convicted Birmingham pub bombers in ringing terms: the longer the case had gone on, he said, the more convinced he was of their guilt.

The Appeal Court's judgement, delivered in the Royal Courts of Justice by Lord Lane on 13 December, was impregnable, admitting no chinks of doubt or hope.

Mrs Mills appeared again for Silcott, and argued that Mr Justice Hodgson should not have allowed his case to be decided by the jury because it rested on too flimsy a basis. Citing various authorities, she said that none of Silcott's alleged remarks could be taken as amounting to an acceptance of the accusations made by Melvin, analysing each in turn. She also suggested that the origin of the police case was suspect because it came from Andrew Pyke, reminding the court that he had failed to come up to proof at the committal and had not given evidence at the Old Bailey despite being brought to the court under arrest.

Lord Lane wasted no time on Pyke:

> It does not seem to us that the criticism of the source of suggestions made by the police is relevant in the circumstances of this case.

As for the interview record being a dangerous basis for a murder conviction, he was equally emphatic:

> Taking the interviews as a whole, rather than each part of the interviews in isolation, as Mrs Mills has invited us to do, each one of us would, without hesitation, have come to the same conclusion as did the judge, namely that there was here a proper, and indeed a solid basis for saying that there was evidence capable of amounting to an admission to the murder, and also a basis on which a jury properly directed could find a verdict of guilty.

Mrs Mills tried one last tack: the legal principle that if the Court of Appeal thought there was a 'lurking doubt' about a conviction, they could quash it on this ground. In support of this argument, she adduced again the matter of Andrew Pyke, and the lifting of the veil on N. She added that since Silcott ran a greengrocery on the Tangmere deck, he was unlikely to have tried to stop firemen quenching a blaze there, while there was no photographic or scientific evidence.

On the question of the veil, Lord Lane was again withering. In a statement typical of the higher judiciary and its lack of understanding of the real world of criminal justice, he rejected the notion that the identification of N as Silcott was in any way prejudicial. Even if the jury's mind had been filled with the memory of the statements made by Hill and Pennant, this had no effect on the safety of the conviction because the judge told them to forget them:

> The suggestion is that the jury may have used the contents of those [Pennant's and Hill's] statements when considering the case of Silcott. However, the judge gave an impeccable direction as to the inadmissibility of statements made to the police . . . there is

no reason to believe that the jury would, even if they had realised who N was, have disregarded that direction.

There was no lurking doubt, Lord Lane concluded.

Raghip seemed to have the best hope at this hearing, in the form of convincing new evidence which went to the heart of the question posed by Mr Justice Hodgson – was he suggestible? Mansfield applied to call this evidence, a report by Dr Gisli Gudjonsson, a psychologist at the Institute of Psychiatry. Gudjonsson was an internationally famous expert who had carried out pioneering research in the field of suggestibility, devising a series of tests which had often been accepted in English courts of law.

Mansfield disclosed that Raghip had undergone an intelligence test before the trial. A preliminary assessment by a Dr Herridge found he had poor verbal skills and had probably not understood many of the words put to him by the police, but was overall of 'average' intelligence. The main test was carried out in November 1986 by Eric Ward, a psychologist in Kent. He concluded that while Raghip's overall test scores 'reflect a performance level comparable to a mildly mentally handicapped person', he was unlikely to be impaired to this degree because he had done well in picture arranging and object assembly tests.

Ward went on: 'In my opinion, the poor level of performance is a reflection of Mr Raghip's very limited educational experience rather than a lack of intelligence. On his own admission to me, although selected for special school, he did not bother to attend very much.' His reading age was only six, but this might be due to dyslexia. Ward stated: 'Mr Raghip's degree of suggestibility was assessed on the Gudjonsson suggestibility scale. His suggestibility scores were, however, average for a normal individual; they do not reflect any abnormal degree of suggestibility.' For obvious reasons, the defence had not called Herridge or Ward to give evidence at the Old Bailey.

But in 1988, Gareth Peirce arranged for Raghip to be tested by Dr Gudjonsson himself. His findings were quite different. 'Mr Raghip is of borderline intelligence. His overall intellectual abilities fall at the bottom four per cent of the general population giving a mental age of between ten and eleven years. He is illiterate of a reading age of about six years and five months. His memory function is very poor. He suggests attitudinal problems.'

Since the trial, Gudjonsson continued, Raghip had also been tested by the prison psychologist at Wormwood Scrubs, with very similar results. It was 'extremely unlikely' he was trying to fake the results: 'All the available evidence indicates that Mr Raghip was trying to do his best.' Crucially, he went on, his suggestibility scores were those of someone who 'gives in very readily under pressure . . . he is also a very anxious individual who would not be expected to cope well with lengthy and demanding police interviews'. The court, Mansfield said, should call Dr Gudjonsson and hear his evidence.

Once again, Lord Lane would have none of it. Mansfield pointed out that Pennant's lawyers had asked Eric Ward to examine him and the psychologist did not think the boy was suggestible; the lawyers had then asked Dr Tunstall to repeat the tests, with the result that his interrogations were eventually thrown out. The same would have happened, Mansfield argued, if Raghip's defence had commissioned a report from Gudjonsson in time.

Lord Lane dismissed the argument. All the tests on Raghip, he said, had come to much the same conclusion about his intelligence: it was low, but 'not mentally abnormal'. The only important differences were over the question of Raghip's suggestibility. But as far as Lord Lane was concerned, it mattered little who was right: 'The fact that this young man is more susceptible to suggestion than others does not by any manner of means make him abnormal mentally, or put him outside the experience of a juryman when assessing his fellow human being.' There was, he said, no basis on which Gudjonsson's evidence could be admissible because expert evidence could only be called to help juries 'in areas where ordinary human experience does not reach'. Suggestibility might vary, but courts had no need of experts: 'The jury had ample opportunity to gauge the degree of intelligence and susceptibility of Raghip when he gave evidence.' Even if the judge and jury had had all the reports in front of them, this would have made no difference to the outcome of the trial, Lord Lane said. 'The jury were in as good a position, if not better, than the psychologist to judge how amenable this young man was to suggestion.'

Finally, Lord Lane rejected Raghip's application for leave to appeal on grounds that his interviews contained no evidence that he was guilty of murder. The jury had been properly directed as to the difference between murder and manslaughter, and to the intent required for the more serious offence; it was a matter for them.

Braithwaite got equally short shrift. The argument about the denial of access to a solicitor under the PACE Act was again not put, although by this time Mr Justice Hodgson's ruling in the case of Samuel was a year old. The main point made by Kamlish was that his confession was not evidence beyond doubt that he attacked Blakelock: he might have hit another officer. Mr Justice Hodgson, he said, had been unfair to the defence on this point in his summing up.

Lord Lane, perhaps understandably, disagreed: 'It seems to us the judge made a great deal less of the strength of the prosecution case than he might have done.' He had put the case as fairly as possible. He added: 'Braithwaite's defence was an exceedingly difficult one to run, namely "I was not there but if, which is denied, I was there, I did not do what is alleged against me". It is not surprising the jury came to the conclusion they did. His application too is refused.'

It was a dark afternoon as we left court, almost the shortest day of the year. The deep shadows of the Gothic law courts matched the sombre mood. Bill and Mary Silcott walked away with resigned, sad dignity, stopping to exchange a few words with Sharon Raghip and Braithwaite's mother Patsie. There seemed to be no hope left.

For Mark, Engin and Winston, this was the worst of times, the bottom of the pit of despair. They were serving twenty and thirty years for a crime for which they had not been responsible, and at a hearing at which they had not even been present the Lord Chief Justice of England had dismissed their appeals out of hand.

Gareth Peirce says: 'It was a dreadful, dreadful judgement. The trauma for them was unimaginable. It was like experiencing the worst kind of accident, or a terminal illness – that is the scale of it.'

Mark Braithwaite describes losing the application for leave to appeal as 'a blow so great, I can't begin to explain what it felt like. It seemed as if I could just go mad. Up till then I still felt some faith in the legal system. That was the end of it. The worst thing was seeing how my son was suffering. When I went inside, he was a baby, and I was very worried about him because he suffered from eczema so badly that some nights there'd be blood on the pillow. Until that appeal I always thought I'd soon be out to look after him, but now it looked as if he was going to grow up without my ever seeing him except inside a prison visiting room.'

Engin Raghip says: 'I still thought the appeal system would work. I hadn't done it, so it would be put right.' One of the things that kept him going was meeting some of the other 'political prisoners' of England's infamous miscarriages of justice: Richard McIlkenny of the Birmingham Six, the three convicted of killing Carl Bridgewater, and others. 'The penny began to drop. I began to see what we were up against.'

At the same time, Sharon Raghip was becoming an active campaigner, and as her husband found comfort and solidarity from others wrongly imprisoned, she made common cause with their relatives, such as Breda Power, the daughter of Billy Power of the Birmingham Six. Sharon says: 'I used to feel so helpless, particularly at the end of a visit. You didn't want to know what the time was but you had to, because you had to prepare yourself for getting up and walking away. That was the hardest thing, to get up and walk away from an innocent man. Whatever campaigning or writing letters or whatever you're doing, you don't feel you're doing enough. You can't enjoy anything in your life without feeling guilt.'

Yet slowly, the campaigning was having an effect. The *New Statesman, Time Out* and other magazines ran articles calling for the case to be reopened, reviewing the weakness of the evidence and the doubts it raised. Andrew Hall, who worked indefatigably to keep the case alive, lobbied Barry Sheerman, the Labour home affairs front bench spokesman, and aroused his concern. Other MPs, led by Bernie Grant, continued to write letters to the Home Office, to table questions and early day motions, to meet the relatives of the jailed men. Trade union branches passed motions; there were well-attended public meetings. The Tottenham Three were beginning to be spoken of in the same breath as the Guildford Four and the Birmingham Six.

In the summer of 1989, Winston Silcott was elected honorary

president of the London School of Economics. It happened in a slow news week, and all the old tabloid venom spewed out. Eventually, after a tumultuous student meeting, the decision was reversed by a narrow majority. But the incident touched Winston deeply and was something of a turning point in the recovery of his spirits. The campaigning was not in vain. Let the leader writers of the *Sun* and the *Star* do their worst, someone out there cared.

15

A Different Approach to Justice

Lord Lane's judgements in the 1988 appeals of the Birmingham Six and the Tottenham Three were last public gasps of the old regime in English criminal justice. Underpinning them was the higher judiciary's automatic inclination towards the police infallibility principle. In the lower courts people were acquitted. But once a case reached the Court of Appeal, the reluctance of the judges to disturb the jury's verdict had little to do with their innate faith in jurors. Virtually all criminal appeals were won on points of law; the reluctance to quash convictions was particularly marked in cases fought on new evidence.

On the rare occasions when a case was referred back to the court a second or subsequent time after new evidence was submitted to the Home Secretary, this reluctance was still stronger. As for journalists or campaigners against miscarriages of justice, they sometimes incurred the Appeal Court's open disdain. The BBC programme *Rough Justice* almost went under for ever after the judges criticised its methods in 1986. Lord Lane's infamous remark about the Birmingham Six in January 1988, that the longer the case had gone on, the more satisfied he was of the six men's guilt, was a barely coded rebuke to Labour MP Chris Mullin and his many allies in the cause of proving their innocence.

In October 1989, the *ancien régime* imploded. The legal establishment's belief in the police infallibility principle sustained a blow from which it has not recovered: the release of the Guildford Four. The four, Carole Richardson, Paul Hill, Gerard Conlon and Paddy Armstrong, had all confessed. The shock and dismay on Lord Lane's face as he heard Roy Amlot say that apparent police malpractice meant the Crown could not sustain their convictions was genuine.

The police, Lord Lane said, in freeing the Guildford Four, must have lied; and with those words, he set in motion a chain reaction of events which has not come to an end. His own loss of faith in the infallibility principle was soon to be revealed as he sat in a series of appeals stemming from a Police Complaints Authority investigation of the West Midlands Serious Crime Squad and freed men serving long sentences for armed robbery. But the effects were much wider. The old complacent confidence had gone. When lawyers working for the Birmingham Six submitted further new evidence to the Home Office in 1990, Douglas Hurd wasted little time in ordering a new investigation by an outside police force. He had already set up a judicial inquiry under Sir John May into the Guildford Four and related Maguire family cases. Not only the police, but the conduct of Crown lawyers, the Home Office and forensic science service were coming under scrutiny.

The attitude of the mainstream media had also changed. In 1988, a high-powered team from the BBC television documentary features department spent several weeks looking at the Blakelock case, announcing its intention of making a substantial programme to question the murder convictions. It was headed by Roger Courtiour, whose stock was riding high following an acclaimed series he had made about Customs and Excise, *The Duty Men*. For reasons which were not made clear, the BBC hierarchy called a halt and the film was never made. Late in 1989, a different team from the same department, attached to the series *Inside Story*, began covering the same ground. This time, the corporation bosses gave the green light.

The programme, broadcast at the beginning of June the following year, was an important landmark in the case's slow unravelling. Presented by Charles Wheeler, one of the greatest reporters of the age in any medium, and produced by Steve Hewlett, the film reconstructed scenes from the trial, laying bare some of the weaknesses of the evidence. In respect of Engin Raghip and Mark Braithwaite, it disclosed important new evidence about their states of mind when they were interrogated.

In March 1990, Mark Braithwaite's solicitor, Danny Simpson, asked Paul Salkovskis, a psychiatrist and researcher at Oxford University, to examine him. Braithwaite, it will be recalled, had complained several times of feeling claustrophobic in his cell and at the trial said this was why he took the unusual step of twice asking for further interviews shortly after interrogation sessions had come to an end. His claustrophobia was mentioned in the custody record.

Interviewed by Salkovskis, a specialist in the study of claustrophobia, Mark went into more detail. What had been easily passed over at the trial emerged as a nightmarish experience. Dr Salkovskis' report described a series of 'acute panic attacks, during which he feared that he would choke, collapse and die . . . he behaved in a characteristic way, requesting that the hatch in the door be opened, and seeking opportunities to leave his cell, i.e. to go to the interview room'.

The cell, Mark told Salkovskis, was poorly ventilated and unbearably hot. It had no window, only thick glass panels which could not be opened. Salkovskis concluded that Mark's description of his symptoms was fully consistent with those of a genuine sufferer. His mother, whom Salkovskis interviewed, was also claustrophobic, and the condition had probably been inherited. He concluded: 'I am convinced beyond reasonable doubt that Mr Braithwaite suffers from claustrophobia, and that he experienced an acute panic attack associated with his detention in a cell . . . the fear he described as occurring during his detention was of extreme magnitude . . . and is likely to have played a key role in his requests to speak to interviewing officers. Furthermore, his ability to answer questions accurately is likely to have been impaired; difficulty in thinking and "thought blocking" is a well-documented consequence of panic.'

The new evidence in Engin Raghip's case added to what had already been said about his suggestibility in the Court of Appeal. Eric Ward, who examined him before the trial and did not find him significantly suggestible, had completely changed his mind in view of the later tests by Dr Gudjonsson, and also in the light of a scientific paper by Gudjonsson published in 1989. Ward added that at the time he tested Engin's IQ and suggestibility, he had not been aware of earlier tests by his local education authority carried out in 1980, 1981 and 1982. These confirmed Gudjonsson's results. Now, Ward said, he 'would agree with the conclusion in the report by Dr Gudjonsson, and with the proposition that Mr Raghip was impaired to a significant extent in his intelligence and social functioning'.

Ward's reappraisal did not address the point made by Lord Lane, that the jury was well-equipped to judge Engin by his performance in the witness box and that expert evidence was unnecessary. But it was clear that had Ward held his modified opinion at the time of the trial, he would have been called as a witness. In all likelihood Mr Justice Hodgson would then have ruled Engin's confession inadmissible.

In the new, post-Guildford climate, the *Inside Story* documentary made a considerable impact. 'After that,' says Sharon Raghip, 'I really began to think my husband might be coming out. The response I got when I wrote to MPs was perceptibly different.' On the evening of the transmission, *Newsnight* broadcast a discussion about the case, in which no less a figure than Lord Scarman stated his belief that the convictions should be overturned. A few weeks later, Channel 4's *Hard News* commissioned me to make a twenty-minute film about media coverage of the case and its prejudicial impact at crucial stages of the trial.

Gareth Peirce submitted a petition based on the new evidence of Mr Ward to the Home Office C3 department, which deals with miscarriages of justice. It was supported by representations from Michael Portillo, the Raghips' MP, who happened to be the local government minister. Danny Simpson did the same thing in respect of Mark Braithwaite. There seems to have been some kind of bureaucratic foul-up with Mark's case within C3, and for months the Salkovskis report was not considered. But that December, the first glimmer of light appeared on the horizon. Kenneth Baker, the new Home Secretary, announced that he was referring the case of Engin Raghip back to the Court of Appeal.

The reference of Raghip's case to the Court of Appeal interrupted another legal process which Peirce had set in motion, an application to the European Court of Human Rights. She argued that under the Human Rights Convention, Raghip had not been tried fairly, because of his extended interrogation and state of mind, while it could not be right that an illiterate man could sign away his right to legal advice. His interviews went on longer than those that the Court had already ruled were oppressively long in the case of an IRA suspect detained under the Prevention of Terrorism Act.

When the referral was made, the European Court's commission had got to the stage of asking the British government for its reply to the petition. Now, the Home Office applied to have the action stopped, because the referral meant the points were being dealt with.

This put the Crown in a very strange position. It was telling Europe that Raghip's case was under consideration, so that there was no need for the points raised to be gone through in detail. At the same time, it was telling Gareth Peirce that it intended to contest Raghip's appeal with vigour. As little as a month before the appeal, when compelling new evidence about Silcott had added him and Braithwaite to the hearing, a senior Crown lawyer told her that this was still the position: that the prosecution intended to argue Raghip's guilt.

The scientific technique known as Electrostatic Deposition Analysis, Esda for short, was invented at the London College of Printing around 1979. It works on the principle that when someone writes on a sheet of paper in a pad, the impressions of his words will appear as indentations on the sheet immediately below, and possibly more faintly on further sheets. The difficulty is to make such indentations show up. Esda does this by stretching a piece of Clingfilm-type plastic very tightly over the paper which is laid on a bronze bed in a virtual vacuum. Very fine particles, similar to photocopy toner, are spread across the plastic and then charged with a high-voltage electric current. For reasons which physicists understand imperfectly, the indentations show up clearly. They can be photographed, and studied at leisure.

At first, Esda seems to have been regarded merely as a scientific curiosity, with possibly some applications in verifying literary manuscripts. It was the police who realised its considerable forensic value. In fraud cases, for example, it might be extremely useful to be able to say whether sheets had been interpolated in a sequence of documents, such as chequebooks or ledgers. Eventually, however, defence lawyers also began to take an interest. Interviews recorded contemporaneously on official pads according to the rules of PACE ought to show a clear sequence of indentations: the impression of page one should be on page two, page two on page three, and so on. If a group of sheets in the middle of a sequence do not contain the marks of the page above, or fail to leave indentations on those below, that might be suggestive that a chunk of the interview was added at a later date.

It was Esda that first began to raise grave questions about the work of the West Midlands Serious Crime Squad, even before its disbanding by Chief Constable Geoffrey Dear. In several cases, prosecutions were withdrawn or appeals won when Esda indicated confessions had been fabricated. After the freeing of the Guildford Four, the Avon and Somerset police used Esda to test numerous interview records, witness statements and other original documents from the case and found several examples of interpolation and alteration over and above those which had caused the Crown's case to collapse.

In August 1990, Devon and Cornwall officers, who had been asked to look again at the Birmingham Six, tested an interview with Richard McIlkenny. The police had claimed in court that the interview was contemporaneously written down. In part of it, the questions were recorded as coming from the lips of Detective Superintendent George Read, the officer in charge of the investigation. But according to Esda, six pages had been added later. Within two days of the discovery, the Birmingham Six were on their way back to the Court of Appeal.

The unexpected turn of events in the Birmingham case led to some agonising discussions among the supporters of Winston Silcott. To those who knew him, the record of interview five had always sounded improbable; for his part, he was adamant that it was fiction. Yet the risk was considerable. There were only seven pages to test in interview five. If Esda confirmed the accuracy of the record made by Maxwell Dingle, it would make it that much more difficult to reopen Winston's case. In the end there seemed little to lose. If Esda found evidence of apparent impropriety, the effect would be immense. If not, Silcott's position, after Lord Lane's stony judgement, could hardly be worse. In November 1990, Andrew Hall wrote to the Director of Public Prosecutions, asking for the original interview notes so a test could be made.

It took more than seven months before they were produced.

The news of the Silcott Esda test and its result was broken on the front page of the *Observer* on 14 July. Two days later, the Home Secretary, Kenneth Baker, asked the Essex assistant chief constable, Geoffrey Markham, to lead an investigation and to repeat the test. Six weeks after that, Baker added both Silcott and Braithwaite to Raghip's appeal. On 25 November 1991, we were all once more in court.

It took two months to convict Winston Silcott of the murder of PC Blakelock, but only ninety minutes for Lord Justice Farquharson, with Mr Justice Alliott and Mr Justice Cresswell, to set his conviction aside. Anthony Scrivener, QC for Silcott, needed to call only two witnesses on his behalf.

The first was Robert Radley, who carried out the first Esda test on behalf of Silcott's defence. The holder of a diploma in forensic document analysis, he had been involved in several hundred cases. The first thing he noticed about Silcott's case, he told the court, was that the seventh and last page of interview five, which should have included a countersignature and endorsement by a uniformed inspector, was missing altogether.

Taking the sheets in reverse order, he said that on page six, he found only an impression of Dingle's signature; the same was true of pages five and four. On page three there were no impressions at all, and on page two traces of a page from one of the earlier interviews. On page one, there was a trace of an earlier signature by Dingle. There was also something much more significant. Radley told the court: 'There were impressions of a further apparent page of interview. This page appeared to be numbered five in the top righthand corner. It continued with a series of questions and answers, apparently directed at Mr Silcott.' Did they correlate to any other known parts of Silcott's interviews? Scrivener asked.

'No, they did not,' Radley replied. Then he read the 'phantom' page five disclosed by Esda to the court:

Q: . . . hand what is it?
A: (Put head back, laughs.) If you're so clever, why don't you know?
Q: Let me draw your attention to this photograph (roll 28, no. 16) – shown to Mr Silcott – Are you wearing pink gloves?
A: No reply.
Q: What is in your hand?
A: No reply.
Q: . . . draw your attention to (roll 8 no. 14) . . . to be in a . . . would . . .
A: No reply.
Q: No. 10 (again) you are in a . . . between . . . after see photograph no. 20. Again you appear to be the . . .
A: This is a waste of time, you know.

Across this record, whose existence had until the test remained unsuspected, was one further piece of writing: an endorsement by Inspector Anthony Clavier of Paddington Green Police Station. The number of lines on the phantom page five was the same as on the other sheets, Radley said. His conclusion was that the page five used in the murder trial had been inserted into the interview record. The words on the phantom page did not fit with the existing pages four or six, he went on: 'The discontinuity suggests the possibility, if not the probability, that these pages, four and six, were also replaced.'

The reference to the 'pink gloves' appears to relate to the photograph of a rioter which, as we saw in chapter eight, the police wrongly believed to be Silcott for some time.

David Baxendale, a Home Office forensic scientist asked to repeat Radley's test by the Essex police, also gave evidence. He had come to identical conclusions, he said, and had detected a few additional words on the phantom page. He also analysed the paper used for the interview record to see whether it all came from the same source. All the sheets used for the first four interviews came from one batch, he said. However, 'pages three to six of the last interview record are from a different batch to the remainder of the records'.

Roy Amlot was short and to the point. 'We fully accept the position' revealed by the scientists' evidence, he told the court.

Anthony Scrivener drew the strands together. The new evidence, he said, was sufficient to cast doubt on the veracity of the officers who conducted the last interview, on which the whole case against Silcott had been based; none of the allegedly incriminating passages could now be relied on. Amlot agreed, making the reply quoted at the beginning of the introduction to this book. Lord Justice Farquharson signalled his assent: 'That speaks for itself.'

After Silcott's conviction was formally quashed and he left the court, Michael Mansfield returned to the new evidence and discussed its relation to the case against Raghip. He argued that the actions of the officers involved fatally 'contaminated' the case against Raghip and Braithwaite: 'Policy decisions would be passed to the rest of the interrogating teams,' he said. 'Once credibility at the pinnacle goes, the contamination inevitably goes to the rest.' Raghip, he recalled, had challenged the record of his interview at the trial. One of the core issues was whether it was reliable. 'Had the learned judge known what Your Lordships now know,' Mansfield said, 'there would have been a rather different approach.'

After calling the psychological evidence about Raghip from Gudjonsson and Ward, Mansfield returned to the same theme two days later. He recalled that the principle of contamination had operated in Lord Lane's judgement on the Guildford Four, where he ruled that the doubts revealed over the interviews with Patrick Armstrong extended to the whole case. 'Can we rely on a squad headed by Melvin?' Mansfield asked. Amlot, as we have seen, replied: 'The answer is, unequivocally, we would not have gone on against Braithwaite, against Raghip, against any other defendants, having learned of the apparent dishonesty of the officer in charge of the case.' Bail was granted. Raghip and Braithwaite were free.

The rest of the appeal hearing contained one other significant issue, the question of Mark Braithwaite's being denied a solicitor. By 1991, the precedent set by Mr Justice Hodgson in the case of Samuel had been strengthened and endorsed by a series of similar rulings. They left no doubt that if a police officer wished to refuse a suspect his right to legal advice, he would have to be prepared to prove that the specific client seeing the specific solicitor would pervert the course of justice: that the lawyer would commit a criminal offence.

Stephen Hendy QC, who represented Mark Braithwaite with Kamlish, admitted that the point should have been raised before, at the trial or at the 1988 appeal. But it was being put forward now, and 'it would be a glaring injustice if it were not now dealt with'. Under the pre-Guildford *ancien régime*, he would have had little chance of raising the matter. In case after case, the Court of Appeal declined to hear submissions or new evidence if they had been available at the time of the original trial, taking the view that it was not the court's job to correct the mistakes made by defence counsel. The argument, Lord Justice Farquharson said, was very strong, 'but the question is whether you are allowed to raise it'.

The object of the criminal law, Hendy argued, was to secure justice, and if the point were not allowed, Braithwaite faced a very long time in prison.

'You're really saying justice requires it,' Lord Justice Farquharson said.

'I am, My Lord,' Hendy replied.

Their lordships delivered their full judgement on 5 December, by which time Mark Braithwaite and Engin Raghip had been free for a week. It ran to seventy-four pages and took more than an hour and a half to read, the three judges taking it in shifts.

The contamination argument was fully accepted: the judges had no doubt that had Mr Justice Hodgson known of the new evidence relating to Silcott, he would have withdrawn the cases of Raghip and Braithwaite from the jury.

The ruling on the other main points of the appeal was of great significance. The final release of the Birmingham Six at the beginning of 1991 had been followed by the establishment of a Royal Commission on Criminal Justice. Its remit was to examine every aspect of the investigative, pre-trial, trial and appeal system, and to make recommendations. In dealing with Engin Raghip's state of mind and the denial of a solicitor to Mark Braithwaite, the judgement of Lord Justice Farquharson and his colleagues sent a clear message: that the Court of Appeal was already struggling to come to terms with its previous shortcomings and could adapt without the imposition of root and branch reform.

Not only Eric Ward, but Dr Herridge, the very first psychiatrist who examined Raghip before the trial, gave evidence at the appeal that they agreed with the findings of Dr Gudjonsson. Raghip, Herridge now thought, was clearly in the borderline subnormal range of intelligence, not 'average' as he had stated in his report in 1986. Dr Olive Tunstall, who had examined Mark Pennant, further confirmed the diagnosis.

Superficially, in conversation or in the witness box, Raghip could appear 'street wise' and articulate. This veneer concealed his underlying vulnerability, and after eight police interviews over three days of incommunicado detention, it would have been stripped away. Gudjonsson told the court: 'Mr Raghip becomes abnormally suggestible when placed under pressure . . . his compliance score is well outside the normal range, proving him exceptionally compliant.' His anxiety scores were also high, indicating a 'very anxious individual who would not be expected to cope well with lengthy and demanding police interviews'.

Dr Tunstall added: 'He is significantly impaired in intelligence and also significantly impaired in social function.' Her tests put his daily living skills in the lowest one per cent of the population. Before ruling on this evidence, the judges examined the construction of Tunstall's and Gudjonsson's tests. This was not done in open court, to prevent possible future subjects from being able to fake the results.

The law, as set down in the PACE Act, the judgement said, was clear. Section 76 enabled judges to exclude confessions where there was oppression, or if anything had been said or done to make it likely they were unreliable. Section 77 provided that there was a 'special need for caution' in dealing with the confession of a mentally handicapped person, especially where they had been interrogated without an independent solicitor or other adult being present. For the purposes of the Act, 'mentally handicapped' meant a state of arrested or incomplete mental development 'which includes significant impairment of intelligence or social functioning'.

The appeal judges moved now to attack Lord Lane's 1988 ruling explicitly. By the time of Engin Raghip's first attempt at an appeal, the judgement said, 'it had become the regular practice of judges to admit psychiatric or psychosocial evidence'. One example was that of Mr Justice Hodgson and Mark Pennant. By the time of Lord Lane's ruling, some of these cases had not made their way into law reports. But it was 'particularly unfortunate' that the 1988 appeal omitted any consideration of the case of a man called Everett, who had been released some months previously by the Court of Appeal in circumstances very close to the case of Engin Raghip.

The three judges said they had no doubt that the evidence of Ward, Tunstall and Gudjonsson would have been admissible at the trial, and they believed that Mr Justice Hodgson would have thrown out Raghip's confession. Other factors from the case had to be taken into account: the long series of interviews over such a long time; the fact no solicitor was present; and the denial of contact with his family. The judgement also criticised the failure by the police to comply with paragraph 3, 7 of the PACE code of practice, then in force in the 'dry run' Met force order. This stated that if a suspect was found unable to read, his solicitor, a relative or other appropriate, independent adult should be brought in to help him check his interview notes.

The judges recalled Lord Lane's conclusion that Raghip's vulnerability could be left to the jury, saying:

With respect to the Lord Chief Justice, he is there endorsing the 'judge for yourself' approach in respect of the jury which this court in Everett held was the wrong approach for the judge. The state of the psychological evidence before us as outlined earlier in this judgement . . . is such to demonstrate that the jury would have been assisted in assessing the mental condition of Raghip and the consequent reliability of his confessions. Notwithstanding that Raghip's IQ was, at 74, just in the borderline range, a man chronologically aged 19 years 7 months at the date of interview with a level of functioning equivalent of a child of 9 years 9 months, and the reading of a child aged 6 years 6 months, cannot be said to be normal. It would be impossible for the layman to divine that data from Raghip's performance in the witness box, still less the abnormal suggestibility of which Dr Gudjonsson spoke.

The question of Braithwaite's claustrophobia was not, in the end, advanced before the Court of Appeal. But in dealing with the denial of access to a solicitor, the judges again had important things to say. They resolved the problem that the point had not been made at the trial very simply. If they tried to put themselves in the position of the trial judge, they were sure he would have thrown out Braithwaite's confession if Tansey had made a submission. The old reluctance to consider omissions by the defence had gone. As Lord Justice Farquharson had put it earlier, justice 'requires' a different approach.

The contamination of the cases against Raghip and Braithwaite would have been enough on its own, but their appeals were allowed on these other grounds as well. At the end of their judgement, the appeal judges pointed out some of the lessons of the case. It illustrated the problem solicitors had in big criminal cases, when their spending was almost certainly limited by the constraints of legal aid. If one expert witness was not able to help a defendant, what should he do? 'Should he seek authority to instruct another expert, and possibly a third, if the second is unhelpful? It is of course most unlikely that authority would be given under the Legal Aid Act to instruct more than one expert, and certainly no more than two.' Yet in Raghip's case, the interests of justice had showed the need to consult a third expert, Gisli Gudjonsson. There would be circumstances where, after consulting counsel, it would be right to pay for an opinion by more than one expert.

When the Court of Appeal quashed the convictions of the Guildford Four, the Maguire family and the Birmingham Six, they did so without comment or apology. The best evidence of the breath of intellectual fresh air which blew through this judgement was perhaps to be found at its very end:

In allowing these appeals we wish to express our profound regret that they have suffered as a result of the shortcomings of the criminal process. No system of trials is proof against perjury, but this will be of little consequence to its victims.

16

A Snivelling Journalist Writes

Mark Braithwaite and Engin Raghip gave a press conference after the judgement, in a gloomy cellar attached to the London School of Economics. Measured against the ordeal of six years' wrongful imprisonment, their delight at freedom was muted. Six of the best, most important and formative years of their lives had been thrown away.

Engin told me later: 'Everyone who loved me was punished. They say Mrs Blakelock was a victim; yes, she was, but I was a victim, my wife, my kids were victims. They couldn't print enough money to make up for what we have suffered.'

Mark added: 'My son, Bradley, hasn't had a father in six years. He was born in August and I was arrested in February. Now he won't leave my side for a moment. The system cannot cope with people who are innocent. They say you're innocent until you're proven guilty. The truth is, you're guilty till proven innocent.'

Both spoke movingly of others they had left behind in prison. 'I remember when the Birmingham Six were freed. It was great,' Engin says, 'but I kept thinking as I watched it on TV, it should be us, it should be us!'

One of the more distasteful features of this story was the reaction of the tabloid press, and some quarters of the police, during the period between the disclosure of the Esda evidence and the appeal. The Police Federation mounted an intense rearguard lobbying action, in which the hapless PC Coombes, who was forced to retire because of the injuries he sustained in the riot, played a prominent part.

The *Evening Standard* of 18 July, four days after the *Observer* broke the Esda story, was typical, with Coombes featured prominently on page one under the headline: 'Where is my justice says Broadwater PC'. The piece began:

> The police hero forced to retire this month because of horrific injuries sustained during the Broadwater Farm riot spoke for the first time today of his bitter anger at the growing campaign to release the convicted murderer Winston Silcott. PC Richard Coombes said: 'I get very angry. The thing that angers me most is that people seem to be more interested in the rights of convicted murderers than they are in the victims.'

There was more in an interview taking up the whole of page three, where after a lengthy description of his appalling suffering he was quoted saying: 'I am convinced the convictions are safe . . . I feel justice has been done and I am sceptical when people start tampering with it.'

Columnist Peter McKay claimed on another page that those who were concerned with the safety of the convictions were 'playing games'. He went on:

> Those who say piously that Silcott in jail may mean another murderer may have gone free are hypocrites. These people do not identify killers, even while they are sleeping with them. They build careers out of destroying police credibility so that they might put their own ideas in place. I'd rather have a bent bobby any day than a vicious criminal who has the support of sanctimonious campaigners and snivelling journalists anxious to make their names by freeing murderers.

Three days later, the *News of the World* led its front page with a picture of Keith Blakelock's jacket, claiming that at least eleven people killed him. Coombes was again quoted at length, and the paper opened a twenty-four-hour 'hotline' for information leading to the real killers.

Coverage of this kind had all the appearance of a clumsy attempt to nobble the Essex police and the Home Secretary: to make Kenneth Baker base any decision about referring the case to the Appeal Court not simply on the evidence but on the political consideration of police and public morale.

A similar, grudging tone was evident after Silcott was cleared. *Today,* the *Mail* and *Mirror* all focused not on the details of the miscarriage of justice, but on the failure to find the real murderers: 'Someone is guilty. My Keith didn't stab himself 40 times' was the somewhat indigestible headline in *Today,* based on an interview with Liz Blakelock used by several papers. The *Express* splashed with: 'My anger, by PC widow.'

Here, regrettably, the lead was coming from Scotland Yard. On 28 November, after the release of Raghip and Braithwaite, Commissioner Sir Peter Imbert gave a press conference. The police infallibility principle, expressed in such an extreme form by Peter McKay, was still on display. There was no sign that Sir Peter had considered whether the methods of the inquiry as a whole might have had an effect on the quality and quantity of witness evidence. Appealing for people to come forward, he said: 'It is quite amazing, in view of the number of people who were present and must know something, that there has been such a paucity of useful information.' Yet again, the people of Broadwater Farm were being blamed for the ineptitude, if not the alleged corruption, of Detective Superintendent Melvin and his team. Pressed on the point, Sir Peter said that perhaps he meant 'disappointed' not 'amazed'. In any event, his line was widely echoed in the press next day.

The commissioner cannot be blamed for attempting to limit the damage, but he displayed an alarming – and in one respect, utterly misleading – complacency. Changes since 1985 had made a repetition of the miscarriage of justice much less likely, he said, particularly the tape recording of interviews. Then he added: 'On the question of PACE, much has been said about a dry run being in operation at the time of the case. The dry run was, in fact, suspended in Tottenham at that time because of the severe pressures on the officers in the investigation.' This, as we have seen, would have been news to Graham Melvin, the trial judge, and just about everybody else connected with the case in any capacity. Sir Peter's statement was not, needless to say, challenged. I have made repeated inquiries to ascertain its provenance, but the best efforts of the Scotland Yard press office have not produced an answer.

Next day, however, John Smith, the deputy commissioner, was more forthcoming. He was frank about the impact of the case on the police: 'The appeals have caused us a hell of a lot of anguish.' But he maintained that the 'ethos of the service' was now completely different. The concept of symbolic locations no longer had any currency: 'I haven't heard anyone use the term in a very long time. There is no area where the community is so universally lawless that you can treat them in such a way.'

The police, he said, must deal with people as individuals. Would the investigation now have been done in a different way? I asked. 'Perhaps it wouldn't now be done in that way,' Smith said. The emphasis now was on investigations before anyone was arrested, with a 'minimal reliance on confessional evidence'.

In fairness to the Met, the efforts at internal reform since the Blakelock inquiry have been strenuous. The ethos now, propounded in Sir Peter Imbert's wide-ranging and ambitious 'Plus' programme, emphasises public service as the purpose of policing. Imbert set up a special Plus team to develop reforming measures, with the aim of 'changing police culture'. Potentially, Plus implies a very radical shift: from servants of the state to servants of the people. The Plus 'statement of common purpose and values', posted in every police station, states: 'We must respond to well-founded criticism with a willingness to change.'

Sir Peter could not have been more different in temperament from his predecessor. A superficially shy man, he had the very rare quality of leading through understatement, of mucking in and empathising with his beleaguered 'ground floor'. He was extraordinarily popular in a service where grumbling is second nature; he could inspire not mere loyalty but even a kind of love in some of his subordinates.

One measure of the democratic changes which have come over the Met is the vastly improved relationship with Labour councils.

An elected police authority for London and an independent complaints investigation system are no longer anathema.

Plus, however, is an attempt to effect revolution from above, a process which history suggests is fraught with difficulty. Early in his reign Sir Peter was often compared to Mikhail Gorbachev; one suspects it is a comparison which would not now be welcome. The new philosophy depends crucially on the commitment of middle and senior police managers to make it work. There are, says Alec Marnoch, who led the reform programme with irrepressible energy for three years, divisions where chief superintendents have grasped the nettle. They have realised that if a service philosophy is to mean more than a handy public relations nostrum, they too have to change: to respond to their own junior officers, to be available, amenable to criticism.

The gulf between senior and junior ranks was an important factor in the riot at Broadwater Farm, and in some areas steps have been taken to close it. Equally, Marnoch admits, there are places where police managers pay only lip service to the reforming wave. There, it need hardly be said, the bad old ways have scarcely changed. In divisions such as these, the new recruits coming out of the police college at Hendon are still told gruffly, on starting their work, to forget everything they have learnt, especially about Plus or democratic policing.

Racism, in some divisions, still flourishes internally in the Metropolitan Police – there are several discrimination cases by black officers in the pipeline – and undoubtedly there is still police racism directed at black members of the public. But if the Met, and several other forces, have at least made efforts at reform, there are still big constabularies where the ideas of Sir Kenneth Newman would be thought dangerously advanced. In 1991, I reported on simmering trouble in the multiracial Leeds district of Chapeltown. The attitude there of senior officers was that organisations who criticised their approach had simply no right to do so, no *locus standi*. Using an old policing cliché, they wrote off their antagonists as 'unrepresentative'.

Even among the most progressive police officers, there is still a feeling of hurt that their service has unfairly taken all the blame for the Blakelock case and the other miscarriages of justice. 'You are right in identifying a principle of police infallibility,' says one senior detective, 'but you make the mistake in not looking beyond the police for its origins.'

It is true, he says, that from their earliest days in the job, police officers are taught to speak in certainties, to give evidence in court, even of trivial traffic offences, which does not admit doubt. But the blame should, he says, be laid at the door of an adversarial system of justice in which the legal process, instead of being a search for truth, becomes 'a game of scoring points, a ritual in which the underlying incident can be distorted or forgotten'. The police, he adds, are already so handicapped by the system, particularly by PACE, that they can barely do their job. Number one on his shopping list of reforms, like those of many policemen, is the abolition of the right of silence. If someone says nothing when interrogated, the Crown should have the right to draw inferences in court. It is a seductive proposition – what have the innocent to fear?

But perhaps adversarial versus inquisitorial is the wrong issue. In the inquisitorial systems of continental Europe, there are also miscarriages of justice and abuses of suspects' rights. The answer cannot, in any event, be to give the police more powers in the name of 'getting at the truth'.

These are all questions for the Royal Commission. The last word on the Blakelock case should belong to Sir Derek Hodgson.

From the detachment of retirement, his comments on the quality of the Blakelock murder inquiry now go well beyond those he made in his ruling on Jason Hill. 'The police were interviewing suspects without the faintest idea of what had happened,' he said, 'and the risks of that method I would have thought were obvious. I would have thought the first thing that was essential for any interviewing officer was to acquire as detailed and accurate a picture as possible of what happened on the night.'

Not until Roy Amlot and Michael Mansfield began their 'public inquiry' into the riot during the murder trial was the sequence of events properly established, he says. The result of the shortcomings of the investigative method were devastating: 'I don't think I, nor any other judge, saw any of the ringleaders.'

He remains disdainful of the quality of the police in general, and of their leadership in particular. 'It would be better if they were more like the army,' he says, 'with an officer class from the beginning. There is a great danger in taking attitudes learnt in three or four or five years as a constable into the senior ranks. The qualifications for reaching the level of inspector should be education at least to degree standard. The police are more important than the army. The inspector should be the equivalent of the army subaltern.'

Some of the public hysteria surrounding the murder trial was palely reflected in the grudging, unpleasant tone displayed by reports of the Esda evidence and the appeal. Sir Derek says: 'The pressure on the case was enormous. I have never known any trial, before or since, when I felt under such intense pressure.' The *Sun* picture of Silcott on day two was, he adds, 'the most gross contempt', and he remains surprised that no action was taken by the Attorney-General.

We may have tape recordings of interrogations, and we may have the Police and Criminal Evidence Act. But the capacity of the tabloid press to act as a lynch mob has, if anything, increased since the murder of PC Blakelock.

As we have seen, if the jury had acquitted the Tottenham Three, the fallback position of the tabloids was to attack Sir Derek Hodgson. The 'dirt' must have been kept on file, for two years later the *Sun* had its crack at him with a wildly inaccurate two-page article provoked by a 'lenient' sentence in an incest case. It started with the false information that he lived in a £250,000 house in the country, and continued with the equally wrong claim that he was divorced. 'I suppose this was par for the course,' he says. 'They were repaying me for referring them to the Attorney-General.'

Did he consider the evidence against Silcott was always dangerously thin? He says: 'My own view is that at the end of the prosecution case, a judge should be able to say: "It would be unsafe and unsatisfactory to allow this to go to the jury." But the Court of Appeal does not take that view. The test is not what the judge may feel, but, "Could a jury, properly directed, convict on this evidence." In Silcott, the answer had to be yes.'

With no small degree of candour, he adds: 'It would have taken a man of greater courage than me to cheat on Silcott. Occasionally I have bent the law to say to the jury they couldn't convict on the basis of the evidence before them. I could not have done that here.'

The sequence of miscarriages of justice has made a deep impression on Sir Derek, as it has on many senior jurists. Further recent research by Dr Gudjonsson points to the risk of anybody, even a person of sound mind and normal intelligence, falsely incriminating themselves.

After the Blakelock case, later the same year, Sir Derek dealt with an horrific rape and murder case in Manchester, in which a man who confessed had had to endure the living hell of being remanded as a 'nonce' in Strangeways prison. Nine months later, shortly before his trial, another man was arrested for an attempted rape, and strong evidence emerged that he had committed the earlier crime. The police taped the innocent man's interrogation, and notwithstanding the fact they were being recorded, they threatened and bullied him unmercifully until he cracked. 'It read like the Inquisition,' Sir Derek commented.

'I have no doubt,' he says, 'we should make an end to convictions based on confessions alone. When I say there must be corroboration, I mean it in the plainest terms. I mean there must be other evidence that he did it.'

As for the right of silence, he is emphatic: 'You must keep it. The innocent in our system have a lot to fear.'

The Killing of Anthony Smith

To find Winston Silcott you need a good map. Gartree Prison lies at the end of a web of unsignposted lanes, on a gentle slope of woods and farms in the rolling Leicestershire plain. At weekends, the governor provides a minibus from Market Harborough station, but at other times you must drive. Typical of Britain's oldest post-war jails, its buildings are low-rise, shabby, a little damp. But as high-security lifer dispersal prisons go, Gartree is a relaxed, humane institution. Prisoners may leave their 'visiting orders' at the gate, instead of having to post them in advance; meetings can be arranged at short notice. Inmates rate it much better than Albany or the Scrubs.

'Ah, Winston Silcott,' says the officer on the gatehouse who checks my paperwork. 'If only they were all like that, our job would be a piece of cake!' The supposed beast of Broadwater Farm is now a model prisoner, held in high regard. 'He has a real maturity,' the officer continues. 'That can be a real asset in cooling things at times.' Well, he ought to be mature; Winston is now thirty-two.

To be allowed to see him, as a journalist, I must sign an undertaking not to reproduce what he says. But I can, I think, answer superficially the question people ask: 'What is he like?'

Winston is tall, but a lot slimmer now than the hefty figure who faced the Blakelock jury. Sometimes he wears thin-framed tortoiseshell glasses, which give him a studious look. He never smokes, and abhors contraband alcohol or drugs. His chief sensual pleasure is music, and he keeps a cherished tape collection in his cell. He speaks quietly, but with humour and animation, expressing himself clearly in speech and on paper. Winston is utterly realistic about his situation. Throughout his long incarceration, his lawyers have always consulted him about the next tactical move, not simply in deference to his position as client but because they value his judgement. His 'justice beard' continues to grow, beyond his waist, still bound by its barrister's ribbon; he has a carved African amulet on a leather thong round his neck. The preoccupation which dominates his life is proving his claim to freedom. He has a resigned courage, which even in his gloomiest moods permits a flash of humour.

Winston Silcott is doubly a victim of the miscarriage of justice. The quashing of his conviction for the murder of PC Blakelock affected his life only slightly: he was downgraded from the maximum 'A' security classification to a more privileged 'B'. When Lord Justice Farquharson allowed him to leave the Court of Appeal on the first morning of the 1991 hearing, two days before Braithwaite and Raghip were released, Winston was secretly relieved: he did not have to watch them leave the dock while he was taken back below. The case of which he still stands convicted, the murder of Anthony Roy Smith, urgently requires review.

Anthony Smith, a boxer aged twenty-two with two professional fights behind him, was stabbed at a blues dance at 177 Mare Street, Hackney, early in the morning of 15 December 1984. Two of his friends and cohorts, Wayne Jones and Renton Nelson, took him to the London Hospital in Whitechapel. He had slashes on his face and two deep wounds to his abdomen; one lung was lacerated, and his aorta was half cut through. He underwent an emergency operation in which his wounds were repaired, but he continued to suffer internal bleeding. In all, he had 136 units of blood transfused. Smith died a week later, the immediate cause being cerebral oedema.

The case against Silcott at his trial in February 1986 was formidable. Wayne Jones, who said he had known Silcott by sight for three years, stated that he saw him arrive and go into the main room of the party, which was dimly lit and crowded with about seventy people, while he himself stood outside, on a landing where the bar was. 'After about a minute Smith came from the room. He was covered in blood, holding his stomach with both hands. I noticed the blood on his face first, and then on his stomach. I grabbed him and put him in the car.'

He said he and Nelson went downstairs with Smith, but Silcott followed them, waving a knife. He had a knife out himself, Jones admitted, but only for his own protection. Four months after the stabbing, he picked Silcott out from an identification parade at City Road Police Station. As far as Jones was concerned, before the incident there was 'no ill feeling' between Smith, his friends and Silcott.

Jodie Young, a student, gave evidence of what had happened in the main room. She said she was with a friend called Dawn, listening to the sound system. Silcott, wearing a leather jacket with wool cuffs, came over and started talking – he knew Dawn. The three were together for half an hour. She went on:

> There was no central light. There was only a light where the sound was, and it was quite low. Someone approached Sticks. The smaller guy pushed Sticks, who pushed him back. They were pushing each other and swearing. Then they started hitting each other. There were blows to the little guy's head and chest. There was a lot of blood. The lights came on at the beginning of the fight. The short man was in a state. He had two friends who succeeded in dragging him away. I could not really say what Sticks did. The lights were not on for very long. We tried to get the matter over and done with and start the party again.

No one, it seemed, realised the seriousness of Smith's injuries. Silcott stayed at the party, she said, and later produced a knife from his sleeve, lending it to a friend who wished to use it for taking drugs. This was something which the judge, Mr Justice Rose, thought specially significant summing up the case, and it crept into most press reports of the Smith trial once the Blakelock case was over.

Renton Nelson also gave important testimony. Like Jones, he was at the bar when he heard 'the music jumping, as if there was fighting'. Smith came out, covered in blood, and he helped Jones take him to the car. As they pulled away, he told the jury, a tall man was outside, waving a knife. Wayne Jones shouted, 'Look what you've done,' and the man – whom he later identified as Silcott – replied: 'He deserved it.'

Silcott was arrested two months after Smith's death, on 13 February, and questioned by Detective Superintendent Eric Brown at Hackney Police Station. There were none of the procedural irregularities of the Blakelock case: Silcott's solicitor was present. His replies were evasive. He denied knowing Jones, Nelson or Smith, and said he had not been involved in a fight. Later he was driven to 177 Mare Street and denied having attended the party at all, although he had been to a dance at another address in Mare Street that night, at the Liberation Hall. Silcott told the police he knew nothing about any killing.

At the trial, Silcott gave evidence, as the only witness in his own defence. Here he told a substantially different story, whose discrepancies with his police interviews Mr Justice Rose dwelt upon at length. He said he had been 'confused' about the different addresses, and in fact had been at number 177. He went there mainly to distribute leaflets advertising the discotheque he ran with Delroy Lindo, the Galaxy Soul Shuffle, after asking a cab driver if he knew of anything going on that night where there might be potential customers. He told the court of his conversation with Dawn Taylor and continued:

> I was standing at the door, with my back towards it and a man was going to come out of the room when he came into me. I saw him walking with two other people, who were in front of me. I did not know him. I had seen one of those who was with him before; that was Wayne Jones. He came into my left front side with his left shoulder. I did nothing. I was looking in the other direction. Then, when I looked in front of me again, he was in front of me and started punching me in my face. He was punching with his fists, fast. I did not know what was happening. I was hit three or four times in the face, round my eyes and nose. He said nothing. I had no idea why he was doing this. I started pushing him away a few times. I did not have a knife or a weapon. I only pushed him away. I did not know he was

a boxer. He was stocky in appearance. When I last pushed him he went down on the ground.

Smith's two friends had knives, Silcott said, but made no move to attack him. He denied going downstairs and said he remained quite calm throughout.

On that evidence, Silcott's guilt seemed patent. The prosecution had drawn a picture, barely softened by Silcott's own appearance in the witness box, of a cold-blooded, almost random killing: a callous knife attack on a stranger who seemed to have done little more than jostle him.

The judge told the jury that if they believed Silcott killed Anthony Smith, they had two options other than finding him guilty of murder. If they thought he was acting in self-defence and reacting with reasonable force, in view of the threat to his own life, they could acquit him. In law, self-defence is a complete answer to a charge of murder. If they thought he had not intended to kill or seriously injure Smith, then they could return a verdict of manslaughter. If Silcott had been provoked, causing a 'sudden and temporary loss of control', and if the provocation was such as might cause a similar loss of control in another reasonable person, then manslaughter would again be the appropriate verdict.

The jury was out for 4 hours and 35 minutes. The unanimous verdict was guilty to murder. Mr Justice Rose did little to conceal his own feelings about the case:

> Winston Silcott, you have been convicted of murder on over-whelming evidence. No doubt the stabbing occurred on the spur of the moment, but that could only happen because you were carrying a fearsome weapon which has never been found . . . by that conduct, and by the lies you later told, you showed yourself to be a vicious and evil man. I have no doubt at least three of those who gave evidence for the prosecution were terrified of you. There is only one sentence prescribed by law; that is the sentence which I pass. You will go to prison for life.

Winston Silcott was defended in the Smith trial by Robert Harman QC, whose junior counsel was Nemone Lethbridge. Silcott's solicitors were Anthony Steel and Co., from Kilburn. Most of the work on his case was done by Stephen Christopher, not a qualified solicitor but a legal executive, a more junior level requiring fewer educational qualifications, endowed with fewer rights and obligations.

Three months after being convicted, Silcott decided to change his representation, and engaged Andrew Hall. Even then, months before the Blakelock trial, there seemed to Hall to be strange features to the Smith case. There was, to begin with, his own assessment of Silcott's character: he did not seem to him to be the kind of man who would kill a stranger over nothing.

There was also the matter of Silcott's bail. Mr Justice Rose imposed the strictest reporting restrictions on the Smith trial. By the time it took place, Silcott had of course been charged with the Blakelock killing, and it was vital to prevent the Blakelock jury from knowing anything of Smith's murder. But after the Blakelock verdict, the fact that in May 1985 Judge Robert Lymbery had granted him bail became a matter of bitter public controversy. The main reason was that the Crown case then seemed weak. In her evidence at the committal, in May 1985, Jodie Young had been much less certain of what she had seen, leaving the prosecution without a witness to Silcott fighting Smith.

But the most striking thing, as Hall began to acquaint himself with the case, was a series of clues to a very different version of events. Put together, they seemed to suggest that Silcott, if he had admitted stabbing Anthony Smith, could have made a strong case for having done so in self-defence.

There was, for example, the evidence of Rozanne Walden. She told the court that she heard an argument, then saw a man coming out of the main room with blood on his face. 'I saw a knife,' she said, 'someone was holding it, a man taller than me, but not much taller: I am five foot one inch. The man with the knife went downstairs. I think he was walking with the guy with blood on his face.' The man with the knife cannot have been Silcott, who towered over her by more than a foot.

There was the fact that when Jones and Nelson brought Smith to hospital, both were armed with knives. Smith, too, had a knife in his pocket. When the police came to hospital to begin their inquiries, Jones and Nelson gave false names, and ended up being arrested for attempted murder. Jones told the court, somewhat vaguely: 'For various reasons I did not tell anyone that night I had seen a man with a knife. I did not wish to disclose who I was. I told the police my name, but not what had happened.' The reason, he said, was that he had been in 'a state of shock'.

Later he admitted he had drawn his knife at the party: 'I was carrying a knife and I drew it at the point when Smith came out of the room. I just took it for my protection . . . I put it back in my pocket.'

Nelson also confirmed he had a knife, but insisted he left it concealed.

All of this might, it seemed to Hall, have created openings for cross-examination on the basis of self-defence. Yet the line was never pursued. He was troubled too by the absence of motive: was Jones' claim that there was no pre-history of conflict between Silcott and the victim really true? At last, on a visit to Brixton prison, where Silcott still had months to wait before the Blakelock trial, he consulted him. The story he told was extraordinary.

In truth, Silcott said, he had stabbed Anthony Smith, although he was unaware how badly hurt he was for some time. Far from being a stranger, Smith and his friends had been engaged in an escalating, violent vendetta against Silcott and some of his friends from Broadwater Farm. When Smith attacked him, punching him about the head, he could see that Jones was armed.

Silcott eventually swore an affidavit setting out his story. Smith, it says, was not only a boxer but a hoodlum, a member of a gang feared across north London, the Yankee Posse. It also included Renton Nelson, who was in prison for robbery when he appeared at Silcott's trial, Wayne Jones and an American called Watts. The source of the confrontation between the Yankees and the youth of the Farm was a friend of Winston's brother George, a budding criminal called Mark Nash.

That summer, Nash sold Wayne Jones some stolen chequebooks. Nash told Silcott that he was never paid. Soon afterwards, Jones' home was burgled. The Yankee Posse believed, the affidavit goes on, that Nash was responsible. One Saturday night, there was a party in Fonthill Road, Finsbury Park. Silcott was running the bar. Outside, in the street, Nash ran into Jones, Nelson and Anthony Smith. There was a heated altercation in which Nash hit Smith over the head with a bottle and ran inside, pursued by the Yankees. According to Silcott, the Yankees were 'not prepared to attack him there because they were outnumbered by people from Broadwater Farm, including myself. However, they did make threats against Nash and me, because they thought I was protecting Nash.'

Silcott says he heard that members of the gang came to Broadwater Farm several times in search of Nash. Once they turned up at the Youth Association and threatened both himself and Nash, but again they were outnumbered and backed off. They returned another day when Silcott was absent, but he heard all about what happened: Smith had entered the Youth Association carrying a zip-up holdall. It contained a double-barrelled shotgun. There was a chaotic fight with chairs, with members of the Association trying to restrain both sides, until it was agreed that Nash should fight Smith on the Tangmere deck outside. Nash seems to have won the fight, but a few days later Nash was walking through Wood Green with a friend, Morris Smallwood, when Smith and his cohorts passed by in a car. They got out and attacked. Nash was slashed across the neck with a knife, Silcott says. On another occasion, he goes on, 'I myself was threatened by Wayne Jones at a party in Landsdowne Road, north London.'

At about the beginning of December, Silcott was approached by Danny, a cab driver from Broadwater Farm. Danny, who has asked me not to use his full name, told Silcott that the day before, he had driven two passengers who appeared to fit the description of Smith and Watts, the American, and overheard a bloodcurdling threat: that neither Silcott nor Nash would live to see the beginning of 1985.

Hall's first reaction on hearing this story was disbelief. He assumed, moreover, that those who might be prepared to corroborate it, Mark Nash in particular, would probably be most reluctant to do so. He began to visit Broadwater Farm regularly, looking for contacts, trying to overcome the suspicion attendant on any outsider probing into incidents such as these. At last he tracked Nash down in prison and went to see him. And then, he says, 'it all came pouring out: an incredibly detailed account which supported everything Winston had said. I knew then that he had been telling the truth.'

Nash's version begins with an admission to a criminal offence for which he was never convicted, selling Wayne Jones the stolen chequebooks and cheque cards. The price agreed was £500, Nash says. 'That same night Jones was injured in a fight and went to hospital. I visited him and asked for my money. He said he would give it to me next day. I went to his home but he wasn't there, and I waited in my car. I saw his girl friend arrive at the house laden with goods, which I thought had been bought with the stolen chequebooks. I found Jones and we had an argument, but still he wouldn't give me the money.'

Several months passed, which Nash spent detained in a youth custody centre. He was released on 1 September, he says, 'and I decided to get my own back. I paid two boys £100 each to burgle his house. They broke in and stole a video recorder.' Somehow, Jones got wind of what had happened and threatened Nash outside his home with a gun: 'I was made to get into a car and driven to Jones' home to see if anyone there recognised me as being involved in the burglary. Nobody did recognise me and they took me back to Broadwater Farm.'

Before the incident at the party, Nash says, there were at least two further confrontations. On one occasion, Smith and Jones threatened him at Tangmere, and Silcott came out of his green-grocery and defused the situation. He describes the incident at Finsbury Park: 'I hit Smith with a Lucozade bottle and ran. I ran into the party and an upstairs room where Winston was running the bar. Smith and the others threatened to kill me.' It was principally Silcott's presence, he says, which dissuaded them from taking matters further.

It was the very next day that Smith, Jones and Renton Nelson went to the Broadwater Farm Youth Association armed with a shotgun. Before going to the Youth Association, they visited a flat where Nash had lived some time earlier and threatened the occupants with a gun. At the Youth Association, Smith put his bag containing the shotgun down on the counter used for serving meals to old age pensioners. Nash had taken the precaution of arming himself with a baseball bat, but Smith came at him with a knife. Somehow, the Yankees were held back: 'The people at Broadwater Farm argued that the matter should be settled by a fair fist fight between Smith and myself.' The two fought for over an hour, watched by more than a hundred people. Smith may have had the technique, but Nash was bigger and had more stamina. Smith, Nash says, was beaten and publicly humiliated.

After the incident in which he was slashed in Wood Green, Nash says Silcott told him to go home and stay out of sight. On 10 December, Nash was arrested and remanded in custody on a robbery charge. At some time between then and Smith's death five days later, he says, the Yankees went to his home, threatened his mother, smashed windows and poured petrol over his car, setting light to it and causing serious damage. His mother suffered a nervous collapse.

There was further corroboration of the vendetta. Dolly Kiffin swore an affidavit in which she described the confrontation at Tangmere and the fist fight: 'They fought for a long time, until they were both exhausted and Smith was physically sick.' Michael Scott, Stafford's brother, says that when Smith burst into the Youth Association he reached into his bag with the shotgun, shouting, 'I am going to kill Sticks.' Scott adds: 'After that, it was fairly common knowledge around north London that Smith and the others had been going around threatening to kill Silcott. I remember speaking to him a week later and warning him.'

Danny, the cab driver, told me: 'It was late autumn, November or early December. I wasn't really taking in what these two guys in the back were talking about until I heard one of them say: "Mark Nash and Sticks, they're going to be dead before Christmas." A couple of days later I bumped into Sticks and told him what had happened.'

Winston Silcott's affidavit gives a very different account of the night of Anthony Smith's death to that described at the trial. He went to 177 Mare Street, he confirms, to distribute leaflets publicising his sound system. He saw Smith, Jones and Nelson on arrival, getting out of a car. 'I felt there was going to be trouble because they had seen me, and because I was on my own they would attack me with weapons.' He saw a man he knew, he says, called Stephen White, and before going upstairs asked to borrow a knife.

White recalls: 'Winston came over to me and said, "Have you got a knife?" I said, "Yes" and Winston said, "Give it to me." He didn't say anything else but I realised there had to be some sort of trouble.'

Upstairs, Silcott says, the three Yankees came into the main room. It was very dark, and they appeared not to have seen him. But then, as they were leaving, Smith spotted him: 'He barged me deliberately with his shoulder. I did nothing because I was outnumbered and I was sure they would be armed. Smith started to walk away from me but suddenly he spun round. He hit me three or four times in the face. I pushed him backwards.'

Silcott says he saw something shining in Smith's hand. It may have been the rings which he was wearing, but Silcott thought he had a knife. The next blow cut Silcott's face – he still bears a half-inch horizontal scar across the bridge of his nose. 'I felt a nick across my face and my face was cut. I lashed out with my knife several times and Smith stumbled backwards. I could see by a light in the hall that Jones and Nelson were trying to come back into the room. Smith made his way out of the room. I could see blood on his face and the knife in his hand.'

Stephen White says he cannot be sure whether Smith had a knife, but he did see Jones reach into his pocket for his weapon. Dalton Mitchell, another witness who did not give evidence at the trial, is more emphatic: 'All I remember is Smith barging into Winston and there being a scuffle and Winston pushing him away. Smith very obviously and deliberately barged into Winston: it was no accident. It was very dark in the room, and the fighting was all over in a matter of seconds. I saw Jones behind Smith and I am certain he had a knife in his hand while the scuffle was going on.'

Mitchell adds: 'Jones seemed to rush forward towards Winston but then stopped suddenly. He came close to Sticks but then seemed to freeze. I am also absolutely sure that Smith had a knife in his hand. When he was pushed backwards by Winston, Smith's arm was in the air and I clearly saw a blade waving about in Smith's hand. At this point Jones was also coming behind Smith with his knife.'

This account would surely have cast the trial in a very different light. Acquittal on grounds of self-defence or at least manslaughter on grounds of provocation would have been much more likely verdicts. Mitchell's story might have been the basis for a devastating cross-examination of Wayne Jones, who stated he had drawn a knife but was not pressed on the point at all.

The reason was that, on his own admission, Silcott changed the story he told his lawyers in key respects between his arrest and the trial. Robert Harman knew nothing of this: he conducted the trial on the basis of instructions that Silcott had no knife, and that there was no background of violence between the Yankees and Broadwater Farm.

Initially, however, Silcott's story was very different. A few weeks after the killing, his affidavit states, he gave his solicitors a detailed account, which was taken down in writing. Here, he both described the pre-history of the killing and admitted he had a knife during the fight with Smith, although he claimed he had not used it.

We should pause here and consider Silcott's state of mind. In 1980, he had come close to being convicted of a murder of which he was entirely innocent, an affair that began with his freely telling a police officer he had been present at the party where Leonard Mackintosh was killed. In the ensuing years, the police had tried on several occasions to 'put him in the frame' for crimes he could not have committed, notably the stabbing of PC Betts on Broadwater Farm. It would not have been surprising if his judgement as to the best way to pursue his case was somewhat cloudy. Telling the whole truth would, we can see with hindsight, have been his best policy. To Silcott, locked up once more in Brixton Prison, it did not seem so simple.

In his application for leave to appeal in 1988 Silcott claimed he had actually been advised to change his story by his legal representatives. It is not possible to verify that allegation: Stephen Christopher is insistent that it is untrue. In an interview with Andrew Hall in January 1992, he said: 'The bottom line is that if there was a change it was Winston's idea.'

But whoever was responsible for the change in Silcott's story, it had a huge and serious impact on his case. Whether or not Silcott had a knife was a fact of utmost importance. A change in his account of such magnitude should, at the very least, have been rigorously queried.

The first problem Andrew Hall had in attempting to verify Silcott's claims was that he had no complete set of case papers from Anthony Steel and Co. He had no statement or 'proof of evidence' taken from Silcott at all, and no statements by defence witnesses. The documents which had been supplied arrived in a chaotic, disorganised state, out of date order, contained in grubby plastic carrier bags.

On 29 May 1986 Hall wrote the first letter in what was to become a marathon correspondence, asking for the remainder of the file. It was, he pointed out, essential in preparing an appeal. In the months that followed, there were telephone calls, broken appointments, and frustrating delays.

On 15 October, for example, Robert Layton, a partner in the firm, agreed to release the papers if Hall sent a courier. But the messenger returned empty-handed. Later that day, Christopher telephoned, saying 'it is not practical to release the papers now'. Layton agreed to attend Hall's firm, Hodge, Jones and Allen, with the papers on 21 October, but that day he phoned to cancel. The meeting was rearranged for 27 October, when Layton arrived three hours late, *sans* papers, only to say he had to leave in five minutes. Another appointment was cancelled when Layton had a car crash. By 9 December Hall was threatening to bring the matter to the notice of the Solicitors Complaints Bureau, and an appointment was made for 17 December. Hall went to the office of Anthony Steel and Co. on that day but 'no papers were available for collection'.

So it dragged on. At last, some nine months after taking on the case, Hall got further documents in carrier bags, after enlisting the help of the Registrar of the Court of Appeal, who also wrote to Anthony Steel and Co. Stephen Christopher was interviewed by one of Hall's partners and signed a statement. But it was soon clear that matters were far from resolved.

The only proof of evidence supplied was a statement by Silcott taken shortly before the trial, accompanied by a handwritten version which was headed 'Line that Harman will take'. This said that Silcott had no knife. Since Harman was not engaged until December, it was obviously a very late addition. Anthony Steel and Co. said in response to Hall's inquiries that there was no earlier statement.

However, among the disordered files Hall unearthed what appeared to be two significant letters, the first dated 4 March 1985, from Anthony Steel and Co. to Nemone Lethbridge. It referred to 'statements from Silcott and Nash'. Later the same month, the solicitors told her: 'The defendant has supplied instructing solicitors with a very detailed statement.'

Then Hall noticed some notes in unfamiliar handwriting. Until some time in the spring of 1987, he did not realise their significance. Now he examined them with mounting excitement.

The notes were headed 'Nemone, herewith (please) my contributions re Silcott'. On page one they stated: 'Note: in Sticks' own statement he tells how somebody else, another man, offered him a knife so that he could protect himself and that he (Sticks) took the knife.' Here, it seemed, was corroboration at last of Silcott's story: a clear reference to an early statement in which he described taking the knife from Stephen White.

There were further references to 'Sticks' statement', and on page four a list of the 'previous altercations' between the Yankees, Nash and Silcott. It included remarks on 'party at Finsbury Park, few weeks before murder – Smith punched Nash, Nash hit Smith in face with bottle', followed by: 'Later Smith went to Broadwater farm to have a fight with Nash.'

The last page included a series of quotations from 'Separate statement by Winston Silcott'. It read: 'Somebody said that the three men who were behind me had knives, and at least one of them did . . . a man offered me a knife so that I could protect myself . . . I took the knife . . . at that point somebody turned the main lights on . . . I moved to one side, near to the man who had handed me the knife.'

Andrew Hall showed the notes to Nemone Lethbridge, who identified them as the work of her then pupil, Jean Kerr. She, in turn, confirmed having written them. She said she often prepared summaries of evidence.

In an interview which was noted contemporaneously by a stenographer, whose transcript she later signed, Lethbridge denied seeing any detailed proof in the spring of 1984. All she had at that time, she told Hall, was a brief summary saying where Silcott had been on the night Smith died. At that stage she had 'never seen' detailed statements from Silcott or Nash. Hall questioned Lethbridge about the contents of the Kerr notes:

Q: It appears to refer to proof of evidence in which the client accepts he had a knife.
A: Yes. I don't know what she is referring to there.
Q: And there are other references in the same document. [Quotes section about borrowing the knife.] These quite clearly suggest he had a knife in his possession at the time . . . Is there anything you would like to say about Jean Kerr's notes?
A: I don't remember what she's referring to, that's the difficulty. I had two murder cases at the time that were very similar, both stabbings at blues parties. Jean Kerr did work on both.

Hall pressed her further, asking what she knew about the background of the vendetta, and the threats to kill Silcott before the party in Mare Street. She replied: 'It's all new to me.' But perhaps, she added, there was a further missing document on top of the 'brief proof' about Silcott's movements:

Q: So you are saying there was possibly a statement in existence before the 14 January 1986 in which Silcott said he had a knife?
A: It seems likely but I don't remember it.

And there, very nearly, the matter rests. In 1988, Ed Rees argued Silcott's application for leave to appeal against his conviction for the murder of Anthony Smith at the same time as the Blakelock hearing. Lord Lane refused it on grounds which typified the *ancien régime* in criminal justice. It might, he said, be possible to accept the premise that Silcott's legal advisers had acted improperly. It might also be true that he had acted in self-defence. But his plight was his own fault. If the claims that he had been advised to change his story were true, he nevertheless had acquiesced in that advice and lied about what happened in the witness box. To allow the argument would be to open a floodgate for anybody convicted of a serious offence, who, having run one defence simply fancied the chance to try another line in the Court of Appeal.

Now, however, that the Blakelock convictions have been quashed, and the evidence against Silcott alleged to have been a fabrication, we should consider whether the Blakelock case affected the Smith murder trial.

When Silcott was charged, every newspaper and news bulletin reported the fact. The *Daily Telegraph* of 15 October 1985 was typical. Its story, published under the headline 'PC murder charge pair remanded', began:

> Winston Silcott, a black greengrocer, and a 14-year-old black youth were remanded in custody yesterday charged with the murder of PC Keith Blakelock during the Tottenham rioting on October 6. Silcott, of Martlesham, Broadwater Farm, chatted to relatives in the gallery at Tottenham magistrates court while the charge was read. Magistrate Mr Samuel Kershwen agreed to a plea by Det Insp Max Dingle that the hearing be moved to a more secure court. Miss Nemone Lethbridge, defending, said Silcott agreed to be remanded in custody until November 11. She made no application for bail.

When, four months later, a black greengrocer called Winston Silcott from Martlesham, Broadwater Farm, defended by Nemone Lethbridge, appeared at the Old Bailey charged with the murder of Anthony Smith, it would not have been surprising if the jury had realised he was the same man: had one juror made the link, it would have been enough. If, as Lord Justice Farquharson put it, Silcott was a 'victim of perjury' in the Blakelock case, its effects may well have poisoned the Smith case as well.

The Smith trial was attended by senior police officers involved in the Blakelock inquiry, and the jury was given special protection. Had Silcott not been charged with killing PC Blakelock, it is difficult to believe these measures would have been thought necessary. The impression was being given that here was an exceptionally dangerous man.

There is also the question of the changes in Silcott's story. If it is possible to see how his judgement might not have been perfect in the weeks after his arrest, the pressures on him after he was charged with the killing of PC Blakelock became almost unimaginable. After years of what he regarded as unfair harassment by the police, he found himself faced with an appalling charge, with the only evidence against him a confession which he insisted he had never made. His position seemed absolutely without hope. The police, according to Lord Justice Farquharson, lied about their evidence against Silcott. It may not, in these circumstances, be astonishing that in his desperation, he was prepared to lie about his role in the killing of Anthony Smith.

A recent case in the Court of Appeal in the case of a man called Matthew Richardson suggests that even Lord Lane is now alive to the pressure that murder defendants can find themselves under. Richardson was convicted of a murder in 1986, but it later emerged that he had not told his defence lawyers vital details about his case. As a result, evidence that might have secured his acquittal was never seen by the jury. Lord Lane repeated his comments about the dangers of opening a floodgate to people who wanted a second crack at a case using another defence. But this time, unlike with Silcott in 1988, he ordered a retrial.

We are left, in the end, with a sense of injustice. The Esda evidence in the Blakelock case was an extraordinary stroke of luck; it is not likely to be repeated.

The powers of the Home Secretary do, however, permit him to refer a case back to the Court of Appeal without dramatic new evidence. According to law, he may do so when there are 'considerations of substance'. In evaluating whether the killing of Anthony Smith raises such considerations, the legal principle raised by Mrs Mills in the Blakelock appeal springs to mind: there must, at the very least, be some 'lurking doubt'.

But for the time being, the Home Office seems bent on exacting retribution, not reconsidering Silcott's conviction. In February 1992, he learnt his tariff date for the Smith murder. His earliest review date by a parole board local committee is 2002, which implies that according to normal procedures his earliest possible release date will not be until 2005, twenty years after his arrest for the murder of PC Blakelock. However, the full tariff could be even longer: all those whom the system intends to hold for more than twenty years get a review at seventeen years. Newly-convicted murderers are now entering British prisons, for offences as bad or worse than the killing of Anthony Smith: their sentence tariffs, typically, will be twelve or, at most, fifteen years.

It is likely that the reasons for Silcott's tariff are political, as they were in the near tripling of the recommendation made by Mr Justice Hodgson in respect of Engin Raghip and Mark Braithwaite. Police officers have told me explicitly that as long as he remains in jail, the blow to morale caused by the quashing of the Blakelock convictions remains endurable. That, unfortunately, is the sole point of reference by which many officers continue to judge the Blakelock case: its effect on police morale.

The Smith case, says Andrew Hall, is 'a kind of acid test: whether the new thinking displayed in Lord Justice Farquharson's Blakelock judgement was anything more than another false dawn'. To quote Lord Justice Farquharson again, 'justice requires' that the Smith case be reopened.

Meanwhile in Gartree, Winston Silcott is growing old.

Postscript

In February 1992, Winston Silcott was told he would shortly be transferred to Whitemoor, a prison near Cambridge holding mainly Catergory A inmates. It was a move he was dreading: Gartree was the one prison where he had settled reasonably successfully. He told me in a letter: 'The reports coming back from men who have been sent to this new penal dungeon aren't good. So it looks like I'm out of the frying pan, into the fire. It seems the authorities are hell-bent on carrying out the 30-year recommendation they imposed on me for the PC Blakelock farce.'

Index

Home Office 198, 200, 206, 209, 211–12, 245
Hopkins, Matthew 96
Hudson, Insp. David 42
Human Rights Convention 212
Hurd, Douglas 51–2, 198, 209

Imbert, Sir Peter 17–18, 223–5
Innis, DAC Bob 47
Inside Story 209, 211
Intelligence and Surveillance Units 90–1
Irving, Barry 98
Irwin, Stephen 118

Jacobs, Nicky 109, 123, 142
Jarrett, Cynthia 57–60, 63, 129, 186
Jarrett, Floyd 57, 61, 126, 196
Jarrett, Michael 60–1
Jarrett, Patricia 59–60
Jedd 82
Johnstone, Susannah 118
Jones, Wayne 230–2, 234–40
Judge, Tony 83

Kamlish, Steven 176, 182–3, 201, 205, 217
Kelsey, Perry 125, 127
Kennedy, DI John 163–5, 179
Kent, Jenny 98, 104, 109, 136
Kerr, Howard 116–19, 125
Kerr, Jean 242–3
Kershwen, Samuel 244
Keys, Paul 123–4
Kiffin, Dolly 39, 46, 50, 53, 61, 63, 126–7, 195, 238
Kinghorn, Bernard 116, 126, 169–72

Lacey, John 161
Lambie, Mark 109, 116, 126, 129

trial 130, 133, 136, 138–9, 186
Lane, Lord 201–5, 208–9, 211, 216, 218–19, 243, 245
Laughland, Bruce, QC 141, 143, 146–9
Lawrence, Arthur 70
Layton, Robert 241
Lee, Junior 126
Lee, Sammy 109
Legal Aid Act 220
Lethbridge, Nemone 233, 242–4
Lewthwaite, James 133
Leyton Police Station 140
Limb, Roy 28, 50, 61, 63
Lindo, Delroy 21–2, 24, 26, 39, 49, 89, 92–3, 200, 232
local authorities 35, 224
    see also Haringey
Lockwood, DC Colin 104, 106, 135, 138, 145
London School of Economics 207, 221
Lynbery, Judge Robert 195, 234

McDermott, Det. Sgt Dermot 172, 181, 183
McIlkenny, Richard 206, 213
McKay, Peter 222–3
Mackintosh, Leonard 92, 240
MacLean, AC Jeff 74
McMinn, Simon 121, 137
McMinn, Vernon 137, 139
Maguire family 209, 220
Makanji, Narendra 47
Mangrove Centre 37
Mansfield, Michael, QC 14, 63–5, 136–9, 186, 201, 203–4, 216, 226
Mark, Sir Robert 75
Markham, ACC Geoffrey 214
Marnoch, Cdr Alec 18, 46–7, 53–4, 225
Martin, George 70